WITHDRAWN

Scribbling Women
& the Short Story Form

PETER LANG
New York • Washington, D.C./Baltimore • Bern
Frankfurt am Main • Berlin • Brussels • Vienna • Oxford

Scribbling Women & the Short Story Form

Approaches by American & British Women Writers

Edited by
Ellen Burton Harrington

PETER LANG
New York • Washington, D.C./Baltimore • Bern
Frankfurt am Main • Berlin • Brussels • Vienna • Oxford

Library of Congress Cataloging-in-Publication Data

Scribbling women and the short story form: approaches by American
and British women writers / edited by Ellen Burton Harrington.
p. cm.
Includes bibliographical references and index.
1. Short stories, American—History and criticism. 2. American fiction—
Women authors—History and criticism. 3. Short stories, English—History
and criticism. 4. English fiction—Women authors—History and criticism.
5. Short story—Authorship. I. Harrington, Ellen Burton.
PS374.S5S37   823'.01099287—dc22   2007027973
ISBN 978-1-4331-0077-2

Bibliographic information published by **Die Deutsche Bibliothek**.
Die Deutsche Bibliothek lists this publication in the "Deutsche
Nationalbibliografie"; detailed bibliographic data is available
on the Internet at http://dnb.ddb.de/.

Cover design by diane gibbs

The paper in this book meets the guidelines for permanence and durability
of the Committee on Production Guidelines for Book Longevity
of the Council of Library Resources.

© 2008 Ellen Burton Harrington
Peter Lang Publishing, Inc., New York
29 Broadway, 18th floor, New York, NY 10006
www.peterlang.com

All rights reserved.
Reprint or reproduction, even partially, in all forms such as microfilm,
xerography, microfiche, microcard, and offset strictly prohibited.

Printed in the United States of America

For Mary Rohrberger
in her memory and in honor of her passion for the short story

Contents

Acknowledgments xi

Introduction:
Scribbling Women and the Outlaw Form of the Short Story

   Ellen Burton Harrington 1

A Miniaturization of Epic Proportions:
Harriet Prescott Spofford's "Circumstance"

   Robert Coleman 15

Sexing the Narrator:
Gender in Rebecca Harding Davis's "Life in the Iron-Mills"

   Ruth Stoner 28

The Short Story as Feminist Forum:
Louisa May Alcott's "Pauline's Passion and Punishment"

   Miriam López-Rodríguez 37

The Art of (Dis)Placement: Ruth Stuart and the Characterization of
African Americans at the Turn of the Century

   Susan Prothro Wright 47

The Linked Excitements of L. T. Meade and...
in the *Strand* Magazine

   Winnie Chan 60

Naturalism and the Short Story Form
in Kate Chopin's "The Story of an Hour"

    Scott D. Emmert 74

Strategies of Self-Representation
in "Natalie" by Alice Dunbar-Nelson

    Margot Sempreora 86

Zitkala-Ša and Sui Sin Far's Sketch Collections:
Communal Characterization as Resistance Writing Tool

    Vanessa Holford Diana 98

Laura's Unconscious Rejection of the Short Story
in Katherine Anne Porter's "Flowering Judas"

    Susana M. Jiménez-Placer 112

"Beyond Human Reach": Silence and Continuity
in Katherine Anne Porter's "Holiday" and "He"

    Rachel Lister 128

Flannery O'Connor's "The Temple of the Holy Ghost"
and "Parker's Back" as Dermatology/Theology

    Sue Brannan Walker 142

Cynthia Ozick's "The Pagan Rabbi"
and the Seduction of the Storyteller

    Beth Ellen Roberts 154

Breaking It Down:
Analysis in the Stories of Lydia Davis

    Karen Alexander 165

Silko, Le Sueur, and Le Guin:
Storytelling as a "Movement Toward Wholeness"

    Gayle Elliott 178

Contributors.. 193

Index.. 197

Acknowledgments

I gratefully acknowledge the efforts of the late Mary Rohrberger, the founder of the Society for the Study of the Short Story, who guided me in the concept of this collection; her efforts helped me to bring together the variety of essays from scholars in Britain, Spain, and the United States. The support of the Society for the Study of the Short Story was also invaluable to me as I compiled and edited the collection. Interns for the organization, Marc LaPorte and Missy Roden, provided assistance and clerical support in the early stages of the project.

I am also grateful to the English Department and the College of Arts and Sciences at the University of South Alabama for their support of this project.

And, finally, I offer my thanks to the contributors for their intellectual work and commitment to the project.

Introduction: Women Writers and the Outlaw Form of the Short Story

Ellen Burton Harrington

University of South Alabama

"Scribbling women," the image purloined from an infuriated Hawthorne, now seems to carry within it the later echoes of Virginia Woolf, theorizing why women, ensconced in the homely chaos of domesticity, might choose to scribble popular, less-demanding fiction over precise poetry. In *A Room of One's Own*, Woolf famously laments women's lack of opportunity, education, and creative space, luxuries that might have enabled more female writers and poets throughout history to attain the stature of male authors. The notion of women writers as figurative outlaws in the literary tradition, outsiders stealing time from their plentiful domestic duties to scribble stories, essays, and poems, seems particularly apt in light of the nineteenth-century struggles for greater autonomy for women. Hawthorne's phrase encapsulates the industry of women's literary production in a frustrated swipe at that "damned mob," a phrase that is irresistibly apt to those of us interested in women's writing, since it portrays women's literary production as a force to be reckoned with economically, if not aesthetically.

Hawthorne, elsewhere helpful and generous to the women writers who were his contemporaries,[1] is here railing against the success of best-selling novels by women in the United States:

> America is now wholly given over to a d——d mob of scribbling women, and I should have no chance of success while the public taste is occupied with their trash–and should be ashamed of myself if I did succeed. What is the mystery of these innumerable editions of the 'Lamplighter,' and other books neither better nor worse?–worse they could not be, and better they need not be, when they sell by the 100,000. (Hawthorne 75)

Written from England in January, 1855, Hawthorne's oft-quoted comment to his publisher and friend William Ticknor marks a particular instance of fear in which popular women writers are conflated with a riotous mob overwhelming literary taste with popular "trash."[2] Similar protests occur in England, where moral and ideological questions about the propagation of sentimental and sensational literature, often written by and for women, abound. The presumption seems to be that women writers pander to the masses (the very mob with which Hawthorne conflates them) undermining men aesthetically and economically.[3] Hawthorne's palpable bitterness expresses disapproval tinged with envy; the producers of such "trash" have managed to occupy the "public taste," thus diminishing sales of male worthies like Hawthorne himself.

Writing a year later, the future novelist George Eliot[4] publishes "Silly Novels by Lady Novelists" in the British journal *The Westminster Review*, an essay that denigrates such popular fiction, arguing that its artificial renderings and formulaically perfect heroines damage women's ability to argue for what she terms "the more solid education of women" (106). In addition, she rejects the notion that "lady novelists" should be judged by separate standards from their male contemporaries: "And every critic who forms a high estimate of the share women may ultimately take in literature, will, on principle, abstain from any exceptional indulgence towards the productions of literary women" (Eliot 113). Ironically, both Hawthorne in his complaint about women writers and Eliot in her call for women to produce realistic novels are voicing the same concern about the low quality of women's popular literary production and the threat that these bestsellers hold; this "trash," in Hawthorne's words, might stifle or suffocate literature of quality by selling in the hundreds of thousands.[5] Eliot does not identify herself as a woman writer in her critique, and it is clear that she distances herself from the stereotypical woman writer she portrays. Here and elsewhere, the genre of women's writing is seen as antithetical to worthwhile literary work, a qualified subcategory of published fiction that is, rarely if at all, art.[6]

The period of increasing literacy, publication, and literary production of the nineteenth century in both Britain and the United States was marked by similar considerations about gender and literary quality as many critics routinely considered women's writing as belonging to an inferior class. This distinction commonly led to the elimination of women's work from or the denigration of women's work in anthologies of short fiction published in the early twentieth century, though women were popular writers of short fiction in the nineteenth century.[7] As Joyce W. Warren notes in *The (Other) American Traditions: Nineteenth-Century Women Writers*, women writers that dominated

Introduction: The Outlaw Form

the scene in the mid-nineteenth century have been largely excluded from the twentieth-century canon of nineteenth-century American literature, leaving women writers to be important primarily in relation to men included in the canon, rather than important in themselves (4). Discussing the position of American women writers as "dissenting voices" who were "defined as other by the dominant culture" (15), Warren emphasizes that the exclusion of female writers is not just an aesthetic act, but also a political one, since women writers focus on themes that diverge from dominant culture, valuing sentiment and sometimes imbuing central female characters with the assertiveness and independence of male individualist protagonists. Again, the marginalization of women writers gives them an outlaw status as women whose sentimental viewpoints and financial success were challenging to the dominant aesthetic associated with men. Scribbling women were resisting social expectations merely by writing professionally; their success was a further challenge to these paradigms.

Since the 1970s, feminist critics have disputed the notion, pervasive in those early twentieth-century anthologies, that women's writing is inferior and lacks historical agency. Writing is an act that in itself implies agency, personal expression, and subjectivity, and women's fiction does much more than simply engages sentiment or propagates traditional gender roles. Increasing examination and republication of women's writing that had been lost or marginalized has helped readers discover a women's literary tradition that is in the nineteenth and twentieth centuries that is vibrant and engaging. In her scholarship addressing the scribbling women of Hawthorne's time, Nina Baym disputes the early feminist idea that all women writers fit the stereotype of the silent, disenfranchised woman, "It was obvious to me that if there really had been a damned mob of scribbling women, then at least some women—indeed no small number of them—had not been passive, had not been submissive, and certainly had not been silent" (2). Baym's comment counters the old stereotype of women writers oppressed by patriarchy as being "outside of history;" in her words, they are "marked (and marred) by the histories in which they functioned" (2). Not only are these women writers a vital part of their literary culture, interacting with and influencing male writers and critics (despite the ideological barrier separating their work as women's writing), but they formed a literary community of their own that wrote, revised, and published stories by women.

The project of recuperating and reconsidering women's writing has only recently reached the short story. In the last twenty years, particularly in American literature, a series of short fiction anthologies that make women's writing accessible have been published, ranging from ethnic anthologies to collections of detective stories to erotica by women writers. Thus, the relationship of the woman writer to the "outlaw" form of short fiction, that persistent contender for the position of fourth major genre, has become an issue for consideration. Alongside these fiction anthologies, some critical collections that give women's short stories deserved gender analysis and historical consideration have been published. While the critical assessment of women's short fiction has also begun—and continues in the work in this anthology—there is still much more work to do in the consideration of women writers and the form of the short story.

The Form of the Short Story

> In short, the short story is, of itself, central to the human experience; so are the poem, the novel, and the play, but most naturally the short story.
> William Saroyan, "International Symposium on the Short Story"

Scholars of the short story frequently lament the lack of attention given to short fiction in comparison to novels, poetry, and drama, and try to locate the special significance of short fiction: comparing it to the lyric poem in the tradition of Poe; complaining that its brevity does not give the novel, that "loose and baggy monster," to borrow Henry James's popular description of Victorian three-decker novels, precedence; finding a place for it in the Aristotelian tradition. Pondering the significance of the form, critics like James Cooper Lawrence try to establish a pedigree for the short story that affirms its significance.[8] Starting with the nineteenth-century theories of Poe and Irving, critics grapple with the defining characteristics of the short story, trying to envision the means of characterizing the short story beyond the simple characteristic implicit in its name.

"But in these shorter writings, every page must have its merit." Washington Irving's 1824 comment on short fiction introduces two of the significant qualities that continue to be featured in theories of short fiction: brevity and craftsmanship (64). Irving's complaint that novel writers rescue "pages and pages of careless writing" by relying on the interest of the story and the insertion of "striking" scenes emphasizes his preference for the tighter crafting of the short story (64). Edgar Allan Poe also glorifies the tale over longer prose since it "affords unquestionably the fairest field for the exercise of the loftiest talent" and compares it to lyric poetry in his consideration of its quality (571). Poe's review of Hawthorne's *Twice-Told Tales* is universally cited as the consideration that crystallizes notions of the short story, insisting on unity of pattern, that "certain unique or single *effect*," and emphasizing readerly participation in the construction of meaning. His laudatory review also takes note of the essays in Hawthorne's volume: "In the essays before us the absence of effort [which Poe earlier calls repose] is too obvious to be mistaken, and a strong under current of *suggestion* runs continuously beneath the upper stream of the tranquil thesis" (571). Interestingly, this "repose" and particularly the "under current of *suggestion*" that Poe attributes to the essays rather than the stories are qualities that will come into consideration of the short story later in the century. This "under current" might reflect the quality that distinguishes the symbolic short story from the simpler anecdote in later theories of the short story, grasping at the figurative meaning under the surface of the symbolic narrative. Poe's early considerations about the nature of the short story influence later theorists in their continuing attempts to conceptualize the short story.

The rich periodical culture on both sides of the Atlantic in the nineteenth century encouraged writers to develop short stories for publication as well as novels for serialization, and the short story became a familiar, popular form. Beginning with Brander Matthews in the 1880's, critics have distinguished two basic forms of the short story, though they have christened them a variety of names, one simply anecdotal (or ironic) and the other symbolic (and arriving at an epiphany). Matthews tries to distinguish the form by hyphenating the name and characterizing the form more precisely: "A true Short-story is something other and something more than a story which is short. [...] A Short-story deals with a single character, a single event, a single emotion, or the series of emotions called forth by a single situation" (52). This emphasis on brevity and unity, clearly derived from Poe, is still cited in short story theory and criticism, but it fails to produce Matthews's desired effect, the consideration of the short story as a literary form on par with the other major forms.

Only in the 1960s and 1970s, do critics begin a systematic consideration of the literary and formal qualities of the short story as an art form in the tradition of Poe and Matthews. Most critics note two categories of short fiction, called variously "simple narrative" and short story, "realistic and symbolic," "mimetic and lyric," "anecdotal and epiphanic," "linear and spatial," etc. (Rohrberger[9]). Each of these sets of terms attempts to illustrate an essential bifurcation in the short story form: some stories are simply anecdotes that sketch a realistic narrative in a linear fashion; others (sometimes via a realistic narrative) probe the nature of reality through a symbolic structure and epiphany wherein meaning is realized in the discernment of pattern in the whole. Joseph Frank's influential 1963 article, "Spatial Form in Modern

Literature," a consideration of narrative technique in fiction, proves important to short story theorists Susan Lohafer and Mary Rohrberger among others:

> The words will yield their meaning only at the moment when the design as a whole is perceived. Frank's point is that the conventions of print force us to read sequentially, by clumps of threads, while the meaning of what we read may lie in the handkerchief-text as a whole. Usually this overall spatial design is created through patterns of imagery. (Lohafer 22)

Thus, the "spatial form," in Frank's words, works against linearity in the story by integrating the sequential perception of the story with repeated images that undermine the linear narrative. The spatial short story seems as intimately linked to modernist formal innovation (nineteenth-century symbolic stories may be considered to anticipate modernism) as to the Romantic, metaphysical tradition that also influenced it.

In the introduction to his influential 1976 anthology, *Short Story Theories*, Charles May contrasts the novel with the short story, "The short story, however, with its insistence that beginnings and ends are not so neat and that 'middles' are always a mixed business impossible to judge, has become for the reader fragmentary, static, and irresolute" (5). Here, May acknowledges the way the short fiction tends to undermine traditional narrative structure, leaving the reader to struggle with the "irresolute" and fragmented nature of short fiction. The brief format and patterns of images tend to make the story and the reader "end-conscious" (Lohafer 94). While epiphanies provide, in effect, formal closure, the stories tend to resist narrative closure, allowing the reader to construct meaning through the interaction of the linear narrative and the spatial field of reference in the story.

The reader's experience acquires structural importance in the perception of the significance of the short story retrospectively. The closing epiphany allows the reader to apprehend the meaning of the whole, enabling the reader to move beyond normal perception and inviting the reader to consider as well as experience the metaphysical world. Lohafer explains that the story itself is a kind of "reality warp" for the reader wherein the short length is "the unique prerequisite and determinant of a rhythm definite enough to delay or even displace life's other tides—till it's had its swell" (81). The experience of the short story marks a departure from the reader's typical experience of reality, ideally offering a perception heightened by the density and complexity of the form. In her comprehensive, retrospective paper, "The Short Story: Origins, Development, Substance, and Design," Mary Rohrberger notes:

> This is the accomplishment, perhaps of all great short story writers, the encompassing of time and motion in a present moment, while simultaneously suggesting past and

future. All of the characteristic devices of the short story finally relate to this end: juxtapositions that create montage patterns, the accumulation of details forming networks of images that become metaphors, the layerings of time and place, the meshing of antitheses—joy and sadness, waking and dream, even life and death—tonal reverberations operating paradoxically, as a means for non-verbal expression [...]; and, of course, the epiphany, a point of frozen energy operating just beyond understanding.

Here, the process of reading the short story comes to symbolize the larger grasping after comprehension of the nature of reality itself. And here we come back to Saroyan's quotation at the beginning of this section: in its brevity and the flash of the metaphysical that the form affords, the short story is central to the human condition, even as it encompasses fundamental human alienation.

Outlaws and the Short Story

> Always in the short story there is this sense of outlawed figures wandering about the fringes of society, superimposed sometimes on symbolic figures whom they caricature and echo—Christ, Socrates, Moses [...]
> Frank O'Connor, *The Lonely Voice: A Study of the Short Story*

> There you see what has happened to the woman writer. She has entered literary history as the enemy.
> Nina Baym, "*Melodramas of Beset Manhood*"

Frank O'Connor's frequently cited description of his chosen form in *The Lonely Voice: A Study of the Short Story* in 1963 encapsulates the notion of the short story as the outlet for the alienated individual. This image of the "outlaw" story comes out of notions of it as a form that is far from central to the literary tradition, the presumption that its brevity makes it subordinate to the supposedly more developed novel. The short story has often been connected to marginalized or liminal writers, even though many of the acclaimed authors of the nineteenth and twentieth centuries have written short fiction. The outlaws he mentions are "remote from society" (to borrow O'Connor's description of the short story itself), figures whose significance is writ large in symbolic male figures from Christianity, Western philosophy, and Western culture more generally. Though O'Connor conceptualizes these outlaws in terms of male figures and, it seems, a masculine Western literary tradition, his model clearly has implications for women writers as well.

Baym's description of the woman writer seems particularly apt below O'Connor's comment, calling up images of the threatening, outlaw woman writer riding into town to shake things up. Of course, Baym's comment invokes Hawthorne's exclamation to his publisher, revisiting the notion that scribbling women are the enemy and their sentimental stories are in direct opposition to his quality writing. In the twenty years since Baym's essay was first published, it has become a critical commonplace to identify women writers as a marginalized group, outlaws who have been historically alienated from society's power structures, including literary traditions.

This alienation makes the short story a natural choice for women writers. In *Re-reading the Short Story*, Clare Hanson begins the work of a feminist consideration of the short story, noting the connection between the genre of short fiction and women's "alienated" perspective, and she goes on to further define the perceived liminality of the genre:

> The short story is a vehicle for various kinds of knowledge, knowledge which may be at odds with the 'story' of dominant culture. The formal properties of the short story—disjunction, inconclusiveness, obliquity—connect with its ideological marginality and with the fact that the form may be used to express something suppressed/repressed in mainstream literature. (6)[10]

Hanson thus sketches short fiction as a potentially subversive form; the very notions of the symbolic functioning of short fiction that undermine the linear narrative may be used to oppose dominant culture. As a genre that is open-ended and symbolic, even as the form itself seems to defy facile definition, the short story seems an enticing genre for writers with a problematic social positioning. The modern short story, which de-emphasizes the plot or removes it entirely, moves toward feminism by relinquishing the all-important notion of a linear narrative.

This collection argues that the short story can be considered a feminist form, one that is particularly hospitable to women writers. The form of the short story, long marginalized in literary consideration, invites other outlaws to plumb alienation and repression in the symbolic subtext, enlightening and challenging the reader through epiphany and patterning. The spatial form of the short story, in de-emphasizing plotline and resolution, undermines a simple linear narrative of culture and progress by demonstrating the underlying complexity of apparently simple relationships. The form of the short story, despite its limited length, is not antithetical to the notion of an expansive women's writing, since short fiction is the "genre that might permit the representation of passing time in moments that are significant, but that refuse rhetorical gestures towards enclosed meaning" (Burgan 268).[11] Mary Burgan's comment here evokes the earlier considerations of the elusive literary form by Rohrberger and Lohafer; this resistance to closure and perception of a different reality, one devised through discourse but not bounded by it, offers a re-envisioning of the expansiveness essential to feminine writing. In this vein, Julie Brown suggests that women writers might do best by refusing to define the short story, since "definitions limit, exclude, and deaden our capacity for surprise" (xxi). In other words, precise definition of the form might limit its lively potential; even as Brown encourages increased critical consideration of the short story, she revels in its ambiguities and its liminality, characteristics integral to the form.

The goal of this collection is also to revel in the variety, subtlety, and audacity of women's writing by featuring essays on women's short stories over 150 years in Britain and the United States. Despite the increasing number of critical collections on women writers of short fiction available, few examine American and British literature in the same volume, offering a broader perspective on women's writing and women's experience, and few emphasize form alongside theme. This anthology features a variety of authors and approaches from major periods from the middle of the nineteenth century to the end of the twentieth century. Each essay specifically addresses the author's use of form, though the term is interpreted broadly to mean a wealth of formal and stylistic choices that shape the short story and its meanings. The essays in this volume examine how that fearsome economic force, that multiplicity of "scribbling women," approach, adapt, and resist the outlaw form of the short story.

The period of the "Scribbling Women," from the 1850s and the 1860s, offers a rich body of women authors writing short fiction for periodicals, often under pseudonyms. Each of these essays demonstrates the complex way in which these nineteenth-century writers reveals and comments on gender, while sometimes simultaneously occluding or problematizing the identity of the writer herself. Robert Coleman's essay on Harriet Spofford explores the way that "Circumstance" transcends genre by complicating the colonial captivity narrative formula and its religious implications, emerging as a narrative of multiple, competing thematic possibilities. The fantastical scene in which a heroine saves herself by singing offers a series of potential interpretative possibilities that complicate and displace the demonization of Native Americans that might be at the heart of the narrative. Ultimately, the singing heroine resonates with the beast she charms as well as the women writer herself, using the short story form to condense a narrative of rich possibility into a powerful image. From the context of her position as a translator of Rebecca Harding Davis, Ruth Stoner closely examines the signification of Davis's refusal to gender the narrator in "Life in the Iron-Mills," arguing that critics' tendency to gender the otherwise undefined narrator implies a simplification of the complicated rendering of gender and androgyny that the story offers. Stoner demonstrates that Davis's characterization of the narrator and structuring of the story constitutes an expression of Davis's "radical sexual politics." Miriam López-Rodríguez reveals Louisa May Alcott's use of the gothic thriller short story to write escapist "gorgeous fantasies" that she published under another name, distancing herself from their popular quality as well as their feminist subtext. In López-Rodríguez's reading, Alcott makes a radical critique of conventional roles for women beneath the Gothic conventions of her thriller short fiction.

The following articles, featuring essays on stories from the 1880s and the 1890s, presents a variety of authors and perspectives, from Ruth Stuart's "local color" short fiction set in the American South to L. T. Meade's mystery stories published in the *Strand* in London, from a fresh reading of Kate Chopin's much-considered "The Story of an Hour" to the short fiction of Alice Dunbar-Nelson in 1890s New Orleans. Susan Prothro Wright's essay on plantation fiction examines Ruth Stuart's short fiction as a racist ideological tool that mythologizes a hierarchy of race by sketching defiant characters always in the context of tragedy. Her caricatured black characters long for the security that supposedly accompanied an idealized, enslaved past, perpetuating the stereotypes that attempt to justify continued oppression. Winnie Chan's lively historical consideration of the authorial and textual gender politics of L. T. Meade's stories for the *Strand* introduces readers to the immensely successful adult work of this prolific author of children's stories, in addition to explaining the general historical context for popular short fiction in Britain at the end of the nineteenth century. Using the conventions of the short story that evolved in the late-nineteenth-century *Strand*, Meade "subverted and exploited" the formula, negotiating short story conventions to assure the success of her "linked excitements." In the next essay, Scott Emmert examines Kate Chopin's "The Story of an Hour" as an example of naturalism addressing women's struggles, one that vividly depicts a "sudden loss of freedom" for Louise Mallard. Since the short story form emphasizes and enables the techniques of naturalist writers, Chopin uses the form to convey a woman's difficulty in creating an independent identity in the society of the 1890s. In another look at the "local color" story, Margot Sempreora examines the way Alice Dunbar-Nelson encodes her mixed-race status in an early story. Though Dunbar-Nelson seemed to work to keep politics out of her stories, "Natalie" represents the complexity of a mixed-race heroine's interaction with a white friend, illuminating the intersection of race, language, and gender in the tensions of their homoerotically inflected relationship.

Focusing on the early twentieth century, the next part of this collection addresses women's adaptations of form to better represent women's experience. The short story form becomes a site of resistance in each of these interpretations, the stories undermining and redefining genre as they explore the complexities of women's identities. Examining the stories of Native American author Zitkala-Ša and Chinese North American author Sui Sin Far, Vanessa Holford Diana argues that the technique of narrative twinning functions in terms of form and politics, creating "internal coherence among collective stories while emphasizing patterns of oppression and resistance among marginalized people." Both authors use short story cycles that incorporate autobiography to demonstrate and resist the pressure for assimilation. In her essay on Katherine Anne Porter's "Flowering Judas," Susana M. Jiménez-Placer demonstrates that Porter uses the short story, a form usually dependent on the "arbitrariness of language" to examine the complexity of its heroine. Throughout the story, Laura rejects symbolism and multiplicity of meaning as a means of ordering the chaos of the Mexican revolution that surrounds her. Her repetition of the word "no" charges it with multiple meanings that make it finally representative of the heroine's failed resistance. Rachel Lister also examines short stories by Katherine Anne Porter, "Holiday" and "He," arguing that Porter's variation of narrative perspective works against the sentimental or moralistic responses that her stories might invite. Both stories utilize silence as a tool to work against the discursive elements of the short story, so that they ultimately function as "constructs of the process of storytelling."

The last few articles cover women writers in the second half of the twentieth century, a period that offers increased formal experimentation and feminist awareness. Sue Brannan Walker's essay looks at Flannery O'Connor's short stories, examining the notion of form through the medium of skin and the marks, tattoos, and rashes that might lend it additional significance. Walker understands O'Connor's stylistic choices through the lens of her final illness, her religious beliefs, and the stories' skin, "the body that is text marked by proscriptions, inscriptions, and prescriptions." Beth Ellen Roberts reads Cynthia Ozick's story "The Pagan Rabbi," centered on the struggle implied by its oxymoronic title, as more than a cautionary tale about religion; the story concerns itself with the temptations of storytelling as a creative act. Situating the story in the Jewish storytelling tradition, Roberts demonstrates that balance rather than deprivation is the answer, since storytelling as a creative act is both potentially dangerous and essential to rebirth. Examining the experimental stories of Lydia Davis, Karen Alexander notes that Davis's minimalist texts have been honored in poetry and prose poem compilations, though the author regards herself as a story writer. In Alexander's explication, Davis's writing questions the nature of the short story, examining and troubling the structure and conventions of the story form and narrative itself.

Focusing on the feminism of Leslie Marmon Silko, Meridel Le Sueur, and Ursula K. Le Guin, Gayle Elliott's essay examines the ways in which these authors make use of the short story form as a way of addressing the alienation of the individual with a movement towards unity and community. These three authors define a vision of femininity that challenges a stereotypically masculine individualist viewpoint, enhanced by the libratory possibilities of the short story form.

Each of the essays in this volume works to examine gender and the position of the woman writer in relation to the familiar, contested form of the short story. The varying lengths, styles, subjects and viewpoints of the short stories discussed in this collection are indicative of the wide range of possibilities of the form; in retrospect, the "lady" writer is not a single figure, but a myriad (not, I hope, a "mob") of individual women who often channel their concerns about identity, including gender, class, race, ethnicity, and sexuality, into the paradoxically compressed and elastic form of the story. The work in this volume speaks to the vast potential of the flexible form of the short story, so much more than the sum of its name, and to that of the outlaw woman writer, who need no more be considered as a "lady" at all.

Notes

1 As James Wallace comments in "Hawthorne and the Scribbling Women Reconsidered," Hawthorne is "supportive, if not necessarily deeply admiring" of his female contemporaries (206).

2 Wallace points out that Hawthorne offers something of an apology for his comment in a letter to Ticknor two weeks later (204). Also, it is worth noting that Hawthorne's "scribbling women" complaint comes amidst letters discussing his business and financial dealings with Ticknor; his economic success or lack of it would have certainly been foremost in his mind writing to Ticknor, his publisher.

3 In the introduction to her anthology of American women's short stories, *Scribbling Women: Short Stories by 19th-Century American Women*, Elaine Showalter makes the point that certain women authors in Britain, notably Jane Austen, the Brontës, and George Eliot, had been recognized in the nineteenth century as attaining "high" literary status in a way that women authors in the United States had not, aside from Emily Dickinson. Though the situation for women writers is certainly not the same in Britain as in the United States, critics on both side of the Atlantic express similar concerns about the nature of women's writing.

4 Mary Ann Evans serialized her first novel, *Scenes from Clerical Life*, in Blackwood's Magazine under the pseudonym George Eliot in 1857.

5 As Nina Baym comments in the introduction to her 1988 edition of Maria Susanna Cummins's *The Lamplighter*, "Hawthorne has had his revenge: the standard American

6   For example, in short fiction like "Miss Witherwell's Mistake," Kate Chopin also criticizes women readers and writers in the style of Hawthorne's critique; see Heather Kirk Thomas's article "Kate Chopin's scribbling women and the American literary marketplace."

7   In the introduction to *American Women Short Story Writers*, Julie Brown surveys the inclusion of women writers in anthologies in the United States, as well as their critical treatment therein. Brown notes that short story criticism concentrates on men; using Gilbert and Gubar, she theorizes that women wrote one-third to one-half of the short stories published in America from 1820-1900 (xviii-xix).

8   In "A Theory of the Short Story," James Cooper Lawrence argues that the short story predates all other literary forms, including the epic and the ballad.

9   Mary Rohrberger was kind enough to give me the unpublished text from her presentation, "The Short Story: Origins, Development, Substance, and Design, Or How I Got Hooked on the Short Story and Where It Led Me," at the International Conference on the Short Story in Oslo.

10 Hanson acknowledges the limitations of such a generalized definition. Julie Brown cites Hanson's "first step towards a feminist critique of the genre," but notes that Hanson's anthology does not include an essay that discusses women's short stories (xvi).

11 In Burgan's consideration, this notion of a feminine writing is tied to form rather than gender.

Works Cited

Baym, Nina. Introduction. *The Lamplighter*. By Maria Susanna Cummins. New Brunswick: Rutgers UP, 1988. ix-xxxi.

———. "Melodramas of Beset Manhood: How Theories of American Fiction Exclude Women Authors." *American Quarterly* 33:2 (1981): 123-39.

———. Plenary Remarks. *Legacy: A Journal of American Women Writers*, 19:1 (Jan 2002): 1-4.

Brown, Julie. Introduction. *American Women Short Story Writers: A Collection of Critical Essays*. Ed. Brown. NY: Garland, 1995. xv-xxviii.

Burgan, Mary. "The 'Feminine' Short Story in America: Historicizing Epiphanies." *American Women Short Story Writers: A Collection of Critical Essays*. Ed. Julie Brown. NY: Garland, 1995. 267-80.

Eliot, George. "Silly Novels by Lady Novelists." *Westminster Review* 66 (October 1856). Rpt. in *A Serious Occupation: Literary Criticism by Victorian Women Writers*. Ed. Solveig C. Robinson. Ontario: Broadview, 2003. 88-115.

Hanson, Clare. Introduction. *Re-Reading the Short Story*. NY: St. Martins, 1989. 1-9.

Hawthorne, Nathaniel. *Letters of Hawthorne to William D. Ticknor, 1851-1864*. Newark, NJ: Carteret Book Club, 1910.

Irving, Washington. "On Style and Purpose in the Short Story." *What is the Short Story?* Ed. Eugene Current-García and Walton R. Patrick. Chicago: Scott, Foresman & Co.: 1961.

Rpt. of "To Henry Brevoort." 11 December 1824. *The Life and Letters of Washington Irving.* Ed. Pierre M. Irving. NY: G.P. Putnam's Sons, 1869. 64-65.

Lawrence, James Cooper. "A Theory of the Short Story." *North American Review* 205 (February 1917): 274-86. Rpt. in *Short Story Theories*. Ed. Charles May. Ohio UP, 1976. 60-71.

Lohafer, Susan. *Coming to Terms with the Short Story.* Baton Rouge: Louisiana State UP, 1983.

Matthews, Brander. "The Philosophy of the Short Story." *The Philosophy of the Short Story.* NY: Longmans, Green & Co., 1901. Rpt. in *Short Story Theories*. Ed. Charles E. May. Ohio UP, 1976. 52-59.

May, Charles. "A Survey of Short Story Criticism in America." Introduction. *Short Story Theories.* Ed. May. Ohio UP, 1976. 2-12.

O'Connor, Frank. *The Lonely Voice: A Study of the Short Story.* Cleveland: World Publishing Co., 1962.

Poe, Edgar Allan. "Review of *Twice-Told Tales*." *Graham's Magazine* May 1842. Rpt. in *Essays and Reviews*. NY: Library of America, 1984. 569-77.

Rohrberger, Mary. "The Short Story: Origins, Development, Substance, and Design, Or How I Got Hooked on the Short Story and Where It Led Me." International Conference of the Society for the Study of the Short Story. Oslo, Norway., n.d.

Saroyan, William. "International Symposium on the Short Story, Part Two." Kenyon Review 1st Series XXXI: 58-62.

Showalter, Elaine. Introduction. *Scribbling Women: Short Stories by 19th-Century American Women.* New Brunswick: Rutgers UP, 1996. xxxv-xlii.

Thomas, Heather Kirk. "Kate Chopin's Scribbling Women and the American Literary Marketplace." *Studies in American Fiction* 23:1 (1995): 19-34.

Wallace, James. "Hawthorne and the Scribbling Women Reconsidered." *American Literature* 62:2 (1990): 201-22.

Warren, Joyce W. "Canons and Canon Fodder." Introduction. *The (Other) American Traditions: Nineteenth-Century Women Writers.* New Brunswick: Rutgers UP, 1993. 1-25.

Woolf, Virginia. *A Room of One's Own.* San Diego: Harcourt, Brace, and Company, 1929.

A Miniaturization of Epic Proportions: Harriet Prescott Spofford's "Circumstance"

Robert Coleman

University of South Alabama

Harriet Prescott Spofford's death on 14 August 1921 at Deer Island, Massachusetts, coincides with the modernist re-valuation of Herman Melville's *Moby-Dick* (1851).[1] Over the course of the twentieth century, Hawthorne, Emerson, Thoreau, Whitman, and Dickinson all garner praise for their proto-modernist writings. Spofford is and is not their unheralded contemporary. Her stories were first published in the late 1850s and early 1860s, and she continued writing fiction into the twentieth century. Today, she is best remembered, when remembered, for her short story, "Circumstance" (1860), a frontier adventure tale Dickinson and Howells greatly admired.[2] In "Circumstance," Spofford extends and revises the frontier romance mode within the constraints of short story form. Like the heroine's musical performance in the tale, Spofford's compressed performance paradoxically escapes generic confinements to range at large—much like Melville's whale.

"Circumstance" is a captivity narrative with a twist. The story takes place in the "eastern wilds" of colonial Maine, where an unnamed heroine is attacked and captured by a panther known to the settlers as the "Indian Devil" (84, 85). The creature carries the heroine up into a tree, where she miraculously survives a wintry night by singing. Her enchanting voice signals Spofford's novelty in this story. According to Judith Fetterley, Spofford's fanciful tale is based on fact—"an incident that actually happened to Spofford's maternal great-grandmother"—and fiction—"[l]ike her prototype, Scheherazade, this woman's life literally depends on her art" (264). Fetterley reads "Circumstance" within a tradition of nineteenth-century literature by United States women: "Like Lydia Sigourney's 'The Father' and Harriet Beecher Stowe's *The Pearl of Orr's Island*, 'Circumstance' dramatizes the nineteenth-century conviction that men, despite their lower nature, have a spiritual component that responds to women and by means of which women can tame their beast and raise them to a higher level" (266). In her analysis, Fetterley highlights gender role inversions: the protagonist acts outside the home and imagines her husband happy at home, taking care of their child. In Fetterley's words, "He, not she, is domestic, and she, not he, is out in the world, exposed to the hard fact of real danger" (265). In my reading of "Circumstance," the unconventional plot signals Spofford's distillation and reconstitution of colonial captivity narratives and nationalist frontier romances, which complicate rather than reiterate what Fetterley sees as the "religious dimension of the story": "God, not man, is the true 'savior'" (267).

The most celebrated American captivity tale is Mary Rowlandson's *The Sovereignty and Goodness of God* (1682), a jeremiad about the perils of spiritual complacency in colonial New England: Indian massacres and captivity, the handiwork of an angry God whose disciples' spiritual failings spark His fiery wrath. Popular through the eighteenth century, Rowlandson's eschatological narrative of captivity and deliverance has more recently been hailed by Nancy Armstrong and Leonard Tennenhouse for influencing the novelty of Samuel Richardson's *Pamela* (1740).[3] The possibility of Rowlandson's trans-Atlantic influence is an exciting thesis sure to elicit debate. Beyond debate, however, is the influence of Rowlandson's text and other colonial captivity narratives on subsequent United States fiction. According to Richard Slotkin, "the first tentative American efforts at short fiction and the 'first American novel' (Brown's *Edgar Huntly*) were very much in the vein of the captivity narratives" (95).[4] *Edgar Huntly* (1799) is a marvelous murder mystery rife with sleepwalkers and Indians. The latter are, as far as Charles Brockden Brown's eponymous hero is concerned, much like panthers,[5] an equation also evident in "Circumstance": there is the already mentioned Indian Devil; and, the narrator describes the wilderness as "untrodden save by stealthy native or deadly panther tribes" (84).

As with the anomalies in Brown's fiction, there are many questions to ask about "Circumstance." For instance, why write a frontier adventure in the late 1850s? Given the historical context, the eve of the American Civil War, one might imagine captivity in terms of slavery, but "Circumstance" can hardly be read as either abolitionist or pro-slavery. In looking backwards to the tried and true forms of captivity narratives and their progeny, frontier romances, Spofford eschews the everyday, the present. Is "Circumstance" reactionary and nostalgic, one wonders? Or, can one read Spofford's turn backwards as, paradoxically, an attempt to be forward looking or innovative? Rather than presenting a plantation tale, Spofford constructs an identifiably American story along the lines Brown outlined in his preface to *Edgar Huntly*: she avoids conventions of popular British fiction and presents recognizably American settings, characters, and incidents. In his version of American exceptionalism, Brown seeks not only to "exhibit a series of adventures, growing out of the condition of our country" but also to elicit the reader's fellow feeling and emotions "by means hitherto unemployed by preceding authors" (29). In place of Gothic clap-trap—"Puerile superstition and exploded manners; Gothic castles and chimeras"—Brown proudly substitutes the novelty of "[t]he incidents of Indian hostility, and the perils of the western wilderness," as more appropriate for an American writer (29). Of course, by 1860, Brown's novelty is old hat or, if you like, vestigial.

Not surprisingly, "Circumstance" appears similarly archaic: a story of the wilderness and "Indian hostility." Like Brown, Spofford starts by rejecting gothic conventions. Readers witness the heroine confronted with a ghostly winding sheet and spectral voice that intones three times "'The Lord have mercy on the people!'" before disappearing (85). The heroine coolly dismisses the anomalous vision: "She might have been a little frightened by such an apparition, if she had led a life of less reality than frontier settlers are apt to lead" (85). Like an imperturbable rationalist, she does not flinch when confronting the eerie and unfamiliar. "[D]ealing with hard fact does not engender a flimsy habit of mind," the narrator reports, "and this woman was too sincere and earnest in her character, and too happy in her situation, to be thrown by antagonism, merely, upon superstitious fancies and chimeras of the second-sight" (85). The heroine's self-control might remind us of Leatherstocking but certainly not of James Fenimore Cooper's idealized heroines.

The heroine's prosaic response to the anomalous experience—to continue home and to doubt her senses—highlights the metafictional and generic contrast between "hard fact" and "flimsy habit of mind." The proverbial moralist anxious about women reading fiction would see in the heroine of "Circumstance" the ideal reader: "sincere and earnest in her character," not given to emotion and fancy, all that is captivating in the gothic. Not one to suspend disbelief, the heroine "smiled simply, a little vexed that her thought could have framed such a glamour from the day's occurrences" (85).

This consummate demonstration of self-possession is precisely the problem, however. Any avid reader of fiction recognizes the heroine as a terrible reader, as someone lacking in curiosity and without common sense expectations of genre. "If she had been imaginative," the narrator points out, "she would have hesitated at her first step into a region [the woods] whose dangers were not visionary; but I suppose that the thought of a little child at home would conquer that propensity in the most habituated" (85). Like a magnet, domestic realities will pull her homeward. Her lack of imagination, however, pulls the plot in other—indeed, predictable—directions. As she enters the forest, the space of fairy tale and romance, she is immediately attacked: "Suddenly, a swift shadow, like the fabulous flying-dragon, writhed through the air before her, and she felt herself instantly seized and borne aloft" (85). Assailed by the Indian Devil, "the most savage and serpentine and subtle and fearless [beast] of our latitudes" (85), the heroine discovers the "hard fact" of fantastic captivity.

The "hard fact" includes not only razor-sharp claws and teeth but other predatory sensations; indeed, the panther "lick[s] her bare arm with his rasping tongue" and "pour[s] over her the wide streams of his hot, foetid breath" (86). Imagining her torturous and aching fate, the normally stoic heroine screams, which causes the panther to stop licking her arm. The heroine, according to the narrator, "did not think at this instant to call upon God. She called upon her husband. It seemed to her that she had but one friend in the world; that was he; and again the cry, loud, clear, prolonged, echoed through the woods. It was not the shriek that disturbed the creature at his relish [...]. It must have been the echo, most musical, most resonant [...]" (86). When the panther resumes flicking his tongue across her arm, she begins to sing in order to pacify the Indian Devil.

Her singing is her salvation in more than one sense: first, pragmatically, her eloquent voice mesmerizes the panther; second, metaphysically, the heroine's performance shifts from secular ditties to spirituals, which initiates her return to Christ. In the process, she recognizes her spiritual failings can account for her predicament just as Rowlandson interpreted her captivity as the result of her spiritual delinquency.

According to the narrator, "She asked herself, as she sang, what sins she had committed, what life she had led, to find her punishment so soon and in these pangs—and then she sought eagerly for some reason why her husband was not up and abroad to find her. He failed her,—her one sole hope in life" (90). This last sentence is ironic. The "He" of "He failed her," of course, is her husband; it is she, however, who has failed Him, her God. Indeed, He, her God, "is her one [soul] hope in life." Hence, while singing does not separate her from the panther, it does remind her of other separations: from her family and from her God. In recognizing these separations, the heroine as well as Spofford's readers must wonder how long her singing can last. This is a physical and mental test of endurance.

One might see in the heroine's singing—the shift from secular songs to Methodist hymns—the realism/romance or "hard fact"/"flimsy habit of mind" oppositions. The narrator's description of the heroine's performance emphasizes rhetorical self-control: "Her voice, at first faint and fearful, gradually lost its quaver, grew under her control and subject to her modulation; it rose on long swells, it fell in subtile cadences, now and then its tones pealed out like bells from distant belfries on fresh sonorous mornings" (87). Here, we see the art Fetterley mentions; we also see in this art echoes of aestheticized rhetorical power akin to the representations of savage eloquence in nationalist frontier romances.

Unlike the broadbrush depictions of Indians in Rowlandson's captivity narrative, Cooper's Indians in *The Last of the Mohicans* (1826) are elaborated through extended dramatic tableaus of their oratory. The theatricality of his "good" and "bad" Indians grants them varying degrees of aesthetic sensibilities, which suggest a level of autonomy missing in Rowlandson's representations.[6] Ultimately, Cooper's novel presents a white fantasy of property rights, where Indian autonomy like savage eloquence proves to be evanescent, a lost cause. With a tear or two of melancholic sympathy for the "vanishing" of Indians, *The Last of the Mohicans* praises (it hardly blames) the nationalist order of things.[7]

Cooper's set pieces of Indian rhetoric illustrate what I call literary orality, which both marks the Indians' distance from white readers and romanticizes the Indians for literate consumption. Aestheticizing savage eloquence calls attention to the printed page that contains and re-presents a white construct—Indian speech. I call this construct literary orality because the physical book's typography ironically underscores the incongruity between the book's readers and the eloquent but unlettered "savages." Indeed, in *The Last of the Mohicans*, Cooper sells the reading public a readily recognizable commodity, the Indian-as-orator.[8] In contrast, Spofford offers her readers no Indians, eloquent or otherwise. Indians are neither heard nor seen in "Circumstance." Only tell-tale traces mark their existence: an enigmatic footprint and the smoldering remains of twelve log cabins. Cooper's savage eloquence charmed readers; in "Circumstance," it is the heroine's singing that is bewitching. Through her vocal "spell," the captive captivates her captor. In so doing, her mesmerizing performance inverts enchanting descriptions of Indian oratory in frontier romances such as *The Last of the Mohicans*. In other words, Spofford repackages literary orality and displaces it as the heroine's singing.

A rhetorical sleight of hand, this repackaging "naturalizes" the heroine's re-conversion or spiritual renewal. Understandably terrified as a captive, subject to death if she loses her voice or if the panther begins to behave as expected, her terror miraculously subsides when she segues to the spirituals: "grand and sweet Methodist hymns, brimming with melody and with all fantastic involutions of tune to suit that ecstatic worship,—hymns full of the beauty of holiness, steadfast, relying, sanctified by the salvation they had lent to those in worse extremity than hers" (90).

Like Rowlandson's references to scripture, the heroine's hymns give the "glory to God," but the singing also inspires her in much the same way as listening to a rousing and talented orator. There are at least two audiences here. She could sing anything and please the panther, but once she starts singing the hymns, she also pleases herself. She is born again in a circumstance in which she is likely to die at any moment should she stop singing. Her salvation is a style or rhetoric appropriate and pleasing not only for the beast and for herself but, additionally, for the literary marketplace.

The links between singing and literary orality should call our attention to Spofford's engagement with rhetoric and romance, co-determinant signifiers at the heart of much writing labeled as classic American literature. By the mid-eighteenth century, both rhetoric and romance were understood as archaic—as vestigial as Indians and aristocrats in the modern, mercantile world. Though literary orality may appear reactionary vis-à-vis theories of realism, it is better understood as a progressive attempt by many antebellum writers to revalue romance and rhetoric. Indeed, in the discredited traditions of rhetoric and romance, American writers have often sought an alternative, liberating discourse with which to oppose the hegemony of British novelistic realism. If Cooper's savage eloquence is understood as a turn to romance for powerful rhetorical weapons to wield, then what are we to make of Spofford's inelo- quent, indeed, voiceless, savages? Her silent Indians significantly revise the frontier romances of the 1820s and 1830s, which present potentially disrup- tive and dissident voices. In "Circumstance," Spofford substitutes the hero- ine's singing for aesthetic oratorical set pieces and frames the heroine's performance within a tableau of terror, her hellish captivity. The action of this theatrical scene is a replication of form on the level of content.

According to Valerie Shaw, the short story form "is eternally preoccupied with devising ways to escape its own condition" (16). In such preoccupation, Shaw sees "an independent yet hybrid genre, which connects with other art forms at various points and keeps eluding definition except as an interplay of tensions and antitheses" (16). In "Circumstance," Spofford seeks to escape the consequences of representing savage eloquence; hence, she displaces it in the heroine's singing. Through this displacement, Spofford masks her rhetorical penchant in order to escape detection in a marketplace attuned to realism.

She is like Hawthorne, a classic example of an American romance writer struggling to escape from the hegemony of realism. A decade before "Circum- stance," Hawthorne's *The Scarlet Letter* (1850) turns the frontier romance form inside out. Like Brown, Hawthorne "call[s] forth the passions and engag[es] the sympathy [...] by means hitherto unemployed by preceding authors" (641). But, unlike Brown and Cooper for that matter, Indians only dot the periphery of Hawthorne's seventeenth-century frontier plot.⁹ Like Hester Prynne's scarlet A, the form and content of Hawthorne's novel stand out in American exceptionalist fashion. Hester re-stitches the generic letter of the law, which mirrors Hawthorne's novel refurbishing of the ostensibly threadbare formulas used by Brown and Cooper. By the late 1840s, the form was shopworn and un-marketable like the "decayed wooden warehouses" of Salem, which, as Hawthorne explains in The Custom-House" preface, show "few or no symptoms of commercial life" (4). A good artist and capitalist must hawk a new and improved version; hence, Hawthorne overturns typical race and gender expectations—his Indians are voiceless and reptilian, and as Michael Gilmore argues, Hester behaves very much like the self-reliant masculine heroes of American romance while Arthur Dimmesdale often behaves like the "scribbling women."¹⁰

The powerful gender inversions, particularly, strengthen *The Scarlet Letter's* novelty just as the gender inversions powerfully enhance "Circumstance," as Fetterley points out. Like Hawthorne, Spofford focuses on a frontier woman, although hers is happily married, and she eschews the expansiveness of the romance/novel genre for the formal compression of the short story. From one perspective, her performance illustrates Shaw's observation that "the development of the short story has always been bound up historically with the state of the novel" (4). From another perspective, Spofford's performance reminds us of how the antebellum short story can also be "bound up historically" with captivity narratives as Slotkin has noted. For example, Spofford distils the temporal and geographical shifts of captivity narratives, i.e., the 20 "Removes" in Rowlandson's narrative, into one scene, a hallmark of short story praxis as defined by Shaw: "The suggestive compression of many stories is achieved by summarizing what would, in the realistic novel, be a record of linked events; in place of a discursive sequence of causes and effects, the story can offer a picture" (12).

The "picture" in "Circumstance" is explicitly the heroine's oscillation between despair and the spiritual sublime and implicitly the absent presence of Native Americans. There is a fairy-tale quality to the providential design of "Circumstance." A great and divine force actually rescues the heroine when she is terrorized and faces eminent death. Ironically a fortunate fall, the Indian Devil captivity actually saves her and her family from the Indian massacre. The heroine and her family are homeless but safe. This ending is quite different from the earlier frontier romances, in which the Indians and not the settlers are dispossessed. There is a massacre at the center of *The Last of the Mohicans*, but Cooper's novel closes with white triumph. The devilish Indian, Magua, dies, and the Delaware patriarch, Tamenund, delivers an oration, which "explains" and "naturalizes" white power and possession of the continent:

> 'Go, children of the Lanape; the anger of the Manitto is not done. Why should Tamenund stay? The pale-faces are masters of the earth, and the time of the red-men has not yet come again. My day has been too long. In the morning I saw the sons of Unâmis happy and strong; and yet, before the night has come, have I lived to see the last warrior of the wise race of the Mohicans!' (349–350)

Similarly, at the close of Catharine Maria Sedgwick's *Hope Leslie* (1827), the Indian heroine, Magawisca, eloquently explains why whites and Indians cannot share the colonial landscape: "the Indian and the white man can no more mingle, and become one, than day and night" (349).

The anti-romance ending of "Circumstance" is novel: the nightmare massacre and dispossession sets the heroine and her family adrift in an eerie vanishing landscape. Indeed, even the telltale sign of Indian existence, "a singular foot-print in the snow," appears to be dissolving (96). One might expect Spofford's de-romanticization to signal a realist orientation. From this perspective, the disenchantment may also register the metaphysics of Indian hating evident in colonial texts such as Rowlandson's narrative, in early republic fictions such as Robert Montgomery Bird's *Nick of the Woods* (1837), and in satires like the one in Melville's *The Confidence Man* (1857). Fetterley acknowledges Spofford's racist orientation: "'Circumstance' exemplifies the insidiousness and pervasiveness of the racist imagination in white American literature. Subtle, deadly, and ultimately self-serving, racist assumptions appear in such texts in part because they are so readily available and so easy to invoke, particularly in circumstances in which hostility must be accomplished by stealth" (267).

The disenchantment may, however, signify something more than the metaphysics of Indian hating. Spofford's displacement of savage eloquence illustrates rhetoric's double-edge. Language betrays—it impedes and imparts meaning simultaneously. Is "Circumstance" a disenchanting tale about enchantment or an enchanting tale about disenchantment? The irony illustrates a commonplace of "modern linguistic theory" as defined by Hayden White: "words are merely things among other things in the world," and "they will always obscure as much as they reveal about the objects they are meant to signify," and "therefore, any system of representation is fated to dissolution when the area of things that it consigns to obscurity arises to insist on its own recognition" (232). A realist orientation seeks, ideally, linguistic transparency: words that will not "obscure as much as they reveal about the objects they are meant to signify." The winding sheet symbolizes this predicament. For the realist, it is gothic clap-trap, a gimmick. Opaque, the sheet veils or conceals. Realism as a system of representation will degrade when supposedly moribund romance and rhetoric, "the area of things that it [realism] consigns to obscurity," arise from the dead much like the winding sheet. Spofford obscures through displacement of the explicit representations of savage eloquence common in frontier romances. The heroine's singing, particularly the hymns, masks or obscures rhetoric: for true believers Christian hymns are a-rhetorical, simply the "truth." But, the heroine's ethereal words are, after all, "merely things among other things in the world."

The religious tenor of "Circumstance" sanctions certainty and challenges skepticism. Yet, Alfred Bendixen casts doubt on Spofford's piety in a footnote he appends to "Circumstance": "Spofford's extensive use of old Methodist hymns and Biblical references in this story implies an affirmation of Christian principles which is not characteristic of her other major works at this time" (219). Spofford becomes devout much later in life, according to Bendixen (xxi). The heroine's unselfconscious shift from secular songs to spirituals is, of course, a very self-conscious performance on Spofford's part. It is a rhetorical move that calls into question what Fetterley describes as the "religious dimension of the story," i.e., "God, not man, is the true 'savior.'" In my reading, such a dimension seems tenuous and not certain, a contingent matter of perspective and circumstance.

Where is the heroine's allegiance in Spofford's plot: with her husband or her God? When she realizes her husband will not find and save her, the heroine imagines the worst: to be killed by drowning or dying in combat or from gnawing disease or fire cannot compare with the terror of being killed and eaten by a wild beast. The heroine equates the panther with "the strength of our lower natures let loose" (89) and contrasts that horror with death by fire, which "does not drip our blood into our faces from foaming chaps, nor mouth nor slaver above us with vitality" (89). Here, the terror is physical, psychological, and sexual and rivals Poe. Homelessness defamiliarizes and disenchants the romantic totality. The existential despair of isolation—"The dark, hollow night rose indifferently over her"; "These beautiful haunts that all the summer were hers and rejoiced to share with her their bounty, [...] forgot her now and knew her no longer" (89)—anticipates philosophical alienation in Stephen Crane's poetry and fiction. The anthropomorphism—"beautiful haunts that [...] rejoiced to share with her their bounty"—vanishes, a figment of her imagination, a matter of contingent circumstances rather than certain reality.

This skepticism contrasts with Christianity's transcendent certainty. In the midst of fear, terror, and agony, the heroine is miraculously born again and, thereby, able to replace mortal fear with peace and comfort in God and providence: "How gently all the winter-wrapt things bent toward her then! into what relation with her had they grown! how this common dependence was the spell of their intimacy! how at one with Nature had she become!" (91-92). Here is the spiritual sublime, which re-familiarizes sanctified nature. This powerful reversal signals a possible ending: she can live happily ever after in the spiritual here-after because she pledges allegiance to God. But, Spofford rejects this ending as premature. Indeed, the spiritual climax gives way to earthly authority. Her husband finally arrives, the heroine promptly loses her voice, and in a reversal of fortune, the husband shoots and kills the Indian Devil. The reunited couple returns home to discover their neighbors' tragedy.

Is the spiritual sublime in "Circumstance" a clever satire of religious enthusiasm? Is it authentic spiritual devotion, a return to Christ along the lines of Rowlandson's renewed piety, or is it something akin to the claim of no atheists in foxholes? Or, is the episode of spiritual sublime better understood another way? I cannot separate the heroine from the Indian Devil: while singing hymns, she is as enthralled and as enchanted as the panther. Is hers also a beastly nature? The hymns' theatricality may remind readers of Spofford's own performative gestures. While she may occupy a position of "superiority" vis-à-vis Native Americans, in the literary marketplace she occupies the same lowly position as the Indian vis-à-vis British writers. As for critical prestige, she occupies a similarly subordinate position as a female writer. In this sense, Spofford identifies on some level with the Native Americans.

"Circumstance" emphasizes how performances enchant in the right circumstances. It does not necessarily make sense to suggest, as Fetterley does, that the heroine's

> faith is vindicated and the wisdom of God made plain. She has come through her test of faith triumphant and, though ejected from Eden, perhaps through her sin, perhaps only through her husband's, she has reaffirmed her spiritual nature. And she has been the instrument of her husband's salvation as well; drawn by her voice he has left the doomed settlement and found safety in the woods. (267)

Does "Circumstance" praise God for saving one family while dooming the rest of the settlers? Suggesting the heroine "has been the instrument of her husband's salvation" denies her and her husband agency. The suggestion treats her much as Rowlandson treats Indians—as God's tools. Rowlandson providentially believes "God had an overruling hand" in the actions of the Indians and the responses of the settlers: "the Lord preserve[d] them [Indians] for his Holy ends, and the destruction of many still amongst the English!" (170). In His inscrutable providence, God uses the Indians for righteous revenge, according to Rowlandson: "But now our perverse and evil carriages in the sight of the Lord, have so offended Him, that instead of turning His hand against them [Indians], the Lord feeds and nourishes them up to be a scourge to the whole land" (170). A writer as sophisticated as Spofford hardly seems likely to miss the implications of her ironic identification of the enchanted heroine and the beast.

Rather than Fetterley's eschatological conclusion, I see Spofford tapping into tenuous subjectivity, a condition not unlike the subjectivity that G. K. Chesterton describes in 1906: "'Our modern attraction to the short story [...] is not an accident of form; it is a sign of a real sense of fleetingness and fragility; it means that existence is only an impression, and, perhaps, only an illusion [...]. We have not instinct of anything ultimate and enduring beyond the episode'" (qtd. in Shaw 17). For Shaw, short story compression and duration mirror the "modern experience of being alive" that Chesterton describes (qtd. in Shaw 17). "Circumstance" reflects the "fleetingness and fragility" of "existence" as "illusion" and "impression," of existence as performance and as rhetoric. This sense of what is transitory and frail must be read dialectically against the sense of endurance and strength foregrounded in the spiritual sublime. The transitory and frail are what the spiritual sublime would ultimately obscure. At odds with "the modern experience of being alive," the spiritual sublime constructs the nostalgic fantasy of totality, a would-be "instinct" of something "ultimate and enduring." Spofford handles and manipulates this dialectic in proto-modernist fashion, demonstrating the depth and range of the short story form. Cooper reflects his rhetorical prowess in his Indians' eloquence as much as in Hawk-eye's firepower. Similarly, Melville's linguistic power resounds in Captain Ahab's rhetorical thunder. One can extend the parallels to include not only the mirroring of Hester and Hawthorne's own self-consciousness as an artist but also to Spofford's skillful distillation and reconstitution of rhetoric and romance from the macro- to the micro-level of short story form. In the hey-day of American exceptionalism, one might call Spofford's feat a miniaturization of epic proportions.

Notes

1 In his introduction to Spofford's *"The Amber Gods" and Other Stories*, Alfred Bendixen writes: "By the time of her death on 14 August 1921, Spofford's reputation as a serious writer of fiction was almost completely gone, and her work seemed doomed to oblivion" (xxi).

2 Bendixen discusses Emily Dickinson and William Dean Howells' admiration of "Circumstance" (x).

3   In *The Imaginary Pilgrim: Literature, Intellectual Labor, and the Origins of Personal Life*, Nancy Armstrong and Leonard Tennenhouse argue: "Rowlandson's account of her captivity may seem worlds apart from Richardson's protracted tale of attempted rape—until one considers what each accomplishes by gendering the writing subject" (209).

4   In *Regeneration Through Violence*, Richard Slotkin says, "The great and continuing popularity of these narratives, the uses to which they were put, and the nature of the symbolism employed in them are evidence that they captivity narratives constitute the first coherent myth-literature developed in American for American audiences" (95).

5   In chapter twelve of *Edgar Huntly*, the eponymous hero refers to a panther he encounters as "this savage" and "the savage" (128).

6   The hymns and Biblical verses may remind some readers of Rowlandson's frequent citation of scripture. It makes just as much sense, if not more, to read the singing as Spofford's twist or turn on the trope of savage eloquence found in the popular frontier romances of James Fenimore Cooper and Catharine Maria Sedgwick, whose texts extend and revise Rowlandson and Brown.

7   My point is informed by David Murray's discussion of the "ultimate example of the aestheticisation of the Indians' condition" in *Forked Tongues: Speech, Writing, and Representation in North American Indian Texts* (43).

8   Tony Davies's discussion of eloquence and identity in Humanism informs my analysis of literary orality (78-80).

9   Hawthorne's silent Indians are not represented as being noble savages. Arthur's eloquent preaching, Hester's artistic needlework, and her forest rhetoric, are displacements of romance Indian oratory.

10 In "Hawthorne and the Making of the Middle Class," Gilmore argues that Hester signifies "less Victorian womanhood than the Jacksonian individualist. It is appropriate to use the pronoun 'he' in describing such a person because to Hawthorne's contemporaries, the solitary subject was necessarily a man" (226). Gilmore adds that Arthur Dimmesdale is often "delineated in terms that typify nineteenth-century femininity more than conventional maleness" (229); indeed, according to Gilmore, "Dimmesdale [...] alchemizes into a communal being who looks remarkably like a sentimental novelist" (228); "Dimmesdale's skill at deploying and manipulating sentiment enables him, like the popular women novelists of the 1850s, to bridge the gap between private effect and public occupation" (229). He is like "Stowe and Warner rather than Cooper or Melville," according to Gilmore (229).

Works Cited

Armstrong, Nancy and Leonard Tennenhouse. *The Imaginary Puritan: Literature, Intellecutal Labor, and the Origins of Personal Life*. Berkeley: U of California P, 1992.

Bendixen, Alfred. "Introduction." *"The Amber Gods" and Other Stories*. Ed. Alfred Bendixen. New Brunswick, NJ: Rutgers UP, 1989. ix–xxxiv.

Bird, Robert Montgomery. *Nick of the Woods*. 1837. Ed. Curtis Dahl. New Haven, CT: College and UP, 1967.

Brown, Charles Brockden. *Edgar Huntly; or, Memoirs of a Sleep-Walker*. 1799. Ed. William S. Osborne. New Haven, CT: College and UP, 1973.

Cooper, James Fenimore. *The Last of the Mohicans*. 1826. NY: Penguin, 1986.

Davies, Tony. *Humanism*. London: Routledge, 1997.

Fetterley, Judith. *Provisions: A Reader from 19th-Century American Women*. Ed. Judith Fetterley. Bloomington: Indiana UP, 1985.

Gilmore, Michael T. "Hawthorne and the Making of the Middle Class." *Rethinking Class: Literary Studies and Social Formations*. Ed. Wai Chee Dimock and Michael T. Gilmore. NY: Columbia UP, 1994. 215-238.

Hawthorne, Nathaniel. *The Scarlet Letter, A Romance*. 1850. Vol. 1 of *The Centenary Edition of the Works of Nathaniel Hawthorne*. Ed. William Charvat and Roy Harvey Pearce. Ohio State UP, 1962.

Melville, Herman. *Moby-Dick*. 1851. Ed. Harrison Hayford and Hershel Parker. NY: Norton, 1967.

———. *The Confidence Man: His Masquerade*. 1857. Ed. Hershel Parker. NY: Norton, 1971.

Murray, David. *Forked Tongues: Speech, Writing, and Representation in North American Indian Texts*. London: Pinter Publishers, 1991.

Rowlandson, Mary. *The Sovereignty and Goodness of God*. 1682. *American Captivity Narratives: Selected Narratives with Introduction/Olaudah Equiano, Mary Rowlandson, and Others*. Ed. Gordon M. Sayre. Boston: Houghton Mifflin Company, 2000. 132-176.

Sedgwick, Catharine Maria. *Hope Leslie; or, Early Times in the Massachusetts*. 1827. Ed. Carolyn L. Karcher. NY: Penguin, 1998.

Shaw, Valerie. *The Short Story: A Critical Introduction*. London: Longman, 1983.

Slotkin, Richard. *Regeneration Through Violence: The Mythology of the American Frontier, 1600-1860*. Middletown, CT: Wesleyan UP, 1973.

Spofford, Harriet Prescott. "Circumstance." 1860. *"The Amber Gods" and Other Stories*. Ed. Alfred Bendixen. New Brunswick, NJ: Rutgers UP, 1989. 84-96.

White, Hayden. "Foucault Decoded: Notes From Underground." *Tropics of Discourse: Essays in Cultural Criticism*. Baltimore: The Johns Hopkins UP, 1978. 230-260.

Sexing the Narrator: Gender in Rebecca Harding Davis's "Life in the Iron-Mills"

Ruth Stoner

Universidad de Málaga

In *The Short Story: The Reality of Artifice* Charles E. May charts the origin of the short story, commonly held to have emerged in the midst of nineteenth-century romanticism, from the religious myth of the Middle Ages into the Renaissance, which "marks a shift from the sacred world of Dante's 'divine comedy' to the profane world of Boccaccio's 'human comedy'" (3). Interestingly, it is this shift that also serves as groundwork for both the form and the content of Rebecca Harding Davis's most famous story, "Life in the Iron-Mills." Although Davis never formally theorized about the short story as did so many of her male contemporaries, "Life in the Iron-Mills" is a symbolic link in the evolution of the short story, since it represents—unquestionably better than any other nineteenth-century short story, in my opinion—both a clear break with romanticism and the birth of realism. Davis was obviously well aware of her innovation based on the fact that she ironically compared her realistic/naturalistic world of the working class during the Industrial Revolution to Dante's inferno. "Iron-Mills" is a realistic fictional account of the plight of the immigrant workers in the middle of the nineteenth century, which is now generally recognized by critics as pioneering in subject matter. However, it is my undertaking in this essay to reveal Davis's often overlooked innovation in form, with respect to gender and narration, which in turn is an expression of her radical sexual politics.

Davis's curious narrative style in "Iron-Mills" is a good example of what Margaret Atwood, in an essay titled "Reading Blind," has termed, "the voice of the story" (1396). Atwood's essay attempts to delineate just what she considers to be the particular attributes that make a story good. In this essay Atwood wishes to remind us that stories derive from an oral tradition and that it is this oral quality, the way the teller tells the tale and the way the reader "hears" it, that is most important to the story's value. She then points out the connection between narration and gender:

> Traditionally, both the kitchen gossips and the readers-out-loud have been mothers or grandmothers, native languages have been mother tongues, and the kinds of stories that are told to children have been called nursery tales or old wives' tales [...]. [L]anguage, including the language of our earliest stories, is a verbal matrix, not a verbal patrix [...] . (1397)

"Iron-Mills" is a well-told story in which the author establishes a close relationship—too close for comfort—between narrator and reader. Davis's narrator does not simply address the "Reader" (usually affectionately) as we typically find in many nineteenth-century authors, especially those that she admired such as Stowe and Eliot. The narrator Davis has created goes much farther by admonishing the reader whom he/she derisively addresses as "amateur psychologist," among many other equally abusive epithets (12). Thus, Davis, through an original exploitation of such simple and common literary devices as were direct address and the frame plot at that time, not only questions the Victorian sexual values of the era, among many more apparent social issues, but denounces them both overtly, in the gendering of her characters, as well as covertly, in the obscurity of her first person narrator and the "strength" of her language, giving the story a rich and complex textured effect. The final irony lies in the fact that the author herself was first perceived and lauded by her early readers as male, but later condemned for her unladylike manners when the truth was known, thus making her a victim of the same prejudices she was denouncing.

On the verge of the outbreak of the Civil War and while literally sitting on the Mason-Dixon line, this then unknown writer from the Appalachians bravely sent her extraordinary tale to the most prestigious literary magazine in the country, the *Atlantic Monthly*. As was the custom, writers, especially women writers, published either anonymously or under a masculine-sounding pseudonym. Therefore, it was not at all surprising that when Rebecca Harding was surprised by the reception of a letter of acceptance, together with a fifty-dollar bill and a request to change the title, her only dilemma was focused on securing her privacy. She quickly replied to the editor:

> I would prefer when this article is published—my name would not be given as a contributor. Is it necessary for me to go in search of a name—or shall I need any? If it is not a trouble will you be kind enough to tell me this before it is printed. Meanwhile, permit me to remain,

>   Respectfully yours
>   R. B. Harding (Langford 14)

Thus, the story was published simply "by a new contributor," perhaps unwittingly, perhaps intentionally, concealing not only the name of the writer, but implicitly the sex.

From its first gripping appearance, the critical response took for granted that "Iron-Mills" was the work of a man, not based on its anonymity, but on its style and subject matter. This is reflected in Davis's obituary fifty years later, which described the fame of "Life in the Iron-Mills": "Published anonymously, there was much speculation as to the authorship. It was thought that the author must be a man, the picture being drawn with a stern and artistic realism that gave no hint of a feminine hand" ("Rebecca Harding Davis Dies," *Philadelphia Inquirer* 8b).

Today, a reader may venture to ask just what was considered the nature of a "masculine hand." Could it be something so abstract as "stern and artistic realism?" And that was not the complete extent of the assessment of "Iron-Mills" as can be observed from the reviews published much later, long after the identity of the writer was well known, since she started signing her stories and articles with her real name, including the "Mrs." which would ensure her respectability: "A story of more than ordinary interest, written in a clear, forcible style, such as, were it not for the name on the title-page, would lead to its being ascribed to a masculine pen" ("Literary Notices," Rev. of "Kitty's Choice" 184).

And, if attributing the story to a masculine pen because of its "forcible style" is not enough, some of the reviewers also had no qualms about expressing themselves in no uncertain prescriptive terms:

> full of interest, but written in a style somewhat broad and coarse, especially from the pen of a woman. It does not, in our opinion, add to the strength of a really powerful book, to add profanity to its expressions, and put oaths in the mouths of women as well as men ("Literary Notices," Rev. of "A Law unto Herself" 435).

We find such words as "strength" and "powerful" the most often repeated by Davis's critics, thus leading us to presume that these must be those masculine qualities—the fact that she refused to employ the sentimental rhetoric favored by the majority of the women writers of that era.

But if we quarry a little deeper into the language and rhetorical devices employed in this pioneering work, we discover that anonymity is also applied to the narration; moreover, the sexual identity of the characters in the main plot is singular. The questions of gender, narration and projection have all come to our attention because of the re-publication of "Iron-Mills" in 1972 as the Feminist Press's inaugural piece, edited by Tillie Olsen. The main character, Hugh Wolfe, an illiterate puddler in an iron mill, has a real talent for sculpting, his social status being responsible for turning him into a frustrated artist. In her "Biographical Introduction" Olsen argues that Hugh is a projection of Davis herself, the unrecognized artist. Olsen may have been influenced by Davis's description of the puddler in feminine terms: "In the mill he was known as one of the girl-men: Molly Wolfe was his *sobriquet*" (24). This is the first clear and direct illustration of the amalgamated genders that pervade the entire work.

The analysis is complicated still further by the introduction of the statue that Hugh has sculpted out of the flesh-colored refuse (called "korl") produced by the iron refinement process. This statue is of a big, strong woman, symbol of the working-woman, in striking contrast to the typical slender and delicate marble sculpture which we have come to idealize: "There was not one line of beauty or grace in it: a nude woman's form, muscular, grown coarse with labor, the powerful limbs instinct with some one poignant longing" (32). It seems only logical to then interpret the female statue, in turn, as the projection of the sculptor/artist himself—the worker filled with a longing, searching for a reason to live. However, there is a female character, Deborah, Hugh's cousin, also a worker in a textile factory, who, because of her large and disfigured body, appears to be the actual model for the korlwoman. And both of these female figures, the woman and her projection in the statue, are the only characters who transcend the foul life produced by capitalism, although Deborah survives only as a kind of nun, forfeiting her sexual nature.

The conclusion the reader is likely to come to is a fusion, perhaps better stated as a confusion, of gender that the writer wished to graphically present. Davis intentionally offers the reader no less than three "indefinite individuals," if not to term them "androgynous": Hugh, Deborah and the korlwoman. Jane Rose describes them as "sexual anomalies" (191). Once realizing the nature of Davis's characters, it is then obvious to assume that the seemingly "neutral" narrator of the frame plot is exactly what the writer wanted to create, but in a much more subtle way.

The sex of the narrator in "Iron-Mills" has been a subject of debate for many of the more recent Davis scholars, branching off from Olsen's interpretation of the narrator as a trapped writer, shut up in an upstairs room of the house where the workers had lived thirty years previously, writing secretly by night (69–78). The model for Charlotte Perkins Gilman's "Yellow Wallpaper" is evident.[1] Although Sharon Harris, the leading biographer of Davis, argues a contrary theory, she defines what would be the traditional inference, the tendency of most modern readers to confuse the narrator with the author: "Critics often assume that the voices of Davis and her narrator are interchangeable" (28). This is the stance Walter Hesford, in 1977, takes as a matter of course—he doesn't even question the fact that the narrator could be someone besides the author, using feminine pronouns in all his references: "The Narrator, though secluded above the crowd *she* observes from *her* window [...]" (72, emphasis added). Jean Pfaelzer, in 1981, also coincides with Olsen with reference to the narrator/writer, "looking at the world from *her* window" (239, emphasis added), reiterating the aspect of being trapped in a house. In 1990, Maribel Molyneaux attempted to elaborate this interpretation, alluding to an unknown narrator at the beginning of the story who is later converted into an active participant of the drama and who is at the same time Davis: "By transforming herself in the story's concluding pages into an actor in the story we have witnessed her write, the narrator becomes, as much as any narrator can become, an inscription of the woman writer's own self" (165). Nevertheless, this position requires a transformation of the sex of the narrator from one century to the next, since as long as the story's narrator remained "anonymous," it would be perceived as masculine, yet upon identifying the author it would become a feminine voice. In other words, both Olsen's and Molyneaux's interpretations are subject to the biography of Davis and do not take into account the 1861 reader.

Another study of Davis takes a similar traditional stance, but arrives at a different conclusion. Rose, in 1990, declares that on writing "Iron-Mills" Davis supposed that the reader would imagine a male author and therefore a male narrator:

> Davis mediates gender coding in her narrative technique, which attempts to transcend female restrictions by acquiring male license. To this end, she often assumes a masculine narrative voice, as she does in "Iron-Mills." Her narrator's sex is not designated in this tale; and therefore, particularly in 1861, it would be assumed to be masculine. (191)

This position would be that of the objective, omniscient narrator, who relates the story in the first person but does not maintain a direct relationship with the main plot. We might call "it" the "mysterious stranger" as some critics have done, but still assuming "it" is masculine. Or, as an unknown "neutered" artist that has rented the house, as William Shurr in 1991 proposes (245).

Nevertheless, the narrator of "Iron-Mills" is related to the workers—not merely a voice from nowhere that is going to tell an old story: "As I stand here, idly [...] fragments of an old story float up before me [...]" (13), but as a character who resides in the same house that the Wolf family did, who knows their private life and who at "present" has the statue of the korlwoman in her library, "hid behind a curtain" (64). Molyneaux correctly observes that the narrator, by the end of the story, turns into a writer.

This fact has led other scholars to reject the autobiographical link and to search for the narrator's identity among the characters of the main plot. It cannot be Hugh because he commits suicide and would therefore not be around to tell the story. But even apart from the fact that he does not survive, it is obvious that the narrator is not from the same social class as the workers, since the language employed by the narrator is middle class, refined, not the particular vernacular that Davis places in the mouths of the Welsh immigrants. Based on the function of the dialects and the Christian elements, Shurr, in 1991, posits the identity of the narrator by resorting to a rational and very original argument against the common opinion that the narrator is Davis. Shurr argues that since there can be no link between Davis and the workers, it is impossible to place her within the house. This allows him to search for a narrator among the upper-class characters of the story, substituting the philanthropist Mitchell for Davis. Mitchell is one of a group of polished dilettantes who visit the factory one night, as if it were a museum, comparing it to the Inferno. These gentlemen, who in some respects represent the old order of Romanticism, discover Hugh's sculpture and it is Mitchell who identifies with the potential artistic talent of the worker: "Mitchell alone is described as the one who 'saw the soul' of Wolfe" (250). Although all of the visitors speak of saving the workers, no one is prepared to do anything, except to plant the false hope of a dream in the head of a man who is destined to die a ghastly death. So, Shurr hypothesizes that Mitchell, through a Christian conversion experience motivated by his guilt over Hugh's suicide, donates his property to the poor and goes to live in the working-class neighborhood to continue creating art. However interesting this theory may be, there is no hint of any of this in Davis's narrative.

In 1995 Richard Hood points out how distorted Shurr's theory seems and offers a much more logical hypothesis that Deborah is the narrator: "only Deborah can claim both the experience *of* the story and the ability to tell *about* the story" (78-80). Deborah, with the help of the Quaker community appearing at the end of the story, has the opportunity of becoming educated without losing the lessons of life in the factory; her link to the house is obvious. But the perception of masculinity for the 1861 readers continues to cast a shadow over the question of gender. Nonetheless, the fact that Davis included a hopeful ending that depended on the Quaker community, exemplifies, in my opinion beyond a doubt, that she was making a political statement, not only concerning Capitalism and the American Dream, but concerning women's position in society, since the Quakers happened to be virtually the only religious group that allowed women a public voice. Davis's supplying the strong working woman with a voice seems a likely interpretation knowing what we do about Davis.

Returning to Sharon Harris's argument, she clearly does not share the theory that Davis is the narrator, explaining, "at significant junctures in the text, she [Davis] separates herself from the narrator" (28). Harris goes on to illustrate the impossibility of a direct connection between the author and narrator: "Three times in the first pages of 'Life,' [...] the narrator refers to *her* 'idle' thoughts and actions; these asides are the first significant clues that Davis and her narrator should not be considered one voice" (31, emphasis added). Again considering the fact, confirmed by the language, that the narrator is from the same social class as the reader of the *Atlantic Monthly*, Harris takes advantage of so much "iron" and conceives of an ironic turn—the reader her/himself is at the same time the narrator: "recognizing at last the ironic twist of Davis's narrative structure. The author's desire all along has been to place the reader in the role of one who 'knows' [...] the reader must become the active participant who unveils the realities of life [...]" (55-6). Thus, Harris explains the symbolism of the statue behind the curtain as the necessity of the readers to hide the workers from view. This theory is attractive since it does not imply the identity of the (anonymous) author; but even more because it places a literary device, the active reader, associated with Modernism, at least one century before the accepted appearance in the 1920s.

In a recent article on "Iron-Mills," Sheila Hughes dodges the gender question with the now politically correct, "the korl figure has been preserved and stands near the narrator, in a corner of *her/his* library" (115, emphasis added). But this solution is not as satisfying as it may seem. As Judith Fetterley warns in a re-edition of the story, the force is in the narration: "As readers, we are rarely allowed to forget the presence of this narrative voice or to escape from the pressure it places on us to realign our vision and our values. Much of the energy of the text relies on this implicit dialogue between narrator and readers" (310).

Davis's narrator is, therefore, a good example of what Charles E. May terms, "the juxtaposition of objective with subjective points of view [...] in which the narrator seems at once immediately involved and aesthetically detached" but which he ascribes as unique to certainly one of Davis's disciples of naturalism, Stephen Crane (13).[2] Davis's innovative narrator, as has just been shown, is much more complex than Crane's and saw the light of publication and critical acclaim before Crane was born.

As Margaret Atwood concludes her essay on what constitutes a good story, what she looks for in a story is exactly the same thing that children look for when they listen to tales, "They want their attention held, and so do I" (1398). Through her unique narrator Davis succeeds brilliantly in holding the attention of the reader and providing an unforgettable reading experience. But words are not enough. Davis the artist, as well as the moralist, makes use of the symbolic and transcendental sculpture to embed a vision of a new sense of gender on her readers. Interpreting "Iron-Mills" with the seeming intention of the author to intrigue the gender and to conceal her own identity in anonymity, together with some understanding of the difference between a Victorian and a twenty-first-century audience only contribute to the richness of "Life in the Iron-Mills." My conclusion is that Rebecca Harding Davis was a very private woman with a notion of gender that was far too complex and "modern" for the year 1861. Her contribution to the development of the short story, in form as well as subject matter, should no longer be overlooked. In his discussion of the development of the short story, May summarizes what he considers to be the most significant nineteenth-century contributions and credits Poe and Hawthorne with "psychological obsession" (8); Davis provides "philosophical obsession" through her focus on the most important social issues and currents of thought, a focus both aesthetic and didactic, subjective and objective.

Notes

1   In fact, Davis herself suffered from nervous depression and was treated by the same "rest cure" as Gilman. However, the onset of Davis's illness was a couple of years after publishing "Iron-Mills," although the cause seems to be the same as Gilman's, the overwhelming domestic duties in marriage that prevented her from obtaining personal creative satisfaction. For further details, see Harris.

2   Stephen Crane was a friend of Davis's son, Richard Harding Davis, himself a famous writer. For more information on the Davis-Crane connection see Langford.

Works Cited

Atwood, Margaret. "Reading Blind." *The Story and Its Writer: An Introduction to Short Fiction.* Ed. Ann Charters. Boston: Bedford Books, 1991. 1395–99.

Davis, Rebecca Harding. "Life in the Iron Mills." *"Life in the Iron Mills" and Other Stories.* Old Westbury, NY: Feminist Press, 1985.

Fetterley, Judith. *Provisions: A Reader from Nineteenth Century American Women.* Bloomington: Indiana UP, 1985.

Harris, Sharon M. *Rebecca Harding Davis and American Realism.* Philadelphia: U of Pennsylvania P, 1991.

Hesford, Walter. "Literary Contexts of 'Life in the Iron-Mills.'" *American Literature* 49.1 (1977): 70-85.

Hood, Richard A. "Framing a 'Life in the Iron Mills.'" *Studies in American Fiction* 23 (1995): 73-84.

Hughes, Sheila Hassell. "Between Bodies of Knowledge There Is a Great Gulf Fixed: A Liberationist Reading of Class and Gender in *Life in The Iron Mills.*" *American Quarterly* 49 (1997): 113-37.

Langford, Gerald. *The Richard Harding Davis Years: A Biography of a Mother and Son.* NY: Holt, Rinehart and Winston, 1961.

"Literary Notices." Rev. of "Kitty's Choice." By Rebecca Harding Davis. *Godey's Lady's Book* 88 (Feb 1874): 184.

———. 1878. Rev. of "*A Law unto Herself.*" By Rebecca Harding Davis. *Godey's Lady's Book* 96 (May 1878): 435.

May, Charles E. *The Short Story: The Reality of Artifice.* NY: Twayne, 1995.

Molyneaux, Maribel W. "Sculpture in the Iron Mills: Rebecca Harding Davis's Korl Woman." *Women's Studies* 17.3-4 (1990): 157-177.

Olsen, Tillie. Introduction. "*Life in the Iron Mills*" *and Other Stories.* By Rebecca Harding Davis. Old Westbury, NY: Feminist Press, 1985.

Pfaelzer, Jean. "Rebecca Harding Davis: Domesticity, Social Order, and the Industrial Novel." *International Journal of Women's Studies* 4 (1981): 234-244.

"Rebecca Harding Davis Dies at Her Son's Home." Obituary. *Philadelphia Inquirer.* 30 Sept 1910: 8b.

Rose, Jane Atteridge. "Reading 'Life in the Iron-Mills' Contextually: A Key To Rebecca Harding Davis's Fiction." *Conversations: Contemporary Critical Theory and the Teaching of Literature.* Ed. Charles Moran and Elizabeth F. Penfield. Urbana: National Council of Teachers of English, 1990. 187-199.

Shurr, William H. "*Life in the Iron-Mills*: A Nineteenth-Century Conversion Narrative." *American Transcendental Quarterly* 5 (1991): 245-258.

The Short Story as Feminist Forum: Louisa May Alcott's "Pauline's Passion and Punishment"

Miriam López-Rodríguez

Universidad de Málaga

Although better known for her novels for young readers such as *Little Women*, American author Louisa May Alcott (1832-1888) wrote in a wide range of genres including novels for adults, poems, melodramas, newspaper editorials and short stories for children and adults, having published well over 100 short stories during her lifetime. All these works made her one of the most popular writers of her time; in fact, literary historian Fred Lewis Pattee has described one of Alcott's collections of short stories for children, *Flower Fables; or, Fairy Tales* (1855) as among the "leading short stories of [its] decade" (164). However, from the moment of her death until the mid-twentieth century, Louisa May Alcott, like so many of her contemporaries, such as Harriet Beecher Stowe, Rebecca Harding Davis, Sarah Orne Jewett, Mary Wilkins Freeman, had been ignored by the academic world for a number of reasons: she has been ignored because of her gender, underrated for writing for the young, and misunderstood by those who considered her writing too Victorian. This began to change slightly in the 1940s when Leona Rostenberg, after carefully reading Alcott's diaries and some of the periodicals of her time, discovered that many of the short stories for adults published anonymously or under the pseudonym A.M. Barnard were in fact the work of Alcott.[1] Although Rostenberg mentioned the titles of the identified stories, she did not publish them; in 1975 and 1976, her partner Madeleine B. Stern finally published them for the first time under the author's real name in the collections *Behind a Mask: The Unknown Thrillers of Louisa May Alcott* and *Plots and Counterplots: More Unknown Thrillers of Louisa May Alcott*. These short stories represent an innovative contribution to the genre since they offer a common element: the substitution of a *femme fatale* female protagonist in place of the expected *ingénue*.

These thrillers, in striking contrast to the novels Alcott wished to acknowledge, immediately attracted the attention of critics—especially feminists—as they portrayed women who were far from the Victorian ideal of "True Womanhood," as defined by Barbara Welter:

> The attributes [...] by which a woman judged herself and was judged by her husband, her neighbors and society could be divided into four cardinal virtues—piety, purity, submissiveness and domesticity. Put them all together and they spelled mother, daughter, sister, wife—woman. (152)

From that moment onwards, the academic world began to show interest in Alcott's short stories for adults, which came to be classified as examples of nineteenth-century feminism. Nevertheless, the rest of her work continued to be ignored by scholars such as Madeleine Stern, Elizabeth Evans Sachs, and Karen Halttunen who felt that Alcott only dared express her reformist ideals when protected by the mask of anonymity (Stern and Shealy xi; Stern, *Plots* viii-ix; Sachs 35; Halttunen 242).

Recent research on Alcott's work has already proved her novels were far from advocating nineteenth-century patriarchal convention (López-Rodríguez). In fact her heroines seldom embraced the cardinal virtues of piety, purity, submissiveness and domesticity, being much closer to the radical protagonists of the short stories for adults than Alcott critics have been willing to admit. Although there are differences between the two genres—novels for adolescents and short stories for adults—I argue that the similarities between the two groups of female protagonists are far greater than the differences.

Just as she did in her novels for the young, Alcott sugar-coated her radical criticism of patriarchy, muffling it in the conventions of the Gothic thriller—very close to those of the melodrama and the modern soap opera—in order to secure the publication of stories which undermined many of the notions sanctioned by the ruling class. Obviously, she succeeded, as the original analysis critics made of the thrillers focused so much attention on the murders, mind control, madness, hashish experimentation, opium addiction and other sensationalist elements, while defining their female protagonists as simple violators of society's conventions without any feminist agenda. However, these women are more than ruthless daredevils, they represent Alcott's boldest criticism of patriarchal society and the role it allots women. To illustrate this point her thriller, "Pauline's Passion and Punishment" (1863, reprinted in Stern's *Behind a Mask*), offers an excellent opportunity to focus on Alcott's creation of a radical female protagonist: the way Pauline behaves, the motivation behind her behavior, the way her behavior compares to that of her foil and how the men in the story react to this behavior.

But even before entering into the specific analysis of this short story, something should be said about Alcott's choice of the short story genre and the Gothic-thriller subgenre, since the choice in itself is a political statement. From the business point of view, the short story has four main characteristics that made it very attractive to a writer like Alcott, who depended economically on the success of her writing. In the first place, being shorter than the traditional novel, these stories adapted far better to Alcott's other indispensable domestic duties, therefore making it easier for her to work on them while cooking, cleaning and sewing. Secondly, this very shortness made it easier than novels for the women readers, who, after all, were the prospective audience who bought the magazines in which the stories were published. Thirdly, short stories were easier to sell to publishers at a time when most periodicals included short stories and serialized novels.[2] Alcott herself explained this in June 1862 in a letter to her close friend Alf Whitman: "I intend to illuminate the Ledger with a blood & thunder tale as they are easy to compo[z]e & are better paid than moral & elaborate works of Shakespeare" (Stern, *Behind a Mask* vii). Books were generally beyond the budgets of most households and lending libraries were few at that time. And, fourthly, apart from the original publication as an independent piece of work, short stories offered the writer the possibility of gaining further economic benefits through later collections. These four features made the short story a very practical genre, indeed, and exemplify Alcott's profound grasp of her audience as well as of the business world.

Alcott's choice of subgenre the thriller, one of the earliest popularized genres in America together with tales and sketches (Voss 4), must have been motivated by Alcott's need to find a vent for her tensions, for the stress accumulated in years of being told she was not the woman her father and patriarchal society expected her to be, what Stern defines as "a psychological catharsis" (*Behind a Mask* xiv). Gothic thrillers have often been defined as escapist literature for readers who want to break away from the monotony of their civilized lives. This is also true of the author who finds it extremely suffocating to adapt herself to the model of womanhood sanctioned by her society. It is this very fact that explains Alcott's sympathetic portrait of her female "villains," since, not only does she refuse to criticize and punish her women protagonists, although the title would seem to suggest this, she offers a forgiving image of them. As Kim Wells explains, this is Alcott's way of showing "her admiration for their ability to guide their own fates rather than to let others rule them." In spite of this admiration, Alcott did, so to speak, keep up appearances to the end by having her Gothic thrillers published without giving away her identity. As she commented to a friend:

> I think my natural ambition is for the lurid style. I indulge in gorgeous fancies and wish that I dared inscribe them upon my pages and set them before the public [...]. How should I dare to interfere with the proper grayness of old Concord? [...] No, my dear, I shall always be a wretched victim to the respectable traditions of Concord. (Stern, *Behind a Mask* xxvi)

The dominant culture in nineteenth-century America dictated very strict social rules about what was right and wrong, about what women could do and could write about. Daring to break these conventions meant, in the most extreme cases, social isolation. But even when things were not taken so far, it meant not having one's work published. To stay within the limits of what was socially acceptable, women writers with liberal ideals could either silence that reform part of their ideology or, as Alcott chose, publish their work anonymously or under a pseudonym or as subversively embedded in a superficially "safe" narrative. Of course, there was still the risk of being found out—but this was far less dangerous than the risk of writing openly against the norms of society. Remaining at home, writing children's literature and performing the role of dutiful daughter and sister allowed Alcott to write the stories that defied prevalent notions of true womanhood, marriage, interracial relations, drug use, and so on. As Madeleine B. Stern stated in her introduction to *The Feminist Alcott*, the heroines in her thrillers "may never have concerned themselves with voting privileges, but they ruled or sought to rule in men's domain. They grasped privileges denied them by half the human race, and whatever the degree of their success, they courageously challenged the status quo" (xxi-xxii).

"Pauline's Passion and Punishment" was first published, anonymously, in *Frank Leslie's Illustrated Newspaper* in 1863.[3] Set in a Cuban coffee plantation, it tells the story of Pauline Valary, a middle-class woman who lost family and fortune long ago and since then has made a living working as the companion of a young girl. The plot itself begins when Pauline receives a letter from her fiancé Gilbert Redmond who announces that soon after leaving Cuba he married an American heiress. Furious at Gilbert's infidelity, Pauline asks for help from her young Cuban friend, Manuel Laroche who, being madly in love with her, offers to kill the traitor. But Pauline has better plans for Gilbert:

> Such revenge is brief and paltry [...]. There are fates more terrible than death; weapons more keen than poniards, more noiseless than pistols. Women use such, and work out a subtler vengeance than men can conceive. Leave Gilbert to remorse—and me. (Alcott 110)

Here, Alcott presents two of the key ideas found in all her short stories for adults: first, that women get revenge in a different way than men, less bloody but not necessarily less painful and, second, that women do not behave in that way unless provoked by men, that is, women are basically good at heart and it is only men's unfaithfulness that turns them into revengeful creatures. It is men with their ungentlemanly behavior who transform generous hearts into spiteful ones: "It is weak, wicked, and unwomanly; yet I persist as relentlessly as any Indian on a war trail. See me as I am, not the gay girl you have known, but a revengeful woman" (Alcott 114).

And it is precisely this element, women taking justice into their own hands, that constitutes Louisa May Alcott's main innovative contribution to the Gothic short story. Generally in this subgenre, just as in melodrama, the hero and the villain act while the heroine waits passively to have her fate decided by the men in her life. Alcott changes this, turning the traditional *ingénue* into a *femme fatale*; her heroines know what they want and how to get it, regardless of social conventions. They can control their own emotions and manipulate others' in order to achieve their goals, which was certainly an uncommon feature among nineteenth-century literary heroines.

Returning to the plot and Pauline's plan, the feminist protagonist breaks conventions once more when it is she who proposes marriage to a younger and richer man, Manuel Laroche. Honest enough to confess to her friend that she is not in love with him, she nevertheless manages to convince Manuel to marry her. Thus, she is transformed not into Gilbert's social equal but into his superior, since Pauline's husband is wealthier than Gilbert's wife. The newly married Pauline and Manuel leave Cuba in search of the Redmonds. Finding them in an elegant holiday resort, they stay in the same hotel and attend the same social events. As part of her revenge plans, Pauline makes Gilbert fall in love with her again while Manuel becomes best friend to Gilbert's wife, Babie, and he also manages to push Gilbert into enormous gambling debts. One day, while the two couples are walking near a waterfall, Gilbert pushes Manuel down; childish Babie, who is by then in love with Manuel, holds on to him for protection dragging both of them down into the waterfall. The original lovers, Pauline and Gilbert, are left as survivors—but not necessarily as winners. Alcott writes a surprisingly modern, open ending as we readers are not told what Gilbert and Pauline's future is to be. Nevertheless, we know Pauline has succeeded in her search for revenge as Gilbert has been humiliated, jilted, and now his life is in Pauline's hands as she has witnessed him murder Manuel. In any case, Pauline is portrayed throughout the story as a triumphant ice queen who succeeds in holding control over her life and the life of the other characters. Moreover, she ends up as a wealthy and independent widow—unpunished for her plotting, unrepentant of the deaths caused, offering an ironic twist to the denouement.

A third element common to all of Alcott's thrillers is the use of theatrical elements. Three of the main characters, Pauline, Manuel and Gilbert, refer to the theatre in one way or another, illustrating Shakespeare's idea that all the world's a stage: "I see a future full of interest, a stage whereon I could play a stirring part," "I have played the lover for your sake, now play the man of the world for mine," "[Manuel] played his part," "You possess dramatic skill. Use it for my sake," "I have [...] made this balcony a little stage for the performance of our version of the honeymoon for one spectator" (Alcott 113, 118, 119, 135). Many of her heroines are or have been professional actresses, but, what is more important from the feminist point of view, all of them have to act in order to survive in their society. They know that in their patriarchal world what one appears to be is even more important than what one really is. Therefore, all of Alcott's heroines wear masks as means of survival, giving significance to Stern's title. These women know what is socially sanctioned and therefore they know how to keep up appearances to achieve their goal, just as their author did. They may not be "true women" at heart (they are passionate, brave, independent, etc.), but they know perfectly well what they are supposed to be, so they perform the role society has allocated to them, not because they are afraid of the consequences if they don't but because this helps them obtain their goals. This is Alcott's way of ridiculing patriarchal notions of propriety and stressing the artificiality of women's position in their society.

Again and again, Alcott highlights the hypocrisy of society and its double standards in relation to men and women. This is what forces people, especially her female characters, to wear masks to hide their true nature. Women are in greater danger than men as their reputation can be easily tainted: "I am a deserted woman, and in the world we are going to my name may become the sport of that man's cruel tongue." (Alcott 115-116). But once more the heroines of Alcott's short stories for adults are perfectly aware of this necessity and, instead of merely accepting their fate, they always fight back, using patriarchal conventions about women to their own advantage.

In opposition to Pauline, Alcott offers her readers a female character who portrays traditional womanhood, the passionless Babie Redmond. Even her name exemplifies her expected role of childlike woman. Despite knowing that Gilbert married her only for her money, and in spite of his coldness towards her and his obvious attraction for his former fiancée, she remains passive and is finally punished for it by Alcott. Not even being hit by her husband makes her react; in fact, the only time she takes the initiative there are negative consequences as it causes her own death as well as Manuel's. This single reaction is not caused by awareness of her situation but, on the contrary, by fear and the substitution of her former idol, Gilbert, for a new one in Manuel. The scene is significant as it graphically demonstrates the patriarchal notion that a woman's life is worth nothing without her man, and, moreover, Alcott's notion that such a passionless partner becomes an unbearable burden that can only cause sorrow.

A fourth element of this short story, common to Alcott's writing, is the importance given to certain aspects of the physical description of the two main characters, Pauline and Manuel, and the connection it has with their personalities. Pauline is described as a pale blue-eyed blonde while her husband is a handsome Cuban with dark hair and dark eyes; in spite of the differences in appearance, they are both passionate people. To understand the full significance of this, and why it is a constant in Alcott's fiction, it is necessary to go back in time to Alcott's childhood and the harm caused to her by some elements of her father's ideology.

The transcendentalist philosopher Bronson Alcott held among his eccentric notions the idea that pale, blue-eyed blondes like himself were morally superior to dark-skinned people who, according to him, had a demonic quality in them. Applied to his own family, this notion divided the Alcott household into two well differentiated groups: on one side Bronson with his daughters Anna, Elizabeth and May; on the other side, his wife Abba and Louisa, whose darker skin, chestnut hair and brown eyes labeled them as inferior. His two "demons," as Bronson often referred to them, seemed to accept this prejudice as evidence was against them: according to Bronson, fair people were angelic, calm and passionless, while darker looking people were impulsive, passionate, uncontrollable and ruled by the heart rather than by the head. This was clearly the case of Abba and Louisa, so both women came to believe Bronson was right in his prejudice against them.

However, as an adult, Louisa May Alcott made a point of portraying most of her heroines as blondes who nevertheless lack none of the passions usually assigned to brunettes. Pauline may have a fair complexion, and she may even be able to control her impulses in public, but she is certainly as passionate as her Cuban husband.

From a theoretical point of view, Alcott was faithful to some typical elements of the short story such as unity, compression, significant attention to symbolic detail and the use of the metaphor. A theoretical analysis of "Pauline's Passion and Punishment" shows how the concept of unity—a single character, a single event, a single emotion (May 109)—is preserved with the whole plot revolving around one woman (Pauline Valary), one action (causing

Gilbert Redmond as much pain as possible) and one emotion (seeking revenge). With regard to the brevity of the story, the characters are developed with just a few strokes of the brush, but sufficient to make readers understand who they are and what the reasons behind their behavior are; at least in the cases of Pauline and Manuel, as Gilbert and, above all, Babie are mere outlines. The exposition needed to make the plot understandable is so condensed it even includes the catalyst that begins the conflict so that the climax occupies most of the length of the narration.

And this brings us to the closure of the story. As Charles E. May explains "the shortness of the form seems inevitably to require some sense of intensity or intensification of structure and emphasis on the end" (116). In the case of "Pauline's Passion" the reader is left wanting more. The melodramatic ending leaves the former lovers Pauline and Gilbert standing at the top of the waterfall staring at each other, surprised at this unexpected end of their marriages. Author Louisa May Alcott does not explain what will happen to these two characters: Has Pauline's revenge come to an end? Will Pauline have Gilbert prosecuted for killing Manuel?

Far from considering this open ending an indication of Alcott's inability to finish the story "properly," it could be interpreted as evidence of the "openness" left to Pauline: after having been jilted by Gilbert, after having seen his way of treating his wife Babie and his unwillingness to control his gambling problem, Pauline finally realizes Gilbert is not the charming prince she thought him to be. There is no danger she may fall for his lies again. On the other hand, Manuel's death suitably leaves Pauline as a wealthy widow. Manuel was a charming young man, but Pauline was not in love with him; what was a good companionship agreement could have turned into a bitter marriage had Manuel insisted on having a "real" marriage. Even if he accepted the fact that Pauline would never feel the passion for him that she had felt for Gilbert, it left her in an uneasy situation as she would continue to depend on Manuel financially and would not have the freedom to find true love. However, Manuel's death at the hands of Gilbert makes Pauline a rich single young woman with no worries in the world. The end of her confrontation with Gilbert may not be the one she had planned, but it is equally successful, as he is left humiliated (his wife had fallen in love with Manuel), heartbroken (after realizing he still loves Pauline he is turned down by her), and with an uncertain future (not only because Pauline could have him arrested for murder, but also because Babie's family could show some reticence to hand him over what is left of her inheritance).

In conclusion, Louisa May Alcott creates in "Pauline's Passion and Punishment" a new type of character within the subgenre of Gothic short stories, a strong indomitable woman with courage enough to defy society and to change the way women were treated by men. As Pauline Valary comments on Gilbert's jilting her: "This is an old, old story, but it shall have a new ending" (Alcott 112). This same heroine remains consistent in Alcott's thrillers. In this way Alcott obtained some sort of "poetic justice" by allowing her female characters to challenge society's prejudices and to express the anger she was taught to hide.

Notes

1 For more information, see Leona Rostenberg, "Some Anonymous and Pseudonymous Thrillers of Louisa May Alcott," *Papers of the Bibliographical Society of America*, 37:2 (1943). Cited in Stern & Shealy, xii.

2 See Pattee on the relevance of nineteenth-century periodicals for the development of the American short story, 164–67.

3 All references to "Pauline's Passion and Punishment" are to Stern's edition of 1975.

Works Cited

Alcott, Louisa May (originally published anonymously). "Pauline's Passion and Punishment." *Frank Leslie's Illustrated Newspaper* XV:379–380 (January 3, 10, 1863). Rpt. in *Behind a Mask: The Unknown Thrillers of Louisa May Alcott*. Ed. Madeleine B. Stern. NY: William Morrow, 1975.

Halttunen, Karen. "The Domestic Drama of Louisa May Alcott." *Feminist Studies* 10:2 (1984): 233–254.

López-Rodríguez, Miriam. *Louisa May Alcott, la feminista oculta tras los convencionalismos*. Málaga: Servicio de Publicaciones de la Universidad de Málaga, 2001.

May, Charles E. *The Short Story: The Reality of Artifice*. NY: Twayne Publishers, 1995.

Pattee, Fred Lewis. *The Development of the American Short Story*. NY: Biblo & Tannen, 1975.

Rohrberger, Mary. "Between Shadow and Act: Where Do We Go From Here?" *Short Story Theory at a Crossroads*. Eds. Susan Lohafer and Jo Ellyn Clarey. Baton Rouge: Louisiana State UP, 1989.

Sachs, Elizabeth Evans. "Describing a Sphere: A Definition of Space in American Women's Domestic Fiction of the Nineteenth Century." Diss. U Wisconsin, 1992.

Stern, Madeleine B., ed. *Behind a Mask: The Unknown Thrillers of Louisa May Alcott*. NY: William Morrow, 1975.

———. *The Feminist Alcott*. Boston: Northeastern UP, 1996.

———. *Plots and Counterplots: More Unknown Thrillers of Louisa May Alcott*. NY: William Morrow, 1976.

Stern, Madeleine B. and Daniel Shealy, eds. *From Jo March's Attic. Stories of Intrigue and Suspense*. Boston: Northeastern UP, 1993.

Voss, Arthur. *The American Short Story: A Critical Survey*. Norman: U of Oklahoma P, 1973.

Wells, Kim. "Louisa May Alcott and the Roles of a Lifetime." MA Thesis. Southwest Texas State U, 1998. Available online. *Domestic Goddesses*. <http://www.womenwriters.net/domestic goddess/thesis.htm>

Welter, Barbara. "The Cult of True Womanhood: 1820-1860." *American Quarterly* 18.2 (1966): 151-174.

The Art of (Dis)Placement: Ruth Stuart and the Characterization of African Americans at the Turn of the Century

Susan Prothro Wright

Clark Atlanta University

The plantation and southern local color schools of fiction were firmly established, interconnected literary genres in the United States by the end of the nineteenth century. Plantation fiction, works dedicated to portraying old southern plantations as pastoral paradises, replete with contented "darkies" and benevolent masters and mistresses, was spawned in 1832 with the publication of John Pendleton Kennedy's *Swallow Barn*. Southern local color, exploiting the habits, and mannerisms, and especially the speech of various classes, races, and ethnic groups, followed in the wake of the Civil War and was fathered by George Washington Cable in 1879 with his short story collection, *Old Creole Days*.[1] By the 1890s, black dialect fiction was in high demand, particularly in the North. Popular southern authors took advantage of northerners' taste for the quaint speech and comical behavior of their African American characters, flooding northern magazines with poetry, short stories, and serialized novels saturated with minstrel-like blacks.[2] And Ruth McEnery Stuart, though fairly lost in obscurity today, was one of the most popular local colorists at the turn of the century along with Cable, Joel Chandler Harris, Grace King, and Kate Chopin, placing her in a position that warrants further inquiry into her now out-of-print fiction.

Stuart, a product of the South, though she moved to New York City from Arkansas in 1890 after her husband's death in order to establish firmly her writing career, committed herself to portraying the South, and especially the southern white aristocrat, in the most positive light. Further, her works tend to reassure receptive northern and southern audiences that each region's methods of dealing with African Americans—from marginalization to complete segregation and disfranchisement—were valid and warranted. Presumably in an effort to further reconciliation between the North and South, Stuart peoples her bucolic southern settings with sympathetic white characters whose fundamental values and goals, if not lifestyles, are in concert with those of their intended northern audience. In her fiction, the harmonious relationships between naturally superior whites and satisfied, subordinate blacks are meticulously schematized so that the Civil War, the emancipation of slaves, and the ensuing years of Reconstruction can be set forth as corrupters of a previously ideal society that was based and thrived upon a structured race and class hierarchy.

Robert Bone points out that antebellum southern writers tended to be of the planter class who emulated the English Country gentleman, with the plantation Big House imitating the English manorial estate, and the black slave "replac[ing] the English peasantry" (15). Philosophically, argues Bone, the southern post-Reconstruction author, commonly of aristocratic background, varied little from his forebears: "[w]hat persisted was a vision of the good society, based on an agrarian economy, a stable moral order, and a rigid social hierarchy" (15). Bone traces a line of descent from the eighteenth-century pastoral tradition to the plantation fictionalists who "produced a literature that was agrarian in outlook, sectional in politics, neo-Platonist in philosophy, romantic in idiom, and pastoral in form" (16). Pointing out that local color also tends to be pastoral, Bone suggests that the "prettification of slavery is [...] the point at which the Local-Color School and the Plantation School intersect" (10). Stuart's fiction serves well to illustrate Bone's hypothesis: her short fiction as well as her novels go beyond merely "prettifying" slavery to the point of proposing that African Americans actually profit most from such a system, or one closely akin to it, following the fundamental assumption of the racial conservative who believed that blacks' innate character traits are mitigated by close association with whites, especially aristocratic whites. Joel Williamson describes racial conservatives as "those who felt they knew, rather precisely, just what was the nature of the Negro. Conservatism always began and ended with the idea that Negroes were inferior to whites in every major way. [...They] believed that the Negro was and would remain perpetually inferior to the Caucasian" (108). Williamson asserts, "*Place* was the vital word in the vocabulary of conservatism" (6), and "place" meant a rigid hierarchical order in terms of race, class, and sex: Stuart's fiction advocates a strict racial hierarchy while remaining equivocal on the importance of preserving strict roles for class and sex. Her fiction does not include exotic black women nor brutish black males, as did the plantation fiction of some of her contemporaries including Thomas Nelson Page and Thomas Dixon, but, as Helen Taylor notes, "By the time

Stuart began to achieve national success, southern local color was helping prepare the nation for black disfranchisement and the most violent suppression since emancipation" (88-89).[3]

And Stuart's fiction plays an integral part in that preparation. In addition to publishing seven novels, Stuart regularly published poetry and short stories in popular journals including *The Century*, *Harper's Monthly*, and *The Atlantic*. From the appearance of her first published dialect story, "Uncle Mingo's 'Speculatioms,'" in 1888, through the turn of the century, Stuart enjoyed continued popularity throughout New England and in the South. William Dean Howells admired and published her work. Her reviewers repeatedly credited her as the purveyor of an authentic African American culture and character, especially of southern blacks. Charles Dudley Warner, responsible for the publications of her first two short stories, praised "her pictures of Louisiana life, both white and colored," claiming them "among the best we have—truthful, humorous, and not seldom pathetic, but never overdrawn or sentimental" (qtd. in Taylor 92). And Joel Chandler Harris, writing to Stuart shortly before his death, tells her, "You have got nearer the heart of the negro than any of us" (qtd. in Taylor 100). Southern readers not only viewed Stuart's portrayal of African Americans as accurate, they also felt vindicated by her dialect fiction. Taylor writes that, for Southerners, Stuart's "major achievement lay in interpreting the 'true' nature of the southern black and southern race relations to a previously unsympathetic northern readership" (96). Eulogizing Stuart in 1917, New Orleanian Belle M'Cormick recognized Stuart's ability to "reveal the relationship between the southern master and the southern darky, which was one of affection and friendliness without familiarity. That is something the northerner has never been able to understand" (qtd. in Taylor 96-7).[4] From a modern perspective, Stuart might more correctly be acclaimed for having rendered yet another white portraiture of the African American through the myopic vision of the racial conservative, especially as he or she narrowly defined the proper "place" of black Americans.

In this paper, I focus on Stuart's relegation of post-Reconstruction African Americans to what whites considered an inevitable, low socio-economic status, one that is reinforced in Stuart's stories by the differences between black and white characters, markedly reflected in her black characters' dialect speech, which, as Eric Sundquist argues, "remain[ed] a sign of difference" at the turn of the nineteenth century demarcating a boundary between blacks and whites (300). But Stuart's fiction also consigns black characters to a position of inferiority through character names and their consistent portrayal as child-like, ignorant, and superstitious, though harmless, people. Stuart's reader encounters scores of black men, women, and children who languish in a market economy and long for the security of slavery or, at very least, desire a close association with a paternalistic white. Her African American characters not only recognize and accept their place in the social and economic hierarchy, but they actually prefer it to any possible other.[5]

The story that brought Stuart to the fore, "Uncle Mingo's 'Speculatioms,'" introduces the reader to one of the author's recurrent themes: for African Americans, economic security equates to adequate food and shelter and minimal expenditure of energy to insure both. In short, slavery, at least Stuart's version of the peculiar institution, was the most economically advantageous system for blacks. The story opens with the emancipated slave, Mingo, rummaging through trash as he explains to the story's white male narrator that he is "marketing" (69). Mingo's monologue continues for two pages during which he explains in thick dialect his means of survival: sometimes he fishes in the river and sometimes in the local garbage cans for food: "Well, you see, boss, my markit moves roun'! Some days hit's right heah in front o' my *residence*, an den I goes ter markit wid a drap-line an' a hook; an' some days hit's back heah in de Jedge's giarbage bar'l, an' den I goes wid a hook ag'in—a hook on a stick" (69). Mingo's dialect, like that of other characters in local color stories, was used by Stuart, Kate Chopin, and other turn-of-the-century local colorists to "patronize and amuse" readers (Taylor 157); but in this story, the slave vernacular also clearly sets Mingo apart from the white narrator educationally, and, seemingly, intellectually, just as the endeavor he explains sets him far beneath the narrator socially. When Mingo detects the questioning narrator's disgust at his means of securing food, the former slave admonishes: "Don't you go to heavin' an' a-hawkin' an' a-spittin' over my markitin', boss! I'se clean of I is black, an' I'se pretickilar of I does go to markit pomiskyus!" (69). Mingo's means of survival along with his indignation at being ridiculed by the white, genteel narrator, considered within a scene that portrays a "natural" social/racial hierarchy, sets the stage for Stuart to reunite this misplaced emancipated slave with his former owner and to return the misconstructed social order to its rightful hierarchy.

Uncle Mingo has not fared well during Reconstruction. He expresses his nostalgia for plantation Sundays when, instead of chicken heads, he feasted on whole chicken in his master's kitchen. Mingo's longing for the toothsome provisions from the old plantation is repeated in many of Stuart's stories, creating a curious twist on the *ubi sunt* formula that is certainly intended to assure the reader that it was not only whites who prospered under the slave system—blacks thrived under it according to their capacity.

This motif recurs in a later tale, "Duke's Christmas." In this story, Moses and his grandson, Duke, become separated from their owners during a flood.

Though the two slaves search for their owners for six years, the forced sale of the plantation during Reconstruction prevents Moses and Duke's desired reunion with their "white folks," as both man and boy refer to their former owners. Moses and Duke live on the fish that they catch in summer, but, in winter, when their resources become meager, they survive on an occasional stolen chicken and what Duke can beg. This story takes place on Christmas Eve, and Moses, in vintage Stuart dialect, describes to his grandson what he wants most for Christmas: "You des gimme de white folks's Christmas-dinner plates, time they git thoo eatin', and' lemme scrape 'em in a pan, an' set dat pan in my lap, an' blow de light, an' go it bline" (165). In fact, Moses informs his grandson, "I'd a heap'd ruther have a secon'-han white Christmas dinner'n de bes' fus'-han' nigger one you ever seed, an' I ain't no spring-chicken, nuther" (168). Moses' sentiments are reinforced by his dialect and both serve to buttress the attitude of positive paternalism, one of Redemptionists' favorite themes.

In both stories, the starving freedmen are reunited with "their white folks," thus restoring the natural racial, social, and economic hierarchy. Ultimately, Uncle Mingo returns to an economic condition not unlike that of his previous slave status as he describes it in the story. The white narrator of the story becomes Mingo's caretaker, providing him with food and a cabin in return for which Mingo performs the small, routine tasks of gathering eggs and vegetables. Uncle Mingo's story ends, metaphorically, as it began and continued for him as a slave—in the service of his mistress; he dies on the same day as his former mistress, and his last request is to follow custom: he asks to be buried at her feet. His dying words, "Tell Ole Miss, don't be afeerd [...] I's a-sleepin' at de do," complete Mingo's journey to the orderly antebellum world of his early life (89).

In "Duke's Christmas," Moses and Duke are fortuitously reunited with their white folks through food. To grant his grandfather's Christmas wish, Duke begs for the Christmas table scraps from a genteel white woman. Moses hears the news of the Christmas dinner scraps tearfully, but before discovering the identity of the generous benefactress, he clarifies his acceptance of, indeed preference for, class distinctions, thereby disclaiming any affinity with poor whites while reaffirming the proper hierarchical relationship between himself and the aristocracy: "I wonder what sort o' white folks dis here tar-baby o' mine done strucken in wid, anyhow? You sho' dey reel quality white folks, is yer, Juke? 'Case I ain't gwine sile my mouf on no po' white-trash scraps" (173). Moses' misgivings are laid to rest after Duke spreads the feast, "a heavy pan of scraps," before his grandfather, who recognizes familiar tastes about the remnants (186). Moses and Duke return together to the house where the scraps were begged, and both are tearfully welcomed back into the service of their former mistress. As lagniappe for young Duke, the boy is also reunited with his father, "the stylish black gentleman who answered the door-bell, silver tray in hand" (188). Moses' good fortune in being virtually returned to his antebellum slave status ironically pales in comparison to Duke's fortuitous Christmas gift, his introduction to life in the antebellum Big House, all of which is emphasized as much by Moses' vernacular as it is by his message. Eric Sundquist describes the "great flowering of regional as well as racial dialect writing during the realist period" as "one marker of class and regional alienation from the centers of power and at the same time a sign of anxiety about [...] reputedly simpler, more humble pastoral phases, as both the plantation and the agrarian mythologies held—of American life" (303-04). Motives for white authors such as Stuart utilizing dialect arguably are more complex than this, however. As Taylor accurately assesses the use of dialect in turn-of-the-century local color fiction, "A standard national language must define dialect as provincial and subordinate, and thus construct particular groups (a race, class, sex, etc.) as obsolescent, marginal, even irrelevant" (88). Stuart artfully applies black dialect in her stories in this way.

The "ambition" of Stuart's black characters may range in degree from absolute indolence to simple fantasizing to the performances of various menial jobs, but all of their aspirations are directly related to their association with whites. Stuart's black characters, then, think like white racial conservatives whose proslavery argument was adapted to accommodate every social, political, and economic development affecting African Americans after the Civil War, including Emancipation, Reconstruction, Redemption, and apartheid in the 1890s. At the core of the conservative argument lay the concept of white paternalism that assumed black complicity. Williamson explains the theory, taking it to its illogical end: "blacks in freedom would cease to exist in America [...]. The black man alone without the white man's supervision was, after all, only poorly productive. Under slavery he had been compelled to work enough to feed himself, if freed he would starve" (84). Stuart's depiction of wretched black characters who, without their white mentors and benefactors, are aimless creatures living in and for the moment, is ahistorical; and yet it is the portrait that served not only as fantasy, but as fact and history for many readers.[6] The African American's version of the story continued to be suppressed, and the reason for this can be reduced to one of economics. As William Julius Wilson points out, "For the ruling elite, 'black freedom' signified not only a threat to white supremacy but also meant the loss of a guaranteed cheap and controlled labor supply for the plantations" (52). The ruling class's way of dealing with this potential economic disaster was to legislate the Black Codes, which C.

Vann Woodward maintains were largely "concerned with forced labor and police laws to get the freeman back to the fields under control" (qtd. in Wilson 53). Later, working-class white farmers, in an effort to eliminate the increasing black labor competition, introduced Jim Crow segregation laws in the South. The white working class depended on "an ideology of biological racism" to enforce these laws; in addition, it benefited "by its gradual transformation of increasing labor power into increasing political power" (Wilson 61). African Americans became players in a socio-economic high-stakes game that they were doomed to lose because they lacked autonomous political power. They did not stupidly tie themselves to their former owners, but they sensibly sought to align themselves with the economically powerful. At first, that included the professional and planter classes; later, it was the working class. Ultimately, the two classes, for their mutual economic best interest, joined forces against blacks.[7] Stuart and other fictionalists who wrote the story of the Reconstruction and Redemption South shared that interest.

Perhaps this explains Stuart's insistent, almost dogged depiction of dependent blacks. In a short story titled "Egypt," Stuart demonstrates that even though some blacks are not temperamentally or intellectually suited for slavery, it is still the economically preferable system for them. The narrator of the story tells us that Egypt, the protagonist for whom the story is titled, is "a woman of superior faculty, with a genius for leadership, which in a position of authority would have made her invaluable" (109). Since a black woman in authority in the slave South is oxymoronic, the reader is not surprised at the narrator's addition to the character description: "the chief trouble with Egypt seems to have been that she was a person of ideas—bothersome things for a slave woman" (119). The reader is advised that not only has Egypt "always been troublesome on the plantation [...] difficult and cantankerous with her kind," but her inability to capitulate to authority also causes her unending problems with the plantation's authoritarian German overseer (108). This, in turn, creates problems for her owner, Pomeroy, who must constantly arbitrate the grievances between his overseer and his slave. Egypt's qualities, combined with her "most stubborn idea [...] that she would never marry a slave man" (110), lead to her emancipation, but not to her welfare.

Egypt is common-law wife to Ajax, a fellow slave whom the narrator describes as a "slight, commonplace little fellow [...] of a lower order than [Egypt]" (111), but, as he is the object of her affection, she determines to buy him out of slavery based on the logic that if one of the two of them should be sold, the other would be free to follow. Because Egypt feels unsuited to gang field work, she persuades her owner to "hire-out" her labor, and with some relief at the prospect of ridding the plantation of a troublemaker, Pomeroy agrees to hire-out Egypt for twelve dollars a month. Egypt determines to save any extra earnings for the purchase of Ajax. As Egypt leaves the Pomeroy plantation for New Orleans, the narrator advises the reader that she will never voluntarily return to it, for "there are those to whom freedom is a birthright, while some are born slaves and must needs have masters [...;] it is not a question of race or condition" (117). The narrator can be speaking only philosophically here, for certainly the American South's slave system to which Egypt belongs was based first on race, with the tacit understanding that all black people are inferior to all white people; and, when that argument became inconvenient as a result of miscegenation, "condition" became the basis of slavery, with children following the status of their mothers.

Enterprising as she is, during her six-year effort Egypt laboriously accumulates the amount necessary to buy Ajax's freedom but affords herself only the meanest living conditions. Egypt becomes ragged, emaciated, toothless, and gray-haired as a quasi-free woman. Overwork and undernourishment ultimately result in her complete physical collapse. Pomeroy is advised by an emissary that Egypt had "drapped dead at her ironin'-boa'd an' hadn't resurrected for two hours" (136), prompting his personal solicitous response and free treatment by his own physician for Egypt.

After the physician restores Egypt to health, she informs her master that although she has saved enough money to buy Ajax's freedom, she desires, instead, to purchase him for herself. The rub is that in order to own property, she herself must be free. Pomeroy willingly emancipates her. The upshot of this seemingly magnanimous gesture on Pomeroy's part proceeds from the axiom mentioned earlier in the story—some people are intended to be owned. Egypt proclaims Ajax one of these, and her master concurs. Both base their position on Ajax's intemperance, the latest incident of which has prompted Egypt to direct the miscreant to his bed, with the strict maternal instructions, "an' don't get up tell I tell yer" (144). Her maternalism for Ajax parallels her master's paternalism for her, both relationships serving as expressions of the burdensome but lovingly accepted duties involved in parenting. Egypt takes on the responsibility of owning Ajax in an effort to "lookout fer 'im an' keep him straight" (145). She tells Pomeroy, "Dat nigger ain't fitten to be free. He needs a marster [...]. You sell him to me, an' I'll look out fer 'im an' keep him straight. He's all right so long as he don't have no chance to play fool [...]" (145). The irony of this situation rests partly on Egypt's own characterization of Ajax as suited to slavery, as well as her own inability to take adequate care of herself as an independent person; she is fortunate enough to have been able to rely on the beneficence of her owner when her health fails. The fact that both dependents in the two relationships are black adults promotes the validity of those ideas expressed in the racial conservative's notion of paternalism. Finally, the reader is left to ponder what lies ahead for this newly freed woman and her human acquisition. From all indications—Egypt's ailing health and her impaired earning ability combined with the encumbrance of a man who drinks and does not work (Pomeroy sells Ajax at a six-hundred dollar loss because of his indolence)—we can assume that the price of freedom is high indeed. In fact, one wonders if certain readers might have been persuaded that Egypt was, after all, better placed in slavery.

Stuart does allude to the historical reality that profoundly *affected* African Americans after the Civil War; however, her impulse is to trivialize even the most oppressive of these realities. In the story "Queen o' Sheba's Triumph," Stuart rather casually dispatches a freedwoman who is feckless enough to think that she can migrate from Broom Corn Bottom, Arkansas, to New York City and survive at such a distance from her suitable antebellum-like southern environment. Though the story does not illustrate the larger economic picture inscribing its plot, it is underpinned by strategies employed by southern whites to recover and maintain the South's economy after the Civil War, and those strategies, once again, require the African American to maintain a subservient role in the South. Stephen Steinberg points out that although the strategies may have been employed by southern whites, they were, at very least, tacitly supported by northern whites. Steinberg writes that after the war

> [t]he South was unable, despite considerable effort, to attract immigrants to the cotton fields, and came to realize that it was utterly dependent on black labor. On the other hand, as long as the North had access to cheap foreign labor [i.e., immigrants] there was no reason to raid the labor supply of the South, especially when its own economic well-being depended upon an abundant supply of cheap cotton. (175-6)

Steinberg adds that even before the war was over "the North was practically obsessed with a fear that emancipation would unleash an 'invasion' of southern blacks to the northern states" (177), thus causing unwanted competition for jobs, especially the menial jobs filled by immigrants, particularly Irish immigrants. (Wilson points out that this is not the entire story. Blacks could "easily find service jobs" and "in many parts of the North it was fashionable to hire Negro domestic help instead of European immigrants," 65.) Until the beginning of the First World War, when immigration came to a virtual halt causing northern labor shortages, no real opportunities arose for blacks in the North. But when those opportunities did arise, hundreds of thousands of blacks migrated to the North, creating a potentially disastrous economic scenario for the South (Steinberg 202-03). Predictably, southern whites, recognizing what the future held for them without the cheap labor of African Americans, appealed urgently to blacks "not to abandon their 'natural home' in the South and warn[ed] of the perils awaiting them in the North" (Steinberg 203).

With this historical perspective in mind, the contemporary reader can review Stuart's short story, "Queen o' Sheba's Triumph." This story relies on a paternal-sounding narrator, one who is more educated, worldly, and knowledgeable than the story's southern black protagonist, Sheba, and thus is more capable of emphasizing the social and economic hardships facing black southern migrants (as well as European immigrants) who move to New York City. Today's reader might safely assume that the story served well to convince nineteenth-century readers that Sheba is incapable of existing outside her economically, socially, and racially prescribed place in the post-Civil War South. Queen o' Sheba Jackson has lived her life on a postbellum Arkansas plantation in apparent Arcadian bliss. The narrator states that she is spoiled by "space, air and freedom," low wages counter-balanced by few responsibilities, the prestige of being a celebrated cook, and the benefit of free health care: she receives the "personal attention of the home doctor whose habit it was to 'lump' the servants' bills in with the yearly accounts of his white patients whom they served" (57). She also is accustomed to her association with "quality" white folks (she came to New York attired in the expensive second-hand clothes of the white judge's daughter) as well as her "second class" social standing on the southern plantation (56). Sheba is warned of the city's evils not by whites but by her relatives, friends, and her "church"; although it takes her only hours in New York City to realize that the admonitions were correct, her pride prevents her from returning home.

Like Egypt, Sheba becomes ill, but in New York, she no longer has any white caretaker to provide for her. She forfeits her health becoming emaciated and prematurely toothless, and loses a "third class job" as cook for a blue collar working family, sinking finally to "the very lowest social order" (61) as th only black among a number of Harlem boardinghouse live-in servants. Most of Sheba's fellow servants, it is interesting to note, are Irish immigrants. Only one among them, Maggie, speaks to Sheba "like [she is] a human" (62). Sheba's plantation dialect, though rarely in evidence in the story, prevents her from being hired in better New York households as well as from having any close association with the northern blacks: in the case of the former, "her speech would not go not at all with them. When it was not too slow it was altogether too swift, which is to say that the picturesqueness of her drawl was insufficient to compensate for its acceleration under provocation" (56); and in the case of the latter, those African Americans who were in close proximity to Sheba "had Eastern pronunciations, and were no company whatever" (63).

And Sheba's subsequent loss of social and economic "place" in New York City has devastating results.

After two years, Sheba is wasted. Her "triumph" is that she dies in style. Falling prey to the sales pitch of a fast-talking insurance agent, Sheba spends most of her earnings on funeral insurance so that she can be assured of a service complete with paid mourners, four carriages, an oration, and a burial plot. When she learns that her friends and family from Corn Bottom plan to attend a convention in New York, she is distraught over their discovering her actual estate. Her initial optimism gone, Sheba assumes that a black cat passing within her vision is a sign of her impending death. Her "spirit" turns to bitter bemusement and a wish for a "timely" death—one that will deliver her from the accusing eyes of her hometown visitors: "Miaou away much as you like," she tells the cat. "I on'y wusht to Gord you'd fetch me de fatal message about de middle o' nex' week. I'd show dem Broom Corners a sight" (74). To insure her own expedient demise, Sheba arranges for a sham funeral so that her impoverished state will go undetected. In a farcical funeral ceremony, which her friends and family attend, Sheba, sitting among them as a veiled mourner, is overcome with emotion and dies of a heart attack. Sheba takes the racial conservative's argument of the dependent African American to its illogical conclusion: the further the black person is from the white person, the lower he or she sinks, perhaps not morally, as authors such a Thomas Nelson Page and Thomas Dixon suggest in their plantation fiction, but, certainly, economically.

In 1898, when "Queen o' Sheba's Triumph" was published, Stuart may have offered Sheba's tale as a reassurance to those who would most benefit from the African American's strict adherence to place: specifically northern blue collar workers whose jobs might be in peril, southern agrarians who needed field hands, and others who utilized blacks for menial and domestic help. Stuart's story was timely. As a result of the later-nineteenth-century southern population explosion, whites began competing with African Americans for "traditional" black jobs. The end result of this circumstance, writes Gunner Myrdal, was that "few [blacks] in the South had opportunity to improve their economic position" and "the difference in desirability between South and North widened as Southern [blacks] became more educated and came to know the outside world" (qtd. in Wilson 65). Unfortunately, as the desirability of the North increased for blacks, northern discrimination against blacks was increasing as well.[8]

Stuart's depiction of African Americans at the turn of the nineteenth century was not responsible for the socio-economic condition of blacks at that time, but her fiction, like that of other plantation and local color fictionalists, provides "reasonable cause" for securing the African American in a separate and unequal position in society. Stuart's use of black dialect played a significant part in what Taylor calls the condoning of "hegemonic culture" of "bourgeois white supremacy, which marginalizes and renders anachronistic black language and thus black social reality" (88). And though Stuart continues her Southern fiction well into the twentieth century, her characterization of African Americans does not fundamentally change—her black characters remain comic, ignorant, ingenuous, and dependent.[9] Stuart's black characters' place in American society remains static: forever children, they remain endlessly in need of white guidance, protection, and financial aid. This is not a rendering of the heart of African Americans, but of the mind of the white racial conservative. And that mind was essentially a collective one at the end of the nineteenth century, despite the stories being produced by African American fictionalists, most notably Charles Waddell Chesnutt, whose collection of dialect stories, *The Conjure Woman* (1889), illustrated, as Sundquist argues, that black dialect tales were "alive with powerful knowledge and cultural meaning generated on hidden but distinguishable African American planes of discourse (301).

Notes

1   Rubin for a historical survey of the development of the plantation and local color schools of fiction, especially pp. 177-257.

2   See Lamplugh for more on the northern reception of the serialized short works of Ruth Stuart and other southern fictionalists. Lamplugh argues, "Each author further refined the *efforts* of his predecessors, until their black cardboard creation moved with the precision of a skillfully fashioned puppet from one ludicrous or sentimental situation to another" (179-80).

3   Helen Taylor suggests that Stuart's males are actually "feminized," a depiction that might diffuse the fear engendered by the portrayal of aggressive black males in other plantation ficitionalists' works, but one that reinforces the stereotype of the indolent African American male who is not worthy of responsible, better paid employment (102).

4   See Taylor for a thorough reception study of Stuart's fiction (94-102).

5   See turn-of-the-century African American female author Frances Ellen Watkins Harper's novel *Iola Leroy, or Shadows Uplifted* (1892), for a counter version of black Americans' experiences during Reconstruction. See also W. E. B. Du Bois, *Black Reconstruction in America* for a historical account of emancipation, reconstruction, and redemption from an African American's perspective.

6   Stuart's awareness of the use of fiction as a historical chronicle is made clear in her novel, *The River's Children: An Idyl of the Mississippi*, when the narrator, intrudes upon the thoughts of the black protagonist, Hannah, who is fondly remembering her antebellum life: " ...the old woman's memory is not so far afield, although as a historian she might need a little

editing. But such even as this is much of the so-called 'history' which [...] dishonors the world's libraries to-day" (84).

7 See Wilson, especially pp. 57-9, for a concise rendering of the efforts of Populists and Democrats to disfranchise African Americans during the last decade of the nineteenth century.

8 See Wilson, pp. 62-5, for more information on this topic.

9 See, for example, Stuart's three novels after the turn of the century: *Napoleon Jackson: The Gentleman of the Plush Rocker* (NY: Century, 1902). *George Washington Jones: A Christmas Gift that Went A-Begging* (1903; rpt. Freeport, NY: Books for Libraries P, 1972); and *The Rivers Children* (NY: Century, 1904).

Works Cited

Bone, Robert. Down *Home: A History of Afro American Short Fiction from Its Beginning to the End of the Harlem Renaissance*. NY: Putnam, 1975.

Du Bois, W. E. B. *Black Reconstruction in America*. 1935. NY: Atheneum, 1992.

Lamplugh, George R. "The Image of the Negro in Popular Magazine Fiction, 1875-1900." *Phylon* 57 (1972): 177-89.

Rubin, Louis D., et al. eds. *The History of Southern Literature*. Baton Rouge: Louisiana State UP, 1985. 177-257.

Steinberg, Stephen. *The Ethnic Myth: Race, Ethnicity, and Class in America*. Boston: Beacon, 1981.

Stuart, Ruth McEnery. "Duke's Christmas." *Solomon Crow's Christmas Pockets and Other Tales*. 1896. Freeport, NY: Books for Libraries P, 1969.

———. "Egypt." *The Second Wooing of Salina Sue, and Other Stories*. n.p.: Garrett P, n.d.

———. "Queen O'Sheeba's Triumph." *Holly and Pizen and Other Stories*. NY: Century, 1899.

———. *The River's Children: An Idyl of the Mississippi*. NY: Century, 1904.

———. "Uncle Mingo's 'Speculatiom.'" *A Golden Wedding and Other Tales*. NY: Harper, 1893.

Sundquist, Eric J. *To Wake the Nations: Race in the Making of American Literature*. Cambridge: Belknap, 1993.

Taylor, Helen. *Gender, Race, and Region in the Writing of Grace King, Ruth McEnery Stuart, and Kate Chopin*. Baton Rouge: Louisiana State UP, 1989.

Williamson, Joel. *The Crucible of Race: Black-White Relations in the American South Since Emancipation*. NY: Oxford UP, 1984.

Wilson, William Julius. *The Declining Significance of Race: Blacks and Changing American Institutions*. 2nd ed. Chicago: U of Chicago P, 1980.

The Linked Excitements of L. T. Meade and... in the *Strand* Magazine

Winnie Chan

Virginia Commonwealth University

In his short preface to the *Longman Companion to Victorian Fiction*, John Sutherland mentions only a handful of authors by name. Predictably, most of the names belong to familiar, canonical writers. Of the rest, Sutherland opines, "I would not condemn anyone to the lower reaches of Victorian fiction. Life is too short and eternity scarcely long enough to read the 197-strong output of Annie S. Swan or all of the 251 works of L. T. Meade deposited at the British Library" (1). Having published more than ten titles annually during several of her forty years as a professional writer, Elizabeth Thomasina Meade (1854-1914), now listed in many library catalogues as Mrs. Toulmin Smith, is in fact probably underrepresented in the British Library. Most recently, Meade has been recovered as chiefly a children's writer, in the 1890s founding and editing the girls' magazine *Atalanta*, as well as probably inventing the girls' boarding school novel, of which she wrote dozens. Apart from their abundance, it is perhaps owing to their obvious sentimental value that her books for children are the volumes that have survived to represent her oeuvre.

During her lifetime, however, Meade enjoyed enormous popularity as a writer for adults, not just within hard covers, but also—and perhaps more importantly—in periodicals, the mass media of the day, where she was just as bewilderingly prolific. She commanded the high rates and high visibility of the most respectable popular magazines, most notably the *Strand*, which in the 1890s arguably created, all by itself, a culture of the short story in Britain where none had theretofore existed. Dated January 1891, the superbly marketed first issue hit the bookstalls in time for Christmas 1890. With its express intention of publishing no fiction but short stories, the *Strand* would develop the genre alongside the detective stories that its own Sherlock Holmes would make into a phenomenon in its first year, catapulting the new monthly into a position to dictate what constituted "the short story" in Britain. In so doing, the *Strand* exerted an enormous influence on the shape of the modern short story, an influence that goes unrecognized because the magazine's mass cultural success was, from the beginning, already denying it legitimacy as a literary influence.

Not surprisingly, then, is such a constant presence in the *Strand*'s pages as L. T. Meade never mentioned in connection with the short story's development, for the supposedly obvious reason that her sensational commercial success depended on her deference to market-tested formulae. Yet even while working within them, she pushed their limits with proto-feminist plots and subtexts, as her undeniably formulaic stories in the *Strand* nonetheless demonstrate. There her work occupied an almost regular space from 1893 to 1903, in six series (a number rivaled only by Conan Doyle) of short stories based on scientific detection. When Meade broke into its pages, the *Strand* had already entrenched itself in the British popular imagination as the most reliable place to find a "first-rate" short story, consistently selling over 300,000 copies each month. By comparison, it took Marie Corelli, whose *The Sorrows of Satan* (1895) ranks as the bestseller of the nineteenth century, an entire year to sell 100,000 copies, a figure that includes all of her titles (Masters 6). Thus, while much of Meade's surviving work within hard covers was for children, in her time her short stories for adults would have brought her much greater and more constant exposure than any one of her novels did. Moreover, her stories in the *Strand* provoked such a demand that every one of them was republished in book form. Though her androgynous initials cloaked what the period's chatty, New Journalistic interviews revealed to be an ordinary wife and mother, Meade played the new, dynamically commercialized short story market brilliantly, placing stories in the most widely read and best-paying periodicals.

Perhaps inevitably, her success attracted a violent backlash. At the height of her popularity, an anonymous Arnold Bennett dismissed her series of short stories as "linked excitements." His disparaging coinage nevertheless aptly describes the commercial form and cultural function of the short story that Meade shaped. Of course, Bennett's phrase refers to the series of linked short stories popularized by Sherlock Holmes, as well as those perpetuated by Meade and others within the *Strand* and its many imitators. Seeking credibility with the *Strand*'s predominately male readership of socially aspirant, middle-class professionals, Meade also found herself compelled to link her name to the pseudonyms of scientifically credentialed male collaborators in each of her series. As she did so, she exploited and subverted the popular conventions that the *Strand* had begun to fix in the British popular imagination as "the short story." Linking Meade to the *Strand*'s wide readership, these inclusive conventions emphasized the inevitability of objective truth at stories' ends, their extraordinary events verified and ultimately delivered onto the page by a narrator flamboyant in his ordinariness and respectability.

In the late nineteenth century, the market for short stories suddenly became a lucrative, competitive field—and Meade played it expertly. Though she wrote hastily and thus often depended on superficial expedients to resolve potentially fascinating complications of plot, she performed no small feat in getting her work in the *Strand*. In a biography of P. G. Wodehouse, whose stories about Jeeves sustained the *Strand*'s popularity in the early years of the twentieth century, David Jasen observes, "Just as *Punch* was the ultimate goal of every writer of humorous articles, so the *Strand* was that of every short-story writer" (qtd. in Jackson 93n). In Meade's time, advice books for aspiring writers confirmed this assessment. The author of *How to Publish* (1898) numbers the *Strand* among "[t]he better-class magazines in this country" and helpfully notes to "young authors" that the monthly "never allow[s] price to stand in the way of securing a first-rate article or story [...]. The work of well-known authors is in all cases a matter of arrangement; that of others is remunerated according to its intrinsic worth" (Wagner 119, 159). This famed liberality with contributors was both cause and effect of the *Strand*'s power within an increasingly competitive marketplace for the short story.

Indeed, the *Strand* was a British institution built almost exclusively on fragments of fiction. When, in 1949, the *Strand* announced that it would cease publication the next year, a columnist in the *Times* eulogized the venerable monthly as "a popular influence of great importance in that lively period of English story-telling [...] which reached its height in the 'nineties'" ("Farewell"). Before the decade the *Times* named had ended, few could deny either the *Strand*'s popular influence or its great importance. In initially abandoning serial fiction, the *Strand* broke with a longstanding convention of British periodical publishing. The British public's demand for long, expansive fiction had, for much of the nineteenth century, deprived short story writers of a market, and so it makes sense that publisher and founding editor George Newnes referred to the absence of a serial only obliquely in the *Strand*'s inaugural issue. His noncommittal "Introduction" to the first number ventured only to promise "stories and articles by the best British writers, and special translations from the first foreign authors," but it was apparently well known that the new monthly would dispense with serials (1: 1). Though based in his belief that his readers were too busy to keep up with a magazine from month to month, Newnes's refusal to publish long, serial fiction seems to make little sense, because the *Strand* had, from the outset, published nonfiction in installments. An early "Illustrated Interview" with Cardinal Manning stretched over two issues, and even in the early numbers the conductors did not flinch at indefinitely lengthy series. These included Arthur Morrison's "Zig-Zags from the Zoo" and Henry W. Lucy's long-running chronicle of Parliament, complete with caricatures, "From Behind the Speaker's Chair." However, these features concentrated on specific groups of animals or parliamentary personalities, and they did not require reference to previous installments, as fiction tends to do.

Serendipity struck in the fusion of the short story with the serial, when, in June 1891, "A Scandal in Bohemia" inaugurated *The Adventures of Sherlock Holmes*. Though issued within the past three years, *The Sign of Four* and *A Study in Scarlet*, book-length works that had featured the detective, had attracted little notice. The appeal of Doyle's famous series of short stories lay in its continuity without cumulative effect. The result, a set of connected stories, forged a community of readers without necessitating a cohesive, loyal readership—which, paradoxically, the *Strand* attracted anyhow. At the end of his life, Doyle claimed to have envisioned the short story series as just such an expedient. He recalled,

> A number of monthly magazines were coming out at the time, notable among which was "The Strand" [...]. Considering these various journals with their disconnected stories it had struck me that a single character running through a series, if it only engaged the attention of the reader, would bind that reader to that particular magazine. On the other hand, it had long seemed to me that the ordinary serial might be an impediment rather than a help to a magazine, since, sooner or later, one missed one number and afterwards it had lost all interest. Clearly the ideal compromise was a character which carried through, and yet instalments which were each complete in themselves, so that the purchaser was always sure that he could relish the whole contents of the magazine. I believe that I was the first to realize this and "The Strand Magazine" the first to put it into practice. (*Memories* 90)

Doyle's self-congratulatory recollections reveal the easy conflation of commercial calculation with populism. Just as "the reader" merges seamlessly into "the purchaser," Doyle's "ideal compromise" made the bonds among character, reader, and magazine fast in several senses of the word, and other magazines rushed to duplicate it. These connected, but not cumulative, fictions presupposed an inconsistent reader, thus gratifying a consumerly attitude toward reading.

Capitalizing on Doyle's serendipitous compromise, Meade replicated the formula in her work for the *Strand*, but with a difference. Surely, her first series, *Stories from the Diary of a Doctor*, seemed too obviously derivative of the stories that Dr. John H. Watson was narrating just pages away. However, "Clifford Halifax, M.D." and his successors in Meade's later series were not observers continually exclaiming their awe at the detective's ingenuity; they were themselves the detectives, recounting the crimes they solved through the latest Victorian science and, more often, pseudoscience. As Sally Mitchell proposes, Meade may well have originated the medical mystery (54). Meade's innovations, as well as her conformities, reinforced the *Strand*'s conventions for the short story.

With its editorial policy of publishing no fiction but short stories and its phenomenal success in selling itself through them, the *Strand* could not help shaping what the British reading public came to regard as "the short story." While in the late nineteenth century most magazines published short fiction, none did so exclusively, and, accordingly, none took it seriously as a literary endeavor. The *Strand*'s publisher and founding editor, George Newnes, had already found fame and a seat in Parliament as the publisher of *Tit-Bits*, the penny weekly that popularized what detractors called "a literature of snippets." Not surprisingly, reviewers complained that the *Strand*, though a much more culturally aspirant cultural production, was too much like *Tit-Bits*. The new monthly's exclusion of serials certainly figured in this perception. At first, the *Strand* relied heavily on stories translated from the Continent. Lengthy headnotes to stories by Maupassant, Balzac, Pushkin, and other writers from countries with long traditions in and critical idioms for the genre attest to Newnes's educative aims in exposing to a British public this unusually concentrated fiction. However, because their lapsed copyrights seem to have determined their publication, the stories themselves tended to belie their sophisticated headnotes.

By no coincidence did the *Strand* develop its homegrown conventions for the short story through repetition in detective stories. As Julian Symons has observed in his little treatise on detective fiction, "the detective story was first generally a short story and only a latterly a novel" (8). Symons's booklet traces the formulaic development of the detective story, which parallels that of the short story in general. The artificiality of both lends them to exaggeration. Not surprisingly, commentary on the short story, more than other literary genres, is typified by how-to manuals, which proliferated throughout the 1890s and the first quarter of the twentieth century, almost simultaneously with the demand for short stories in journalism. These manuals emphasize the stories' endings, just as supposedly more respectable commentary does. This more general tendency coincides with the detective story's accumulation of clues toward the solution. As Doyle reflected of Poe, "To him must be ascribed the monstrous progeny of writers on the detection of crime—'*quorum pars parva fui* [of which I was a small part]!' Each may find some little development of his own, but his main art must trace back to those admirable stories of Monsieur Dupin, so wonderful in their masterful force, their reticence, their quick dramatic point" (*Through* 114-15). Meade was no smaller part of Poe's monstrous progeny than was Doyle.

The quick drama of the *Strand*'s short stories, regardless of whether or not they were detective stories, pointed to an infallibly objective truth. Where the stress in the short story has evolved to fall customarily on the end, the stress in the *Strand*'s short stories fall on an infallible "truth," the substance of which is usually a confession or other form of revelation at the end. The brevity of the short story inclines its details and plot toward concentrating on one idea, and the story derives its intensity from this idea, usually revealed at the end, which illuminates all that comes before it. James Joyce, of course, manipulated this tendency to innovative effect in the epiphanies of *Dubliners*. As Susan Lohafer has noted in her structuralist theory of the form, the short story "is the most 'end-conscious' of forms. Readers of short fiction are the most end-conscious of readers. Perhaps the reason is that the end is generally not given before they have had time to be curious about it, nor is it then withheld for very long" (94). This explanation is not unique to Lohafer, and in fact is integral to Poe's pioneering definitions of the genre and practically all the commentary that has followed since. The fact that commentators never question this assumption is important in that it is such a widely held assumption. Writers certainly subscribed to it to the extent that it became a convention in itself. Readers of the *Strand* were trained to be end-conscious, because the end resolves the story through a revelation of truth, which unifies more than just the story.

In these stories the word "story" is typically synonymous with a true "confession" or "secret" to which, significantly, only a select few are privy. Those thus privileged include doctors, lawyers, detectives, journalists—generally, those in (or rising into) positions of social authority, significantly conferred by the century's rapid professionalization. In various permutations of an essay on the cultural work of Sherlock Holmes, Ronald Thomas has provocatively observed that "the property rights to someone's story are transferred to the official or unofficial agent of society who is empowered to see and identify the body of the criminal, speaking for the whole society in assigning a story to that figure" (Thomas 660). In Meade's stories, more even than in Doyle's, culprits cannot seem to help relinquishing their stories:

> "Still, I will confide in you; I will tell you everything. To know that someone else shares my terrible secret will be an untold relief." (16: 129)

"I have something to confess," she said, in a hollow whisper. "Send the nurse and—and Dr. Mackenzie out of the room." (7: 267)

"I must tell you my story. I will do so as briefly as possible. . . . I cannot help myself. The truth for the first time passes my lips." (12: 672)

And so on. Because Meade gives her narrators such magnetic power over the truth, the first story in each of her series always begins with the narrator establishing in meticulous detail his credentials, which invariably involve medical training. Such credentials complement the authority traditionally conferred by social class. As one of Meade's fictive witnesses insists, "I trust you—you are a perfect gentleman—gentlemen can always be trusted" (9: 656). It matters to whom the truth is revealed. The truth may be a confession or a rational explanation of a mystery, but the conditions of its exposure work on the same principle of privileging a perspective with which readers were likely to identify or to which they might aspire. After all, revealing the truth—to the right man, of course—affirms the social order.

By virtue of their reliance on confessions, the *Strand*'s stories concerning detection almost invariably depict characters transmitting a story faithfully. Unlike real witnesses, they always know in what order to relinquish the information, and, though some of them may conceal part of the truth, they seldom contradict each other. Often the recording narrators report the story's provenance in an earnest, scientific fashion. Moreover, in stories that do not involve detection, the conflation of the detective story's conventions with those for the short story in general induced writers to have their narrators record such absurd details as "the doctor told me his story, which I am enabled to give practically verbatim, for I wrote it down in my diary the same night" (Platts 13: 392). This convention became so common in the *Strand* that H. G. Wells, ever the astute player and critic of the literary marketplace, parodied it in his stories for the monthly, where one of his narrators asserts, "Since that occasion Mr. Bessel has at several times repeated this statement—to myself among other people, varying the details as the narrator of real experiences always does, but never by any chance contradicting himself in any particular. And the statement he makes is in substance as follows [...]" (Wells 16: 572). The story he tells is, as usual, true, but Wells's reference to "the narrator of real experiences" connects it to the readers' real experiences of storytelling. Like a chain of custody that documents the handling of evidence, the stories portray the perfect replication of "truth" leading to its revelation.

Whoever controls access to the "truth," those privy to it always included the *Strand*'s readership, and thus the story form cultivated in the *Strand* privileges the reader, whom it positions in a community of surveillance. Some stories end with less fortunate culprits helplessly seeing their secrets revealed in a newspaper article, quoted in the hackneyed last paragraph of the story. For those more fortunately placed in society's pecking order, their secrets remain hidden, accountable to a higher justice (as determined by the story's social authority) and accessible only to the *Strand*'s readers. The truth is hidden from the fictive public, the plot under tension between publicity and suppression. For example, Watson cites needs to avert a scandal in "The Beryl Coronet" and to preserve national security in "The Naval Treaty." Indeed, the truth about important people will be the secret revealed only to the *Strand*'s half million privileged readers for sixpence. The headnote introducing Meade's series with "Robert Eustace," *The Brotherhood of the Seven Kings*, reinforces the privilege of reading the stories: "It is to the courtesy of Mr. Norman Head that we are indebted for the subject-matter of the following hitherto unpublished revelations" (15: 86). In making readers the collective confidant of Mr. Norman Head, globetrotting gentleman, amateur man of science, and confidant to aristocrats, the series forges an exclusive community of confidants to extraordinary events.

While technically still a framed tale, this dominant revision of storytelling contrasts with earlier forms of British storytelling. In the first third of the century *Blackwood*'s had also built a significant reputation through its own distinctive form of short fiction that, unlike the *Strand*'s, does not seem to have attracted many imitations. Presented as confessions of criminals or the testimony of witnesses to horror, stories in *Blackwood*'s gratified readers' morbid tastes. This intimacy in positioning readers as insiders or confessors also exaggerated the stories' horror, in light of the insistence upon the narratives' authenticity. The *Strand*'s introduction of a mediating narrator, or even multiple narrators mediating each other in recounting extraordinary events, thus seems to occupy a middle ground between traditional third-person narration and later impressionism, the next step in a progression toward the unreliable narrator. In series such as Meade's, as in individual stories, the outer frame-narrator is usually removed from much of the action and occasionally even the historical period. However, his rationality and objectivity in discerning the truth protect him from unreliability. Would a rational person believe a criminal, or someone who had seen a ghost? Indeed, the *Strand*'s stories often center on debunking a mystery, thus marking a dramatic departure from more traditional forms of storytelling.

Far from undermining the stories' credibility, the painstaking documentation of their mediation(s) is supposed to enhance their authenticity. Even in those stories that do not feature detectives, it is as if the stories establish their indirect transmission not to undermine the story's credibility, but to establish provenance. Formally, the stories foreground their telling, tediously recounting their transmission in ways reminiscent of the early novel's artifice of posing as a found document or "history" to achieve verisimilitude in the eighteenth century. Its chief improvement, the meticulous documentation of the mediations through which the story is transmitted, mitigates the effect of competing subjectivities, which therefore do not undermine the narrator's reliability. Unlike self-consciously artistic short story periodicals like the *Yellow Book*, or later the modernists who seized on the short story's artfully limited perspective to explore subjectivity, the short stories of the *Strand* exploited multiple subjectivities to document a story's transmission.

The analogy to documentation confirms the increasing belief in the infallibility of scientific method and its credo, the reproducibility of results. The magazine prided itself on keeping readers abreast of the latest science, an interest it gratified not only in clumsy (in the 1890s, at least) science fiction but also in scientific articles and in illustrated interviews and thumbnail biographies of men of science. From the outset "Curious Inventions" and "Zig-Zags from the Zoo" occupied an almost regular space, and as the decade progressed, technological innovation prompted articles on photography, microscopes, telescopes, and x-rays, as well as such pseudosciences as physiognomy, graphology, and chiromancy. As Arnold Bennett would scoff, Meade's series do rely on some absurd contortions of the latest Victorian science (*Fame* 137-138). Her scientific heroes perform the grisly, then-routine procedure of trephining the skull, in addition to the indispensable techniques of hypnotism and physiognomy. They can even cure cancer through inoculation, as the headnote to one story insists: "[This story is based on the results of a series of investigations made in France with the modified virus of malignant disease. There is every reason to believe, from the experience gained, that in this direction lies the future cure of maladies of this nature.]" (10: 290). The scientific preoccupation, combined with the stories' and their readers' emphasis on a verifiably consistent, rational "truth," bears out Walter Benjamin's remarks in "The Storyteller," which contends that the rise of print produced a cultural shift that changed storytelling from a primal act to a quest for information, superseding storytelling for enchantment. As one of Meade's narrators puts it, "I simply want to be in possession of facts" (6:169).

Though she was, as Sally Mitchell asserts, a New Woman, Meade apparently considered gender a liability for a woman writing in this genre, in this setting, for this readership (Mitchell 54). As Reginald Pound, the monthly's penultimate editor, recalls, "[w]hile posing as a family magazine, The *Strand* primarily appealed to men [...]. Some issues went to press with no story or article of compelling interest to women" (70). Writing for a world of men, the author of *A World of Girls* (1886) capitulated to their presumed expectations even in her self-identification. Having married Francis Toulmin Smith in 1879, L. T. Meade was in fact Mrs. Smith for all but thirteen years of her long career. Of course, her pseudonymous, androgynous initials belonged to a *fin-de-siècle* fashion that included H. G. Wells, E. Nesbit, W. W. Jacobs, A. E. W. Mason, and many forgotten others. For a woman publishing in the *Strand*, however, the ambiguous initials take on additional import. As a woman Meade stood little chance of credibility either as a scientific writer or as a creator of convincingly authoritative male narrators. The evolution of Meade's nomenclature in the *Strand* is therefore especially suggestive. Her first story in the *Strand* was credited to "The Author of 'The Medicine Lady.'" The next month's story was ascribed to the same novel's "Authors," whose identities are finally revealed a year later, in the second series, as "L. T. Meade and Clifford Halifax, M.D." The pseudonym of a coroner for the Metropolitan Police, "Halifax" provided scientific material for two series of his purported recollections as well as those of "Paul Gilchrist." Even after Grant Allen, notorious for his New Woman novel *The Woman Who Did* (1895), had introduced into the *Strand* Girton girl detectives, Meade continued to fashion male scientific detective-heroes for her narrators. With the help of "Robert Eustace," who went on supply Dorothy Sayers with scientific information, Meade would invent the adventures of "Norman Head," "Paul Cato," and "Dixon Druce."

With surprising frequency, these masters of forensic science match wits with Meade's women, who stop just short of defeating them—and thus of upsetting the stability of objective truth and male authority reinforced in the *Strand*'s iterations of the short story. Reginald Pound cites L. T. Meade as chief among the *Strand*'s tokens to provide for "women's fiction needs" (70). Ever the shrewd judge of her readership, Meade did not explicitly address her scientific crime stories to women. Yet her perfunctorily "beautiful" women threaten to subvert the *Strand*'s formula for short stories. While some of her women help to save male victims (or are themselves the victims), most of Meade's women in the *Strand* are villains. From her first story in 1893, in which a blackmailing mother-in-law drives a country doctor to attempt suicide and murder, to the story that concludes *The Sorceress of the Strand* in 1903, where two ingenious villainesses face off and kill each other, Meade's women are more than a match for her men. Most likely modeled on Doyle's Professor Moriarty, Meade's Madame Koluchy (Norman Head's archenemy in *The Brotherhood of the Seven Kings* [January–October 1898]) and Madame Sara (Dixon Druce's archenemy in *The Sorceress of the Strand* [October 1902–March 1903]) are, significantly, expert in the latest science, which they use not to preserve social order, but for personal gain. Outwardly, too, their expertise aspires to no higher purpose than artifice: Madame Koluchy consults the aristocracy on beauty, while Madame Sara professes herself a "beautifier," a cosmetic dentist who works magic at her posh office in the Strand. Ultimately, though, the narrating authority reveals the evil truth behind the woman's artifice.

Until the predictable end, such characters and plots threaten to undermine the *Strand*'s dominant form for the short story, a form that reinforces a social order maintained by middle-class men. While both series necessarily end with the villainesses' deaths, Meade does not allow the narrator to prevail over them. With grand spectacle, Madame Koluchy apparently dies, but by her own hand: "At the bottom of the well lay a small heap of smouldering ashes. These were all the earthly remains of the brain that had executed some of the most malignant designs against mankind that the history of the world has ever shown" (16: 429). But since the preceding story in the series details the malignant design by which she fakes her own death, she may well not have died, ending the series less conclusively than either Meade had ostensibly intended or the *Strand*'s readers would have grown to expect. As for *The Sorceress of the Strand*, readers do get to see Madame Sara die, but not because the authorities get to punish her; rather, her womanly jealousy and greed provoke another ingenious villainess to kill her. If Meade saw a contradiction between her villainesses' keen scientific reasoning and their irrational motives, she never acknowledged any. Indeed, she often attributed ridiculous motivations to women. One repentant consumptive confesses to trying to scare her husband to death because "the terror of dying alone, worked such a havoc within me that I believe I was scarcely responsible for my own actions" (7: 16). Another pretty penitent confides, "I am a woman—a woman does not always reason, but strongly believes in instincts" (7: 173). In every case, order is restored, as it must be in popular fiction. But though she yields the truth in an inevitable confession, the woman does not pay for her wicked, ingenious, and gloriously repeated crimes.

In these inconsistencies that at first risk violating but then capitulate to readers' presumed expectations, as in the ostentatious collaborations with men of science, Meade was negotiating a perilous market with high stakes. Throughout the 1890s, no other woman published regularly in the *Strand*, the most lucrative (and therefore enviable) place in the increasingly competitive field that constituted the culture and commerce of the short story. While Pound indicates in his memoir of the *Strand* that Doyle's rate of payment expanded geometrically throughout the 1890s, he never mentions that Meade ever made more than five guineas per thousand words, the standard rate at the *Strand*, whose commercial success enabled it to afford such largesse. Even at that rate, Arnold Bennett considered her overpaid. As he complained anonymously in the *Academy* in 1900,

> The name of Mrs. Meade, who began by writing books for children, is uttered with a special reverence in those places where they buy and sell fiction. She is ever prominent in the contents bills, if not of one magazine, then of another. She has the gift of fertility; but were she twice as fertile she could not easily meet the demand for her stories. With no genius except a natural instinct for pleasing the mass, she has accepted the form from other hands, and shaped it to such a nicety that editors exclaim on beholding her work: *"This is it!"* And they gladly pay her six hundred guineas for a series of ten tales. (*Fame* 136)

The suggestive juxtaposition of her "gift of fertility" and her undeserved rate of payment reveals the *ad feminam* nature of Bennett's objection. Her dazzling success in "the most successful modern journalism" seems to be what galls most. Still basking in what he would recall as his "Yellerbocky days" and aspiring to be an arbiter of culture, Bennett had not yet become the middlebrow Mr. Bennett that Virginia Woolf excoriates in "Mr. Bennett and Mrs. Brown" (*Truth* 65).

Before he himself succumbed to the allure of mass cultural success, Meade's formulaic work in the short story exemplified for Bennett "The Fiction of Popular Magazines." Of this,

> the most characteristic form [is] that which is to be found equally in each magazine, and which may, therefore, be said to speak the final word of editorial cunning. This form, without doubt, is the connected series of short stories, of five or six thousand words each, in which the same characters, pitted against a succession of criminals or adverse fates, pass again and again through situations thrillingly dangerous, and emerge at length into the calm security of ultimate conquest. It may be noted, by the way, that such a form enables the reader to enjoy the linked excitements of a serial tale without binding him to peruse every instalment. (*Fame* 135)

While Doyle, Grant Allen, J. E. P. Muddock, and other men also exploited the short story series in the *Strand* and other magazines, it is Meade that Bennett singles out for abuse, and he was not alone in identifying Meade with periodical fiction—particularly its deleterious effects. A survey in the *Nineteenth Century* in 1906 found that she was, along with Edna Lyall and Marie Corelli, among the three most popular authors among young girls, who made a monthly habit of the *Strand* and even lesser magazines. On this evidence, the surveyor concludes that

> Parents should sternly forbid the reading of more than one magazine per month, for the indiscriminate reading of magazines is perhaps more harmful than anything else; it creates a distaste for reading anything but 'snippets' and the lightest of literature,

and gives the reader an air of superficial knowledge that is far worse than downright ignorance. (Low 286)

A decade of Meade's linked excitements was more than enough for these critics, whose verdict was, with justification, that this genre of connected snippets created and gratified unthinking consumers, rather than readers.

Giving the public what it wanted, Meade's short stories link her inextricably to the *Strand*, and therefore to the development of the modern short story as a phenomenon of mass print. Her stories for the legendary monthly won such popularity that, despite belonging to a genre tied to the impermanence of periodical issue, every one of them achieved permanence within hard covers. The *Stories from the Diary of a Doctor* were repackaged for the *de luxe* Strand Library, a distinction shared with the *Adventures* and the *Memoirs of Sherlock Holmes*. The OCLC lists a translation of *The Brotherhood of the Seven Kings* in Urdu. Taking a sober view of this sort of success, Reginald Pound, the *Strand*'s penultimate editor, concluded of its most faithful contributors that "[o]ccasionally, they may have raised their eyes to gaze on the summit of Parnassus. Mostly, they remained content with the surer profits to be earned by toiling on the lower slopes" (105). Among the most industrious and ablest of toilers, Meade necessarily conformed to but could not resist subverting the conventions of a supremely commodified form. The story of Meade's short stories in the *Strand* is ultimately one of a woman's triumphant negotiations with a bewilderingly dynamic literary marketplace.

Works Cited

Benjamin, Walter. "The Storyteller: Reflections on the Works of Nikolai Leskov." *Illuminations*. Ed. Hannah Arendt. Trans. Harry Zohn. NY: Harcourt Brace Jovanovitch, 1968. 83-109.

Bennett, E[noch]. A[rnold]. *Fame and Fiction: an Enquiry into Certain Popularities*. London: Grant Richards, 1901.

———. *The Truth about an Author*. NY: George H. Doran Company, 1911.

Doyle, Arthur Conan. "The Adventure of the Beryl Coronet." *Strand* 3 (May 1892): 511-525.

———. "The Adventure of the Naval Treaty" *Strand* 6 (Oct.-Nov. 1893): 392-403, 459-68.

———. *Memories and Adventures*. Boston: Little, Brown, 1924.

———. *Through the Magic Door*. Toronto: William Briggs, 1900.

———. "Farewell to the 'Strand.'" *Times* December 14, 1949: 11C-D.

Jackson, Kate. *George Newnes and the New Journalism in Britain, 1880-1910: Culture and Profit*. Aldershot: Ashgate, 2001.

"A Literature of Snippets." *Saturday Review* 87 (1899): 455-456.

Lohafer, Susan. *Coming to Terms with the Short Story*. Baton Rouge, LA: Louisiana State U P, 1992.

Low, Florence B. "The Reading of the Modern Girl." *Nineteenth Century* 59 (1906): 278-87.

Masters, Brian. *Now Barabbas Was a Rotter: the Extraordinary Life of Marie Corelli*. London: Hamish Hamilton, 1978.

Meade, L. T. and "Robert Eustace." "The Doom." *Strand* 16 (October 1898): 416-429.

———. "The Mystery of the Strong Room." *Strand* 16 (August 1898): 123-137.

———. "At the Edge of the Crater." *Strand* 15 (January 1898): 86-98.

"The Authors of 'The Medicine Lady'" [L. T. Meade and "Clifford Halifax"]. "The Horror of Studley Grange." *Strand* 7 (January 1894): 3-16.

———. "My Hypnotic Patient." *Strand* 6 (August 1893): 163-177.

———. "An Oak Coffin." *Strand* 7 (March 1894): 255-269.

———. "Ten Years' Oblivion." *Strand* 7 (February 1894): 159-174.

Meade, L. T. and "Clifford Halifax." "Little Sir Noel." *Strand* 9 (June 1895): 649-663.

———. "The Strange Case of Captain Gascoigne." *Strand* 10 (Sept. 1895): 290-304.

———. "The Panelled Bedroom." *Strand* 12 (December 1896): 664-677.

Mitchell, Sally. "Children's Reading and the Culture of Girlhood: the Case of L. T. Meade." *Browning Institute Studies* 17 (1989): 53-63.

Newnes, George. "Introduction." *Strand* 1 (January 1891): 1.

Platts, W. Carter. "The Doctor's Yarn." *Strand* 13 (April 1897): 392-400.

Sutherland, John. Preface. *The Longman Companion to Victorian Fiction*. Burnt Mill: Longman, 1988.

Symons, Julian. *The Detective Story in Britain*. London: Longmans, Green, 1968.

Thomas, Ronald R. "The Fingerprint of the Foreigner: Colonizing the Criminal Body in 1890s Detective Fiction." *ELH* 61 (Autumn 1994): 660.

Wagner, Leopold. *How to Publish a Book or Article and How to Produce a Play: Advice for Young Authors*. London: George Redway, 1898.

Wells, H[erbert]. G[eorge]. "The Stolen Body." *Strand* 16 (November 1898): 566-576.

Naturalism and the Short Story Form: Kate Chopin's "The Story of an Hour"

Scott D. Emmert

University of Wisconsin, Fox Valley

When writing about American literary naturalism, most scholars focus on the novel. Although in their discussions of naturalism critics may include short stories by certain writers, such as Stephen Crane and Jack London, statements about the structural properties of naturalist fiction derive exclusively from a study of novels. This close attention to the naturalist novel has yielded valuable insights, to be sure, because naturalist writers created new ways to tell stories. For example, the plot of decline in which a character degenerates physically, socially, and even morally over an extended period of time is a naturalist invention, as David Baguley indicates when he identifies two types of plots of dissolution developed by French naturalist writers (22). In its origins and uses, however, the plot of decline comes to America as a way of structuring novels only, and as Philip Fisher and June Howard indicate, such a plot served most obviously to give form to Theodore Dreiser's *Sister Carrie* (1900) and Frank Norris's *Vandover and the Brute* (1914) (Fisher 169-78; Howard 63-69). In addition to the plot of decline, Fisher finds the structure of naturalist novels to be dependent upon different "temporary worlds" through which characters carry their desires and seek their identities (138-53).

Short stories, in contrast, cannot easily form narrative with the plot of decline or with a series of temporary worlds. Their length makes it exceedingly difficult to present the span of time needed to make plausible a character's gradual degeneration, and at best a short story may focus successfully on a small number of settings. The short story nonetheless provides advantages to naturalist writers. A story's limited length and formal compression may assist writers as they dramatize the oppositional forces arrayed against naturalist characters. Indeed, often the sense of restriction and entrapment felt by these characters registers with greater inevitability in short stories than in novels. Just as inventive as naturalist novelists, short story naturalists employed their own formal techniques to express the theme of determinism. These techniques—including symbolic characterization, the predictive beginning, and the sudden reversal—can be recognized in Kate Chopin's masterful "The Story of an Hour,"[1] which displays the structural advantages the short story has for naturalist writers.

At first glance, the work of a woman regionalist writer such as Kate Chopin may appear to be intrinsically opposed to the naturalist milieu David Shi has described as "a world full of fists" (223). Although Shi's metaphor emphasizes a violent masculinity, Chopin also wrote about a kind of violence, one directed against the emotions and psychologies of her female characters in a restrictive, male-dominated society. While male characters in naturalist stories by men often meet deterministic forces in the larger world of adventure (e.g., in war or at sea), in the natural environment of desert or arctic wastelands, and in urban squalor, the female characters in stories by Chopin and other women naturalists discover these forces much closer to home—in their bedrooms, kitchens, and drawing rooms, in both the biological and gender limits particular to a woman's experience. In this light, a recent body of scholarship has identified a distinctive kind of naturalism that chronicles the struggles of women against an array of coercive forces not necessarily operative for men.[2]

A basic affinity between the fiction of Kate Chopin and that of other naturalist writers lies in her focus on restricted characters. Recognizing this focus is essential to understanding much of Chopin's work, which has been defined as "the fiction of limits" because "the demarcating limits of human experience" command "the center of attention" (Wolff 133, 127). Along with a psychological determinism that frequently limits her characters,[3] Chopin dramatizes the biological imperatives that circumscribe human behavior. Certain critics of *The Awakening* (1899), for example, argue that Edna's increasing sexual appetite results in her loss of individuality, becoming a greater factor in her death than oppressive gender roles.[4] The desire to portray characters limited by forces beyond their control may in fact provide one explanation for Chopin's interest in the short story, a form that is especially well suited to a depiction of confinement. Critic Andrew Levy has argued that "[a]mong prose genres" the short story "is most like an enclosed space, most concentrated in form. Among *all* genres, it is most 'locked,' requiring the synthetic closure of an impact-filled beginning and a dramatic conclusion" (65). Chopin and other naturalist writers found ways to take thematic advantage of these formal requirements to portray the boundaries imposed by nature and society.

Contrary to long-standing opinion that regarded her as a literary natural who cheerfully struck off stories in a single sitting amid the clamor of her children, Chopin was a deliberate and diligent artist[5] who was drawn to the short story genre. Her output consists of two novels but nearly one hundred stories and sketches, and Per Seyersted notes that her stories usually number around 3,000 words with only a few running longer than 5,000 words. Her partiality for the shorter literary form derives in part from a preference for character and situation over plot and from a desire to control the elements of her fiction to produce a specific effect (Seyersted 116). Part of her desired effect was to provide, as Seyersted puts it, "a more powerful realism" than that available in the novels of Madame de Stael and George Sand while still offering "a true picture of the fundamentals of [female] existence" (98). The drama of the fundamental limits that women face receives a stronger expression in a short story such as "The Story of an Hour" (1894) than in Chopin's famous second novel, mainly because of the story's greater sense of closure.[6]

A tautly constructed drama that admits little ambiguity, "The Story of an Hour" vividly depicts a sudden loss of freedom. The story begins by announcing that Mrs. Mallard's weak heart may be vulnerable to the knowledge that her husband has been killed. Far from dying of grief, however, Louise Mallard weathers a "storm" of emotion and finds herself becalmed in front of an open window. Outside of this window lies an "open square [...] all aquiver with the new spring of life." Louise breathes in the "delicious breath of rain" while her eyes fix on the "blue sky showing here and there through the clouds." From these sense impressions comes a "subtle and elusive" awareness, one she cannot resist, cannot "beat [...] back with her will." First she names it, uttering "over and over under her breath: 'free, free, free!'" And then she experiences a physical revitalization. When first hearing of her husband's death, she felt "a physical exhaustion that haunted her body and seemed to reach into her soul," but in front of the open window, with the word "free" on her breath, Louise feels her own pulse, her "coursing blood" (352–53).

Thus enlivened, Louise can clearly recognize what before had been only an elusive "something." Stretching before her appears to be "a long procession of years to come that would belong to her absolutely. [...] There would be no one to live for her during those coming years; she would live for herself. There would be no powerful will bending hers in that blind persistence with which men and women believe they have a right to impose a private will upon a fellow-creature." Louise comes into a "possession of self-assertion which she suddenly recognized as the strongest impulse of her being" and she looks forward, as she has not before, to a long life (353).

Louise's sense of freedom and her greater awareness of an individual self imply, at this stage of the story, her kinship with protagonists in fiction by literary realists. As Lee Clark Mitchell has persuasively argued, realist characters tend to possess autonomy unavailable to naturalist characters. An essential self often allows such characters to resist, or at least successfully negotiate, external forces. The realist character Huckleberry Finn, for example, is able to defy his social conditioning by refusing to return Jim to slavery. Characters in literary naturalism, in contrast, frequently lack both an essential self and the ability to act independently of "their strongest desires," desires that are produced and enforced by biological or social energies (Mitchell 7). Although Louise's sudden sense of autonomy, her "possession of self-assertion," creates an exultant vision, because she is unable to act on this vision, she is never completely a realist character. This perception of freedom, furthermore, seizes her consciousness against her will. Her feelings possess her uncontrollably, suggesting her lack of self-possession by insinuating the power of an elemental force.

Louise's "freedom" is short-lived of course, for her husband is not dead, and when he enters the house, Mrs. Mallard suffers a fatal heart attack. The story's last sentence ironically emphasizes the false sentiment behind society's view of marriage: "When the doctors came they said she had died of heart disease—of joy that kills" (354). As Emily Toth argues, "The Story of an Hour" offers "a criticism of marriage itself, as an institution that traps women" (10). If, for an hour, she thinks of herself as unique and independent, Louise's fortunes are reversed suddenly, and she dies not out of "joy" but from a traumatic divestment. Louise's heart fails at her abrupt return to "Mrs. Mallard," to her socially constructed identity. In a sense, she is killed by the shock of becoming, finally, a naturalist character.

Naturalist characters may often be interpreted therefore as symbols of human frailty, pressured as they are by conditions and forces that tend to erase differences among people and that deny the exercise of a self-defining free will. Characters in short stories, however, do not require justification for being symbols instead of uniquely represented selves. One reason naturalist novels present their characters in connection with numerous disparate worlds is that movement through these worlds helps to explain why characters change over the course of the novel. They change not in some essential core of being, but in the desires that push them into different sets of circumstances. Conversely, in short stories a character's motivations do not require the level of explanation found in novels; as Sean O'Faolain writes, "The characterization of short-stories is always of the simplest" (153). Because readers of short stories place less emphasis on an extensive elaboration of character, the motives and background of short story characters can be suggested rather than detailed.[7]

Consequently, naturalist short stories allow greater freedom for characters to function symbolically, in contrast to novels in which characters are less easily abstracted from the more abundant referential detail that surrounds them. Taking them as individuals first and foremost, we expect to know a novel's characters intimately. The never-named protagonist of Ralph Ellison's *Invisible Man* (1952), for example, shocks in part because his is the central consciousness in a story of over five-hundred pages. Tellingly, however, characters in naturalist stories are sometimes not even given proper names, or their names—as is often the case in the stories of Ambrose Bierce, for instance—are ironically grand designations, pretensions to individuality belied by a reductive plight.

Still, readers tend not to mind so much if a character is not named in a short story. One explanation may be that readers have intuited that short stories are about incidents, discontinuous slices of time—what Edith Wharton called "situation" (48). Michael Trussler has argued that because a short story, unlike a novel, "emphasizes the integrity of the singular event, the autonomy of the moment," it resists the "totalizing experience" that is expected from a reading of a novel. In novels, the interpretive context, which Trussler defines as the "encyclopedia" of knowledge provided by the text and by the reader, is more equally weighted between text and reader (561–62). By providing less textual evidence, however, short stories require greater interpretive effort. Aware of the need for compression and trusting the reader's greater attention, short story writers are freer to insinuate meanings, to provide less characterization, less explanation.

A symbolic use of detail, including characters, is one method of achieving thematic compression in the short story. Theorizing about the ways stories realize "compression rather than expansion," Charles E. May argues that in short fiction characters become "stylized figures rather than 'real people'" (64). Similarly, Suzanne Hunter Brown maintains that the "[t]echnical factors" of short stories "lead many short story writers to project an individual's nature as an essential given" (199). The naturalists' interest in portraying mostly static characters that lack an essential identity is therefore assisted by the short story form. Interpreted as a symbol, Mrs. Mallard in "The Story of an Hour" has often been seen as representative of married, middle-class women in 1890s America, women who were subjected to a strict set of social codes that governed female desire and identity. Allusively, in one definition "mallard" means male duck: Mrs. Mallard's identity is certainly determined by the socially sanctioned prerogatives of the male, particularly the defining power to name.

The abrupt change in status near the end of the story—the sudden shift from "Louise" to "Mrs. Mallard" and, of course, her swift death—most clearly dramatizes Mrs. Mallard's loss. In place of the plot of decline, naturalist short story writers often employed peripeteia, a sudden reversal of fortune, to emphasize the determined circumstances of their bounded characters. "The Story of an Hour" is similar in this regard to other short stories that are more commonly identified with literary naturalism. Crane's "The Open Boat," for instance, features the unexpected death of the most capable character, and London's "To Build a Fire" stages nature's unforeseen dangers, most memorably the results of a misplaced fire. In these stories, circumstances intrude when characters feel the most liberated, the most confident, or the most secure. By quickly overturning these feelings, each story violently contradicts the illusion of personal control over events.

Although the ending of "The Story of an Hour" may, as Chopin likely hoped, take readers by surprise, it is nevertheless foreshadowed by the opening paragraphs. In fact, the beginnings of naturalist stories often predict endings in which characters succumb to external circumstances. Naturalist stories frequently begin by instantly establishing the dramatic situation, creating immediacy by quickly moving readers over the "ontological gap" that separates the world of the reader from the different reality of the story.[8] The need to interest readers of the periodicals in which naturalist writers published can explain the immediacy of their stories' first sentences. But in addition to appealing to readers beset with rapidly increasing demands on their attention and leisure, the beginnings of naturalist stories have thematic significance. The famous first lines of "The Open Boat," for example, not only place the reader within a particular setting but also within a perception of that setting, thereby announcing the story's epistemological theme.[9]

A more general theme inheres at the start of many naturalist short stories, however, because frequently these stories begin by putting characters in danger or placing them amid confining circumstances. Unlike naturalist novels, whose opening paragraphs do not necessarily foreshadow inevitable decline or dissolution, short story naturalism often seeks to reduce suspense and thereby suggest the inevitability of defeat. While naturalist novels commonly depict a character's decline over time, characters in naturalist short stories are regularly placed immediately in crisis. One senses the protagonist's dire predicament in the opening paragraphs of "To Build a Fire," for instance. And the first sentence of "Before the Low Green Door," a naturalist story by Hamlin Garland, announces the approaching death of the suggestively named Matilda

Bent, an overworked farmer's wife. From their beginnings, these stories confront characters with the insurmountable, implying subsequent reversals of the characters' misguided sense of freedom and foreshadowing an ultimate submission.

"The Story of an Hour" also declares the protagonist's present danger: "Knowing that Mrs. Mallard was afflicted with heart trouble, great care was taken to break to her as gently as possible the news of her husband's death" (352). The story's opening sentence immediately establishes Mrs. Mallard's "heart trouble," but it also presents the presupposition that a wife's life and emotional stability (her "heart") will naturally be threatened by "the news of her husband's death." This sentence indicates both the reality of sudden death and the societal assumptions that affected women in the late nineteenth century. Mrs. Mallard is, from the beginning, confined both physically and socially. Subtly her end has been predicted to allow the story's conclusion to come as a credible surprise. This matching of beginning and ending, moreover, provides a structural and thematic "lock" to complete both the story's narrative trajectory and Mrs. Mallard's fate.

The second paragraph of "The Story of an Hour" introduces another significant element in naturalist fiction. This element may conveniently be labeled the "familiar uncommon," and here it is represented by the "railroad disaster" that has supposedly killed Mrs. Mallard's husband. The desire among naturalist writers to depict the unusual experience found in everyday life[10] led them to combine the probability of realism with the extraordinary qualities of romance, much in the manner of the yellow press of the time, which reported sensational stories as part of day-to-day events. Familiar but uncommon events significant in naturalist fiction by other authors include the real murders that inform Norris's *McTeague* (1899) and Dreiser's *An American Tragedy* (1925), and the incidents of shipwreck found in *Vandover and the Brute* and London's *The Sea-Wolf* (1904). In addition to murders and shipwrecks, railroad accidents captured a great deal of press attention. Similar to today's airplane crashes, these accidents were reported with front-page emphasis. One of Dreiser's first big stories as a newspaper reporter, for example, was a train wreck that occurred outside of St. Louis, Missouri, in the early 1890s. A personally meaningful train disaster for the longtime St. Louis resident Kate Chopin resulted in the death of her father, Thomas O'Flaherty, who was killed in 1855 when a railroad bridge collapsed.

In naturalist short stories, the familiar uncommon may provide a central dramatic situation, as is the case with the shipwrecked characters in "The Open Boat." Though not central, the "train disaster" in "The Story of an Hour" certainly helps to establish the dramatic circumstances. More important, however, is its suggestive purpose, the way it plants in the reader's mind the issue of sudden death in a manner that may be more "realistic" to contemporary readers, and that functions more obviously than the implications of a woman's weak heart. On first reading, this suggestion may not lessen the impact of the abrupt death that ends the story, but in retrospect this detail certainly helps to support the story's theme of the powerless individual.

The formal compression required by short stories emphasizes individual details like this one. Such compression also places greater importance on the ending, which arguably functions differently in short stories than in novels.[11] In addition to providing, as Levy writes, an expected "dramatic conclusion," the endings of short stories often enforce an interpretive re-orientation by requiring readers to "sweep back through the story" and judge its details in relation to the finale (Trussler 572). Short story endings have a "shaping influence" in that they often obligate the reader to re-examine details for missed or misplaced significance (Trussler 573).

The ironic last sentence of "The Story of an Hour" ("When the doctors came they said she had died of heart disease—of joy that kills," 354) shapes our understanding by requiring a re-examination of the story's seemingly straightforward details. In this way, the social determinism becomes clear. Along with grasping the central irony that Mrs. Mallard does not die when she learns her husband is dead but when he turns up alive, readers may discover other, more subtle ironies, including the sense of restriction found in the single setting: Louise feels herself to be free, but she never leaves the house. The ending reveals, furthermore, that the most violent force in the story is not a derailed train but a gendered set of social expectations—a husband who will enforce his "private will" on a wife and a public opinion that rigidly normalizes the oppressive dynamics of marriage. The irony in the last sentence is, of course, available only to readers. As unironic pronouncement its finality is implacable for the story's remaining characters. To them, Mrs. Mallard will be remembered as the tender-hearted wife, and her private suspicion of marriage as a barrier to personal liberty will never be known. In the end, Chopin has dramatized the peril of a socially determined identity while recognizing the difficulty—maybe even, for women in the 1890s, the near impossibility—of opposing society for the sake of individual freedom.[12]

While "The Story of an Hour" provides an example of social determinism, other stories also reflect the influence of naturalism on Chopin's fiction. These stories demonstrate, moreover, an important development in American literary naturalism. In stories such as "La Belle Zoraïde," "Athénaïse," and Désirée's Baby" Chopin registers the biological forces arrayed against her female protagonists, thus clearly falling within the male tradition of American naturalist fiction. Her concentration in these and other stories on sexual passion and the female reproductive role aligns her with the male naturalists' emphasis on innate physical drives—what Dreiser called "chemisms." She marks a stage in the development of naturalist fiction, however, by going beyond natural determinism to demonstrate the seamless connection between a woman's biological imperatives and her social roles. To be sure, Chopin was not alone in her presentation of social determinism, for a fair measure of such determinism shows up in fiction by Stephen Crane. But unlike Crane, whose stories often present separate naturalist dramas, one in nature and one in society, Chopin combines the natural and social worlds to demonstrate the ways in which these worlds remain inseparable for women.[13]

By making this connection Chopin is able to raise issues of miscegenation and heredity to express the taboo subjects of female sexuality and racial "purity." Taboo or "sordid" subject matter was claimed by male naturalist writers, from Emile Zola to Frank Norris, as an important and even necessary foundation for a new kind of fiction. But while male writers tended to confine themselves to a depiction of the lower classes, Chopin portrayed both marginalized and middle-class women who are compelled by similar deterministic forces. Her stories exhibit, therefore, an early signal of naturalism's spread beyond a lower class, male-centered milieu. Thus much of Chopin's short fiction presages Edith Wharton's class-bound women, F. Scott Fitzgerald's doomed social climbers, and the snare of Southern history that traps William Faulkner's characters. She stands squarely within a tradition of American literary naturalism and careful attention to short story craft, and her naturalist stories demonstrate a deft integration of theme and form.

Notes

1   First published as "The Dream of an Hour" in *Vogue* on December 6, 1894.

2   Donald Pizer, for instance, locates a social determinism—the "theme of the entrapment of women within social codes and taboos"—in "a great deal of fiction by women about women" (14). In addition, Susan Ward places a number of nineteenth-century women writers within the parameters of naturalism, among them Chopin, Edith Wharton, Charlotte Perkins Gilman, and Rebecca Harding Davis. Donna M. Campbell argues that both Wharton and Chopin "attempt [a] fusion of naturalism and local color" (148), and she cites a number of studies that consider naturalism in Wharton's novels (205, n6). See also the unpublished dissertation by Linda Ann Kornasky.

3   In a critique of Hamlin Garland's literary theories, Chopin argues for a timelessness in human psychology: "Human impulses do not change and can not so long as men and women continue to stand in the relation to one another which they have occupied since our knowledge of their existence began" ("Crumbling Idols" 693). Nancy Walker argues

that Edna in *The Awakening* "resembles a sleepwalker" who, unable to understand her psychological motivations, "is not really in control of herself" (101).

4   Walker and Karen Simons.

5   Chopin carefully cultivated the public view that she was not an assiduous artist but a widow who casually wrote stories to help support her family. In 1923, Fred Lewis Pattee wrote, erroneously, of her method: "Without models, without study or short-story art, without revision, and usually at a sitting, she produced what often are masterpieces before which one can only wonder and conjecture" (327). Years later, Seyersted quotes her claim that she was a "spontaneous" artist (117), implicitly accepting Pattee's earlier declaration about her lack of revision, while elsewhere demonstrating that Maupassant was clearly an influence. Newly discovered manuscripts, however, reveal her to be "a diligent reviser" (Toth 167). As Emily Toth writes, behind the pretense that her writing was merely "a hobby," Chopin "was actually a very dedicated and ambitious author. She was never a dilettante" (142, 109).

6   Interpretations of *The Awakening* frequently hinge on the extent of Edna's freedom at the end of the novel. Is she coerced into suicide or does she choose death to express her refusal to submit to social norms? The novel's ambiguity inspires critical disagreement on this score. My point here is that the obvious lack of freedom enjoyed by Mrs. Mallard in "The Story of an Hour" lends this story more easily to a deterministic reading.

7   In *The Writing of Fiction*, Wharton also posits an essential difference between the more developed characters in novels and those in short stories: "[T]he characters engaged [in short stories] must be a little more than puppets; but apparently, also, they may be a little less than individual human beings" (47).

8   See Susan Lohafer (55) for a discussion of this term.

9   Writers at the turn of the century clearly understood the need for dramatic openings in their short stories, but they also insisted on the thematic import of a story's first sentences. Jack London, for example, once exhorted himself in a set of notes, "Insist on your [emotional and thematic] *key*" as he worked out the beginning of a possible story (271). Wharton also identified the importance of a short story's beginning in service of unity and theme (*Writing of Fiction* 50-51).

10 For example, Frank Norris in "Zola as a Romantic Writer" argues that "the characters of a naturalist tale [...] must be twisted from the ordinary" (72).

11 See John Gerlach on the function of short story endings.

12 The contemporary aversion to the theme of positive female self-assertion, however thwarted, is indicated by the difficulty Chopin had in publishing this story. Seyersted notes that it was rejected by Richard Watson Gilder, editor of The Century magazine, because he "considered it unethical" (68). Even *Vogue*, which eventually did publish the story, at first rejected it (Seyersted 209n. 59).

13 Helen Taylor emphasizes the interconnected relationship between biology and society that often affects Chopin's characters (161).

Works Cited

Baguley, David. "The Nature of Naturalism." *Naturalism in the European Novel: New Critical Perspectives*. Ed. Brian Nelson. NY & Oxford: Berg, 1992. 13-26.

Brown, Suzanne Hunter. "The Chronotope of the Short Story: Time, Character, and Brevity." *Creative and Critical Approaches to the Short Story.* Ed. Noel Harold Kaylor, Jr. Lewiston, NY: Edwin Mellen Press, 1997. 181–213.

Campbell, Donna M. *Resisting Regionalism: Gender and Naturalism in American Fiction, 1885–1915.* Athens: Ohio UP, 1997.

Chopin, Kate. "'Crumbling Idols' by Hamlin Garland." *The Complete Works of Kate Chopin.* Ed. Per Seyersted. Baton Rouge: Louisiana State UP, 1969. 693–94.

——. "The Story of an Hour." *The Complete Works of Kate Chopin.* Ed. Per Seyersted. Baton Rouge: Louisiana State UP, 1969. 352–54.

Fisher, Philip. *Hard Facts: Setting and Form in the American Novel.* NY: Oxford UP, 1985.

Garland, Hamlin. "Before the Low Green Door." *Other Main-Traveled Roads.* NY: Harper & Brothers, 1910. 293–301.

Gerlach, John. *Toward the End: Closure and Structure in the American Short Story.* University, AL: U of Alabama P, 1985.

Howard, June. *Form and History in American Literary Naturalism.* Chapel Hill: U of North Carolina P, 1985.

Kornasky, Linda Ann. "Women Writers of American Literary Naturalism, 1892–1932." Diss. Tulane University, 1995. *DAI* 56 (1995): 2237A.

Levy, Andrew. *The Culture and Commerce of the American Short Story.* Cambridge: Cambridge UP, 1993.

Lohafer, Susan. *Coming to Terms with the Short Story.* Baton Rouge: Louisiana State UP, 1983.

London, Jack. "The Sleepy Mood of the Doldrums." *Critical Essays on Jack London.* Ed. Jacquelin Tavernier-Courbin. Boston: G. K. Hall & Company, 1983. 271.

May, Charles E. "Metaphoric Motivation in Short Fiction: 'In the Beginning Was the Story.'" *Short Story Theory at a Crossroads.* Eds. Susan Lohafer and Jo Ellyn Clarey. Baton Rouge: Louisiana State UP, 1989. 62–73.

Mitchell, Lee Clark. *Determined Fictions: American Literary Naturalism.* NY: Columbia UP, 1989.

Norris, Frank. "A Plea for Romantic Fiction." *The Literary Criticism of Frank Norris.* Ed. Donald Pizer. Austin: U of Texas P, 1964. 71–2.

O'Faolain, Sean. *The Short Story.* London: Collins, 1948.

Pattee, Fred Lewis. *The Development of the American Short Story: An Historical Survey.* NY: Harper & Brothers, 1923.

Pizer, Donald. "Introduction: The Problem of Definition." *The Cambridge Companion to American Realism and Naturalism: Howells to London.* Cambridge: Cambridge UP, 1995. 1–18.

Seyersted, Per. *Kate Chopin: A Critical Biography.* 1969. Baton Rouge: Louisiana State UP, 1979.

Shi, David E. *Facing Facts: Realism in American Thought and Culture, 1850-1920.* NY: Oxford UP, 1995.

Simons, Karen. "Kate Chopin on the Nature of Things." *Mississippi Quarterly* 51(1998): 243–52.

Taylor, Helen. *Gender, Race, and Region in the Writings of Grace King, Ruth McEnery Stuart, and Kate Chopin.* Baton Rouge: Louisiana State UP, 1989.

Toth, Emily. *Unveiling Kate Chopin.* Jackson: UP of Mississippi, 1999.

Trussler, Michael. "Suspended Narratives: The Short Story and Temporality." *Studies in Short Fiction* 33 (1996): 557-77.

Walker, Nancy. "Feminist or Naturalist: The Social Context of Kate Chopin's *The Awakening*." *The Southern Quarterly* 17 (1979): 95-103.

Ward, Susan. "Naturalism." *The Oxford Companion to Women's Writing in the United States*. Eds. Cathy N. Davidson and Linda Wagner-Martin. NY: Oxford UP, 1995. 622.

Wharton, Edith. *The Writing of Fiction*. NY: Charles Scribner's Sons, 1925.

Wolff, Cynthia Griffin. "Kate Chopin and the Fiction of Limits: 'Desiree's Baby.'" *The Southern Literary Journal* 10 (1978): 123-33.

Strategies of Self-Representation in "Natalie" by Alice Dunbar-Nelson

Margot Sempreora

Webster University

> It is the better self within, the other consciousness [...]
> the original soul struggling for utterance.
> Alice Dunbar-Nelson in a letter to Paul Dunbar, 1899[1]

The 1890s stories of Alice Ruth Moore, a young New Orleans woman of mixed race, constitute a choreography of disguise and disclosure not only in terms of race but also in terms of gender and sexuality. Authorial identity was a complex journey for an ambitious woman writer who possessed the inheritances of her Negro, Caucasian, and Native American races; who received a Western education; who spent her first twenty-one years in New Orleans during a period marked by Jim Crow bigotry and racial violence; and who peddled her stories in a racist and sexist Victorian publishing establishment. Despite the contradictory and competing influences and imperatives affecting her writing, Alice Dunbar-Nelson, as she would finally be known after her marriages, found an authorial identity in the short story genre.

By 1928 Alice Dunbar-Nelson had experimented with every possible genre—novels, plays, poems, scholastic articles, biographical and historical essays, speeches, newspaper columns, peace pamphlets, educational proposals, even film scripts—yet she singled out the importance of the short story, telling an interviewer that she "considers her short stories her most representative work."[2] In what sense does the short story "represent" Dunbar-Nelson? In many ways, Dunbar-Nelson's concept of representation breaks with current practice among women writers and writers of color, in that the young Dunbar-Nelson seems to have excluded race and gender from constructions or presentations of the authorial self. In fact, Dunbar-Nelson's early local color stories lack characters explicitly identified as black, and do not directly take on issues of race, class, gender, or sexuality—issues which are certainly "representative" of her thinking in her later militant journalism and efforts to improve black education. What draws one to the study of Dunbar-Nelson's early Louisiana tales, fourteen of which were collected in *The Goodness of St. Rocque* (1899)—local color tales peopled with white Creoles and Acadians—is the search for the material signs and cultural meaning of that "representation."

Because she appears to delete herself, her desire, and the complexity of her mixed ancestry from the world of her fiction, Dunbar-Nelson's 1928 assertion prompts us to ask in what way her short stories represent her. In what ways did the local color genre allow aesthetic choices in which she felt at home? Whatever Dunbar-Nelson may have meant by "representative," it is true that the plots, settings, and situations of the local color tales allow her to re-present herself autobiographically, historically, even politically, in an encoded translation of her life. In other words, despite their non-specificity of race and their inattention to blacks' or women's concerns, which she later championed in her essays, her fictional accounts do render with some integrity the world of her experiences and thus "represent" her existence. In part, Dunbar-Nelson accomplishes her self-representation through a shifting geography, often at water's edge, which metaphorically renders issues of disguise, passing, suppression, and revision. Additionally, Dunbar-Nelson adapts the genre to include a spiritual and sexual dimension to her female heroines; material forbidden from conventions of plot, action, or explicit character description is embedded in symbolic detail or hinted at through a supernatural dimension that lies just outside the borders of fictional realism.

Analyses by Gloria (Akasha) Hull, Elizabeth Ammons, and Eleanor Alexander explore the issue of Dunbar-Nelson's seeming absence as an identifiable narrator or character from her early Louisiana stories. Relating this absence to Dunbar-Nelson's aversion to the popular genre of plantation fiction, Hull reasons that by not identifying characters as black, Dunbar-Nelson avoided re-inscribing racist stereotypes:

> [T]he reading public [was] conditioned to expect only plantation and minstrel stereotypes. Her strategy for escaping these odious expectations was to eschew black characters and culture and to write, instead, charming, aracial, Creole sketches that solidified her in the then popular, 'female suitable' local color mode. (Hull, *WADN* xxii)

Gloria Hull finds that Dunbar-Nelson's own concept of authorial identity proscribed black characters and themes:

> Dunbar-Nelson was the most uncomfortable of all with mixing race and belletristic literature. Throughout her career, she maintained a sharp demarcation between black concerns and her literary work. Though race was the keynote and unification for practically everything else that she did, it rarely sounded in her poems and stories. (*Color, Sex* 19)

Acknowledging this same "demarcation," Elizabeth Ammons identifies Dunbar-Nelson's choices as political rather than aesthetic, arguing that by writing aracial fiction Dunbar-Nelson was consciously resisting one genre of borrowed language by refusing to "cater to the race-fiction expectations" of the white literary establishment; "Intent on being an artist, Dunbar-Nelson was determined not to be bound by race in any direct way, either linguistically or thematically" (66, 60). Acknowledging this issue from a slightly different angle, Eleanor Alexander sees Dunbar-Nelson's fictional non-black creations as extensions of the author's own created persona. In her book-length analysis of Alice and Paul Dunbar's relationship, Alexander identifies the "colorless" characters of her early stories as alter egos of their creator, aracial Creoles who, like Dunbar-Nelson's created self, "had no place in the racial scheme of the times" (71). Alexander explains:

> Since [Alice] was not legally white and did not consider herself black, she perceived herself as an aracial, mixed race creole. This identity allowed her to circumvent the racial label conferred on her by American society: it enabled her to escape the reproach of birth and blood. (67)

In fact, as Ammons notes, Dunbar-Nelson was inexorably bound by race from birth: whether, as Hull believes, she was guided by her own "ivory tower conception of literature" (*Color, Sex* 23-4); or whether, in response to the limitations on her literary career, she was politically resistant, there can be no question that the racist era in which she wrote affected her aesthetic choices, and possibly determined her strategies of form.

The public's taste for the non-standard, exotic sounds of a particular American locale is made clear by the popularity of dialect poetry by writers such as her first husband, Paul Dunbar. And at the same time it is obvious that Alice Dunbar-Nelson objected to the mainstream injunction to use dialect. Early in her writing career, in her first known letter to Paul Dunbar, she takes this clear position:

> You ask my opinion about the Negro dialect in Literature? Well, frankly, I believe in everyone following his bent [...]. I don't see the necessity of cramming and forcing oneself into that plane because one is a Negro or a Southerner. Don't you think so? (qtd. in Ammons 66)[3]

Following her "bent" meant setting her stories in the place she grew up, a problematic choice for Dunbar-Nelson, as it required returning to the languages which identified race and class—the African-American, Creole and Acadian patois of New Orleans and the Louisiana bayous. Dunbar-Nelson did use "Negro dialect" in more than half of the fourteen tales in *The Goodness of St. Rocque* (1899), her second volume of work; however, she successfully avoided the self-deprecating tones of the minstrel show. In order to locate her unique voice in this autobiographical realm and yet avoid the exclusive use of dialect and stereotypes of race and gender often found in local color tales, this young writer had to not only adapt elements, but also invent new strategies within the genre, such as: shifting points of view, multiple self-translations, encoded racial identity, and symbolic representations of sexuality.

To editors Barbara Ewell and Pamela Menke, Dunbar-Nelson's accomplishment represents a subversion of the mainstream short story genre. In the preface to their collection, *Southern Local Color*, they assert that Dunbar-Nelson, along with contemporaries such as Kate Chopin, "adapted the narrative strategies of local color to address sophisticated problems of morality, emotion, aesthetics, and sexuality" (lviii). That complex subversion is true of one story not included in *The Goodness of St. Rocque*. "Natalie" presents a female character whose exceptional qualities help to reveal Dunbar-Nelson's strategies of self-representation. Published for the first time in 1988 in The Schomburg Library of Nineteenth-Century Black Women Writers, "Natalie" constitutes a proud assertion of linguistic difference rather than a command performance of exotic dialect. In addition, the character of Natalie possesses a vitality and defiance that makes her unique among the heroines of the published collection, characters whom Hull aptly describes as, "usually correct, conventional heroines with none of the verve and bravado that characterized [Dunbar-Nelson's] own life on both public and private levels" ("Shaping Contradictions" 37). There is, indeed, a singular silence about many of Dunbar-Nelson's heroines. Nuns or obedient daughters and wives, her women are limited by the contemporary cultural injunction that a woman must find her place, dignity, and language only within the institutions of marriage or church. However, the unusual qualities of the main character, as well as Dunbar-Nelson's manipulation of story elements in "Natalie" offer an instance of what Dunbar-Nelson may have meant by "representation" in her tales.

"Natalie" makes use of both symbolic detail and the shifting geographical elements of her locale—storms, tides, floods, and rising spring waters—in order to disrupt the status quo and create a female character who combines physical strength, linguistic control, and an undefined but ruling spiritual dimension. This tale of an interracial summer friendship may be read as a metatext of

Dunbar-Nelson's aesthetic predicament, containing all the issues that surface singly or together in other tales—encoded mixed race, language as site of difference, cultural and gender conflicts, and taboo love between women. As it was signed "Alice Moore," "Natalie" was probably written before her marriage to Paul Dunbar, and could have been included in *St. Rocque*, but the story was not published in Dunbar-Nelson's lifetime. One of her strongest stories, "Natalie" should have been part of the *The Goodness of St. Rocque* collection. One wonders if it was rejected by Dodd and Mead, who published *St. Rocque* as a companion volume to Paul Dunbar's *Poems of Cabin and Field*, or, suppressed by the author herself—as a story too expressive of her sexuality and her outrage at America's racism.

Briefly, "Natalie" concerns the innocent circumstance of a summer friendship between two fourteen-year-old girls on the shores of Lake Ponchartrain. Natalie is a "native" of the lake shores, and Olivia a "pale" summer visitor from New Orleans, hungry for the physical pleasures of a summer out of doors. Out of bigotry and snobbishness, Olivia's mother banishes her daughter's new friend, but Natalie's courageous rescue of mother and daughter from the flooding Ponchartrain allows the two young women to continue their friendship.

The locus of Dunbar-Nelson's portrayal of female, non-white power is Natalie, a "native" girl who speaks fluently in both French and English and whose repeatedly-mentioned tan skin and dark features, in ironic combination with her surname, "LeBlanc," indicate that she is to be read as a figure of mixed race. From the unstable borderlands at the edge of the lake, Natalie rules her tale physically, linguistically, and spiritually, performing feats of climbing, rowing, and rescue, and manipulating symbols of metamorphosis to influence and transform the visitor, Olivia: "Down here on the sands at this edge of the beach was Natalie's own kingdom, and woe unto the trespasser who dared within its boundaries" ("Natalie," *WADN* 3: 153). Writing of another such border in the preface to *Borderlands/La Frontera*, Gloria Anzaldúa identifies the empowering magic of these margins:

> Living on borders and in margins, keeping intact one's shifting and multiple identity and integrity, is like trying to swim in a new element, an "alien" element [...]. I have the sense that certain "faculties" [...] and dormant areas of consciousness are being activated, awakened.

Giving her character reign over this boundary kingdom, altering the equation of dominance, or erasing beneath the floodwaters of the Ponchartrain all accepted borderlines, Dunbar-Nelson expands the limitations of her aesthetic space. The "awakened" consciousness of the border-dwelling Natalie allows her to talk back and take charge.

For example, in Olivia's and Natalie's first encounter, Dunbar-Nelson reverses the terms upon which the dark (conventionally submissive) native meets the fair (conventionally dominant) maiden; Natalie, referred to as the "queen," clearly asserts her domain over the land and at the same time establishes her control of language and her superiority to "the blonde": "The queen approached the trespasser and said, 'Who are you and what are you doing here?' She spoke in French and the blonde shook her head and said sadly, 'You'll have to speak English'" (3: 154). While it reaches toward the stranger, Natalie's question asserts her authority, rewriting the conventional equation of dominance (i.e., Anglo over Native) and posing a question about "place" which the story begins to answer. What is it that the visiting Olivia Spiers and her family want from Natalie's domain and from Natalie? The linguistic superiority of the native, established in this opening exchange, is matched by a physical strength which recurs in the story in athletic activities and courageous physical feats. Though Natalie's strong body is problematically used in service to her blonde friend, Dunbar-Nelson manages to break from the stereotype of genetic slave-strength by establishing clear mutual affection between Natalie and Olivia and by aligning Natalie's power with youthful health, teaching, and freedom. When Olivia's mother abruptly interrupts their first meeting, Natalie hoists Olivia up through the underbrush onto the breakwater:

> So, boosted up by Natalie's strong, bared arms [...] Olivia gained the beach smiling, flushed, triumphant, only to be met with a scowl on the face of the overdressed lady.
> 'What do you mean,' she said sharply, 'by acting like a regular tomboy, and running about with such a person already?' (3: 155)

As a dark, French-speaking young woman unknown to Mrs. Spiers, Natalie represents an instability of race, gender, class, and language—a threat doubled by the sexual energy of those bare "tomboy" arms lifting up the flushed Olivia.

In contrast, having been told of his daughter's new friend, Olivia's father eagerly accepts Natalie as a kind of summer trainer who will provide the proper health regimen for his daughter. He countermands his wife's orders:

> 'Let Olivia take off those fancy clothes and get some blood in her face; she looks like a wax doll. Let her [...] get sunburned [...]. Let her go with the natives, they'll teach her more healthy topics of conversation than that fashionable city set.' (3: 156)

Generalizing her into the category "the natives," Spiers removes Natalie's identity to the margins of his family life; his approbation signals appropriation and resembles the turn-of-the-century white reading public's taste for regional tales which allow one to "go with the natives" and escape unhealthy, if fashionable, city talk.

Spiers maintains a significant presence throughout the tale as a listener to Olivia's stories about Natalie. If we read Natalie as a woman of mixed race, Spiers' witness to her adventures suggests the presence of white readers in nineteenth-century black narratives. Discussing this dynamic, Robert Hedin suggests about Charles Chesnutt that the "white audience outside the texts [...] all but forced itself onto the very pages of the black texts." Speaking about Chesnutt's *Conjure Woman*, Hedin goes on to say that listeners such as John, who sits in judgment of Uncle Julius' conjure stories, play a complex role for the black author: "as listeners and observers, the white intruders simultaneously validated and confined the black characters they perceived" (180). Dunbar-Nelson's handling of Spiers' conditional approval of Natalie, who, like Dunbar-Nelson is a daughter of probable mixed parentage and multiple languages, constitutes a metanarrative of Dunbar-Nelson's own restrictive white readership. Of such a dynamic, Hedin suggests:

> Within their texts [i.e., nineteenth-century black narratives] are encoded the very cultural relationships which, outside the texts, serve to shape them. In the intratextual relationship of black character and story to these white presences, black texts reveal both their sense of restriction and their strategies for coping with it. (181–82)

Such restrictions and strategies are apparent in Dunbar-Nelson's text: while Natalie fulfills Spiers' expectations by producing a healthier Olivia, Natalie's relationship to Olivia also suggests a subversive ability to initiate change, to teach, and to transform Olivia. Under Natalie's influence Olivia's health and coloring do improve: "Nothing pleased [Mr. Spiers] better than to see his 'little country girl' so healthy." However, Mrs. Spiers shows concern about her darkening daughter: "[T]he stylish mother grieved to see the unfashionable tan on the girl's cheeks" (3: 158). Ironically, Olivia's "tan" functions as a mutable sign—either of health or of sickness; Mr. Spiers reads health in his daughter's face because he is secure in his control over Natalie's limited role as an exercise coach; on the other hand, the perceptive Mrs. Spiers interprets her daughter's deepened color not only as a misstep of fashion, but also as a sign of Natalie's more profound effect upon Olivia.

The Spiers' conflicting, doubled reading of Olivia's tan not only signifies the complex view of Natalie held by the "white presences" in her story, but also suggests Dunbar-Nelson's complex relationship to her mainstream readers. Her ambiguous treatment of Natalie's race, status, and sexuality represents a kind of hide-and-seek self-translation strategy. Hedin uses the term "double agent" to describe a strategy of the black male writer who "can pass for white in order to keep the tale black" (199). Hedin wonders: "To what extent did the very survival of black stories depend on their central voices not quite being heard accurately or their central characters not quite being seen for what they were to their authors?" (181).

The double agency of "Natalie" extends beyond race to an exploration of sexuality. Through the symbol of Natalie's artesian well, a site of female sexuality, Dunbar-Nelson represents Olivia's initiation into the mysteries of womanhood. On the day after their meeting, Olivia experiences the bubbling spring in Natalie's backyard.

> In Mandeville [...] everyone uses the artesian well [...]. This one of Natalie's fell into a big stone basin, overgrown with scarlet creepers, and waterlillies on the clear pool. Upon the stone beneath the trickling stream there was a glass, and Natalie explained how glasses could be colored by simply letting them stay under the action of the water for a day, then the sulfur and iron would turn the white into a clear amber with iridescent lights throughout. (3: 158)

The basin, scarlet creepers, stream, and glass function as a complex cluster of symbols that suggest female potency and creation. Issuing from a womb-like source, the flow produces "a clear amber with iridescent lights throughout," linking Natalie's power with both sexuality and race. Thus the well, as a site of female sexuality and physical and spiritual transformation, holds the taboo elements of the girls' relationship that are missing from the tale's plot or action.

Dunbar-Nelson's use of symbolic detail informs our reading of other tales as well. Objects or sites such as the artesian well become vessels holding implied action. Such symbols make room in the story for material such as a young woman's ability to control and revise her life or to claim her sexuality. Manuela of "The Goodness of St. Rocque" fondles an amulet worn about her waist to insure the return of a lost lover; Sister Angela, of "The Locket," trembles beneath the convent blankets, where relinquishment of worldly goods and sexual identity have been inextricably bound; she caresses a locket, her only inheritance from her mother. Dunbar-Nelson writes of the novitiate's struggle: "She threw herself across the bed, with her hand pressed against the guilty, accusing thing, trying hard to stifle her wicked thoughts and desires" (3: 79).

The locket leads Angela to claim her birthright as a daughter as well as the love of a former suitor. In contrast, if the relationship between the two young women in "Natalie" followed the trajectory suggested by the artesian well, the result would constitute a depiction of love exchanged across several forbidden boundaries. While their relationship "passes" for girlish friendship both within the Spiers' scenario and within Dunbar-Nelson's tale, the intensity and equality in the "close intimacy between the girls [...] the new found affection that was so strange to [Natalie]" (3: 158) suggests a relationship which, whether or not we read it as lesbian love, represents an insurrection in the social code which Dunbar-Nelson was not willing to pursue.[4] Interrupting the development of their relationship immediately after their experience at the artesian well, Dunbar-Nelson displaces Natalie from her sovereign water territory to the Spiers' front garden, where, inland and out of place, Natalie becomes the trespasser. Mrs. Spiers physically restrains Olivia's affectionate greeting and scolds the two girls for their transgressive verbal conduct:

> "Oh, Natalie," [Olivia] cried joyously, and would have kissed her friend, but the mother held her back.
>
> "Do you mean to tell me, Olivia, that this—this—person calls you by your first name as if she were your equal? Do you allow that?"
>
> Both girls' faces crimsoned; the one with a fair flush of mortification, the other with a darker tint of injured pride and anger. (3: 159)

Dunbar-Nelson's comment on complexion calls attention to a source of the mother's objections—the ominous presence of a darker race. At the same time, Mrs. Spiers' attack on the verbal intimacy between the young women signifies her attempt to reconstruct the linguistic edifices of class and heterosexual womanhood: "In future, girl, [...] I want you to call my daughter *Miss* Olivia. I require that of all inferiors." Mrs. Spiers demands that the private language of friendship be translated into the public language of difference and distance. Her assertion of control over language resonates deeply within a body of work which strategizes to maintain its proper relation to the reading public. Natalie's response to her attacker—"[I]n age and education I am Oleevia's equal, yes, and in birth and breeding, I am superior to Madame herself" (3: 159)—constitutes an instance of "talking back" as bell hooks identifies it; momentarily released from the object-position of Mrs. Spiers' racism, Natalie speaks in a "liberated voice" (hooks 9).

After the encounter in which Mrs. Spiers separates them, the girls do not meet again until the wild flood waters of the Ponchartrain submerge the town; Natalie, now the object of Mrs. Spiers' entreaty, consents to row mother and daughter to Mr. Spiers, who waits anxiously off shore on the New Orleans steamer. In that Natalie's rescue of the pair restores the proper balance of power and brings an apparent closure to the disruptions of plot, it reveals Dunbar-Nelson's strategic use of the local color tale. Natalie accomplishes a "superhuman" feat by rowing mother and daughter safely against the impossible current; the depiction of her physical prowess shifts from health and pleasure to back-breaking service: her "brown arms" pulling at the oars, "her strong back bending," her hands blistered (3: 164-65) as she safely conveys them out of her domain and back to the waiting patriarch. The safe arrival of the women to the steamboat marks the end of Natalie's tale and the symbolic restoration of the edifices of bigotry; we enjoy no celebration of mixed race, powerful womanhood, or women's love. The friends are not heard in the story again and their silence declares the impossibility of an alternative ending, one in which Natalie and Olivia might embrace and acknowledge the transforming power of "this strange new feeling"—their love for one another.

The final paragraph of "Natalie" transports the reader eight years into the future and shifts the setting from Natalie's Ponchartrain kingdom to Spiers' New Orleans world; no longer active in her own tale, Natalie is "rewritten" by Mr. Spiers:

> And when Natalie goes to New Orleans for the Carnival week, Mr. Spiers introduces her to everyone as the 'plucky little girl who rowed my wife and daughter out of a death-trap, by Jove!' (3: 165)

Spiers' version of Natalie's heroism situates her courage, physical strength, and moral superiority within a scenario of service to his family; his language ("plucky little girl") reduces the tale to its least-threatening status—as a summer vacation story, a local color tale.

Handing the story over to Mr. Spiers is a maneuver that allows a tale of race, class, and women's love to "pass" for a mainstream bit of local color fiction. However, the almost supernatural nature of Natalie's actions have disrupted the realistic plot: a young girl who has been rejected and insulted by her friend's mother accesses a physical and moral strength that seem to lie outside the bounds of the local color tale and transforms pettiness to drama and heroism. In addition, insisting on the continuing friendship between the young women, the door between two worlds is left ajar, and the story does not relinquish all its claims to power: the Spiers' mansion has been leveled by the flood, Natalie's kingdom remains intact, and the artesian well flows untouched by Spiers' reframing techniques.

If we see Spiers as representative of the kind of "reader" who, by his presence, reduces and reshapes Dunbar-Nelson's tale to his own formula, what we discover immediately after that realization is that Spiers' condescending appropriation has been corrected by a new era of readers who recognize Spiers' white, patriarchal framing gesture and who understand the story as more complex and larger in its implications. "Natalie" succeeds in "representing" Dunbar-Nelson in its attention to the defiant use of language by a marginalized female character, a positive portrayal of mixed race, symbols of woman's physical courage and powers of creation, and the expression of a generous mutual affection between women. A new reading of "Natalie" allows us to understand Dunbar-Nelson's use of and contribution to the short story.

Notes

1. Quoted in Metcalf (742).
2. References to the short stories of Dunbar-Nelson will be to The Schomburg Library of Nineteenth-Century Black Women Writers edition, abbreviated WADN. This quotation is from Hull's Introduction, page xlii. The two collections of short stories published in Dunbar-Nelson's lifetime, "Violets and Other Tales" and "The Goodness of St. Rocque," are reproduced in facsimile in Vol. 1 of the Collected Works; "Natalie" is published in Vol. 3.
3. Elizabeth Ammons quotes this letter of May 9, 1895, citing Ruba Ora Williams's exhaustive dissertation on Alice Dunbar-Nelson. The letter is located in the Paul Laurence Dunbar Papers of the Ohio Historical Society. Alice Dunbar Nelson's letters are also available from Special Collections, University of Delaware and in a UMI dissertation by Eugene Metcalf, *Letters of Paul and Alice Dunbar: A Private History*.
4. In her chapter, "The New Woman as Androgyne: Social Disorder and Gender Crisis, 1870-1936," in *Disorderly Conduct: Visions of Gender in Victorian America*, Carroll Smith-Rosenberg treats the growing anxiety at the turn of the century over women's friendships, in light of the generation of "New Women." Here the threat of Natalie's and Olivia's friendship is, of course, heightened by differences in race and class.

Works Cited

Alexander, Eleanor. *Lyrics of Sunshine and Shadow: The Tragic Courtship and Marriage of Paul Laurence Dunbar and Alice Ruth Moore. A History of Love and Violence Among the African American Elite*. NY: New York UP, 2001.

Ammons, Elizabeth. *Conflicting Stories: American Women Writers at the Turn into the Twentieth Century*. NY: Oxford UP, 1991.

Anzaldúa, Gloria. *Borderlands/La Frontera: The New Mestiza*. San Francisco: Aunt Lute, 1987. N. pag. in preface.

Dunbar-Nelson, Alice Ruth Moore. *The Works of Alice Dunbar-Nelson*. Vols. I-III. Ed. Gloria T. Hull. NY: Oxford UP, 1988.

Ewell, Barbara C. and Pamela Glenn Menke. Introduction. *Southern Local Color: Stories of Region, Race and Gender*. Athens, GA: UP Georgia, 2001. xiii-lxvi.

Hedin, Raymond. "Probable Readers, Possible Stories: The Limits of Nineteenth-Century Black Narrative." *Readers in History: Nineteenth-Century American Literature and the Contexts of Response*. Ed. James L. Machor. Baltimore: Johns Hopkins UP, 1993. 180-205.

Hull, Gloria T. *Color, Sex, and Poetry: Three Women Writers of the Harlem Renaissance*. Bloomington: Indiana UP, 1987.

———. Introduction. *The Works of Alice Dunbar-Nelson.* By Dunbar-Nelson. 3 vols. NY: Oxford UP, 1988. xxix-liv.

———. "Shaping Contradictions: Alice Dunbar-Nelson and the Black Creole Experience." *New Orleans Review.* 15.1 (1988): 34-7.

Metcalf, Eugene Wesley. *Letters of Paul and Alice Dunbar: A Private History.* Diss. U California Irvine, 1973. Ann Arbor: UMI 1974. 7413820.

Smith-Rosenberg, Carroll. *Disorderly Conduct: Visions of Gender in Victorian America.* NY: Oxford, 1986.

Williams, Ruby Ora. *An In-Depth Portrait of Alice Dunbar-Nelson.* University of California Irvine, 1974. Ann Arbor: UMI, 1975. 75-11, 18.

Zitkala-Ša's and Sui Sin Far's Sketch Collections: Communal Characterization as Resistance Writing Tool

Vanessa Holford Diana

Westfield State College

> Some feminist novelists, especially those who are identified with a marginalized community, have [...] attempted to represent both similarity and difference by constituting a multiplicity of individual female voices that echo one another through experiences and perceptions that are also distinct. These voices are not competing for authentic versions of a narrative or offering multiple perspectives on a single story, but are offering multiple stories, each one contributing to a fuller portrait of a specific community.
>
> Susan Sniader Lanser, *Fictions of Authority*

Zitkala-Ša's *American Indian Stories* (autobiographical stories, short fiction, and essays written between 1900-1921) and Sui Sin Far's *Mrs. Spring Fragrance and Other Writings* (autobiographical stories, short fiction, and essays written between 1900-1914) use the strategy of narrative twinning as a means of achieving communal characterization and resisting the cultural erasure efforts of the assimilation period in U.S. history. Both twin autobiographical experiences of isolation and cultural displacement, as well as self-definition, into their short fiction, a technique that emphasizes through repetition the lethal effects of forced assimilation practices and ideologies on their respective cultural groups.[1]

Through this twinning technique, both tell and retell multiple versions of the same core story from various perspectives, employing autobiographical personae and third person fictional narrators. Annette White-Parks notes that Sui Sin Far "shuffles 'facts' between stories and enters or exits at will [...] anonymously, in masquerade as a character, and invisible to an audience that does not know the difference"; this "shuffling" forms "a common thread among journalism, essays, and short stories across her career" ("Trickster

Authorship" 7). Zitkala-Ša and Sui Sin Far create emblematic autobiography, in which self-representation functions allegorically. Jeanne Smith explains the representational function of autobiography in Zitkala-Ša's work: "the personal is inseparable from the political: Her individual story speaks to and comes out of other American Indian stories" (51). Similarly, Annette White-Parks notes that Sui Sin Far's "sense of exile equaled that of the Chinese North American community about whom she wrote" ("Trickster Authorship" 9). Both short story collections operate in the regionalist tradition, which "allow[ed] the reader to view the regional speaker as subject and not as object [...] through [...] shifting the center of perception" (Fetterley and Pryse xvii–xviii). The compiled sketch genre, a form with which a number of American women writers experimented at the turn of the century, "creates out of accumulated short sections an extended narrative that does not conform to familiar, western, climax-oriented, dramatic structure yet does have its own internal drama, rhythm, and coherence" (Ammons, "Men of Color" 25). Twinning, then, creates an internal coherence among collected stories while emphasizing patterns of oppression and resistance among marginalized people.

Communal Voice in Zitkala-Ša's *American Indian Stories*

The selections in Zitkala-Ša's *American Indian Stories* were written at a time when U.S. "reform" policies toward Native Americans were shaped by an assimilation agenda that aimed "to stamp out Indianness altogether and to substitute a uniform Americanness" (Prucha 250). In light of such goals, any attempts on the part of Native Americans to preserve their cultural practices, beliefs, or community and kinship structures was viewed from a mainstream perspective as a stubborn persistence of un-American "savagery." Government-run schools initiated such culturally violent rules as the banning of Native languages as part of the school's effort to "kill the Indian and save the man" (Trout 598). Zitkala-Ša illustrates the consequences of an assimilationist education on herself and her Native-American characters. Many editorials espousing the reformers' assimilationist viewpoints appeared in periodicals such as the *Atlantic Monthly*, where Zitkala-Ša also published a number of her stories, a placement that suggests that her writing is in direct dialogue with the underlying assumptions of such reform rhetoric.

The structure of Zitkala-Ša's collection emphasizes patterns of suffering among those targeted by the psychological warfare of the assimilationist agenda. Because the collection begins with a series of autobiographical short stories that trace her maturation from a young girl living with her mother in a traditional Sioux community to an adult woman struggling with isolation from both Sioux and mainstream American cultures, Zitkala-Ša's later fictional stories are infused with emblematic autobiography. The fictional stories echo the autobiographical with twinned experiences and images, inviting readers to interpret Zitkala-Ša's autobiographical stories as allegorical representations of many "American Indians' stories," so that when Zitkala-Ša describes her struggles to work through "the problem of [her] inner self" (97), which results from her experiences of assimilation pressures, she simultaneously tells the story of a generation's struggle for agency and self-definition in the face of national patterns of disenfranchisement, abuse, isolation, and corruption.[2] Repeatedly she tells the story of the Native American child who is separated from her or his people for a Euro-American education, comes home a "stranger" or "foreigner," and is unable to re-assimilate successfully into tribal life. This technique can be compared to the oral tradition of telling and retelling variants of a core story.[3]

Zitkala-Ša's own family history corresponds with the family histories of many Native Americans, who, like her, were coming of age during the assimilation era (roughly 1880-1930). Dexter Fisher explains that the Bureau of Indian Affairs' policy for schooling assumed "that Indian children would more rapidly assimilate into American society if they were kept away from the reservation for long periods of time" ("Evolution" 232). Zitkala-Ša herself spent three years away from her mother before her first visit back home. Those three years were the beginning of a schism between mother and daughter that continued to widen over Zitkala-Ša's lifetime. She focuses the early autobiographical pieces on her relationship with her mother, specifically illustrating a growing rift between them, which she attributes to acculturation tactics. In this way, Zitkala-Ša sets up a foundation for the later twinned depictions of inter-generational conflict found in the fictional pieces. In "Impressions of an Indian Childhood," Zitkala-Ša describes her early years and traditional upbringing on the Sioux reservation as idyllic (Fisher, "Transformation" 204), devoting the early pages of her autobiography to her close relationship with her mother,[4] who was at once her protector, teacher, and role model. Zitkala-Ša and the other young girls on the reservation "delighted in impersonating [their] own mothers" (21). Zitkala-Ša's early identification with her mother sets up a striking contrast to the stark images of isolation that will later define her experiences at the Eastern schools. Later, the experiences of her fictionalized victims of acculturation are also characterized by isolation and disconnection.

The moment at which Zitkala-Ša and her mother are separated begins the portrayal of isolation and silence through which Zitkala-Ša critiques assimilation efforts. As the train pulls away and Zitkala-Ša realizes her separation from her mother, she begins to feel the oppression of an inhospitable culture: "I no longer felt free to be myself, or to voice my own feelings" (45). As Zitkala-Ša moves toward the site at which she is promised a role in democratic America, she ironically loses her voice, her capacity for self-representation. That freedom of self-expression was possible when Zitkala-Ša was a valued member in her tribal community, but the school to which she is traveling will be a place where education means not only forgetting that tribal community but unlearning its values.

The incomprehensible rules and regulations of the school also stand in direct contrast to the images of freedom Zitkala-Ša evokes in descriptions of her childhood, when she was "wild with surplus spirits, and found joyous relief in running loose in the open" (21). At the school, she is tied down to a chair and forced to endure the humiliation of a "coward's" haircut, a violent act that causes her to lose her spirit temporarily. Paula Gunn Allen comments on the predominance of images of isolation in Native-American literature: "For us, the whole issue of enslavement is part of the issue of conquest and colonization. In that context, it becomes a theme that shows up frequently in Native-American writers' stories about jail, boarding school, war, and abduction. In all of these stories the underlying theme is about forced separation, signifying the loss of self and loss of personal meaning" (*Spiderwoman's Granddaughters* 8).

Uprooted culturally, removed from her family and tribe, Zitkala-Ša describes herself emblematically as "a cold bare pole [...] planted in a strange earth" (97). The image suggests that she has been removed from all that nourishes her, stripped of that which determines her survival: place and community. But her recognition of that isolation moves her to seek a way to speak her outrage: "Still, I seemed to hope a day would come when my mute aching head, reared upward to the sky, would flash a zigzag lightning across the heavens. With this dream of vent for a long-pent consciousness, I walked again amid the crowds" (97). Determined to give voice to her "long-pent consciousness" and to disrupt—with lightning force—the system that strives to "kill the Indian within," Zitkala-Ša discovers "a new way of solving the problem of [her] inner self" (97). And this solution lies in entering mainstream culture—"walk[ing] again amid the crowds"—to enact the political reforms to which she will devote the rest of her life. In this moment of recognized power, Zitkala-Ša casts herself as a dangerous woman, a characterization that she later twins with the fictional "Warrior's Daughter," Tusee, who, like her, claims the right to self-definition. These layers of female communal characterization are a composite strategy of resistance writing founded on Zitkala-Ša's construction of an emblematic self. Zitkala-Ša uses the intimacy of first-person narration to show Native Americans under siege from forced assimilation practices, and then she goes on—in both the autobiographical and fictional stories—to illustrate various ways of resisting the harmful discourse of assimilation.

The fictional Tusee, whose father is the bravest warrior in the tribe, enacts self-definition through physical disguises. She single-handedly rescues her lover, who has been taken captive in battle, by enticing the enemy captor out of the victory celebration with her womanly charms, murdering him, disguising herself as an old woman, and sneaking into the center ground where her lover is tied. "A Warrior's Daughter" works within *American Indian Stories* to strengthen the allegorical significance of Zitkala-Ša's autobiographical self by building on the alternative definitions of female potential she introduced in her autobiographical pieces. As a creation of Zitkala-Ša's narrative voice, Tusee enacts the triumphant "lightning force" Zitkala-Ša had imagined for herself as a young woman. Zitkala-Ša's narrative twinning are textual acts of disguise paralleling Tusee's. We first meet Zitkala-Ša at age eight, and, as Allen points out, the character of Tusee is similar to the ideal images of female potential evident in Zitkala-Ša's first eight years. As a child, Zitkala-Ša's mother "taught [her] no fear"; she was "as free as the wind [...] and no less spirited than a bounding deer [...] keenly alive to the fire within" (8). Tusee as a child is described in much the same way: "Her childish faith in her elders was not conditioned by a knowledge of human limitations, but thought all things possible to grown-ups" (140). The similarities in the two women's upbringing lead the reader to compare the two women as adults. Tusee defies any ideas readers may have about the "human limitations" of women, and Zitkala-Ša defies any ideas Euro-American readers may have about the limitations, be they intellectual, cultural or political, of a Native-American woman.

While Zitkala-Ša—like her fictional heroine Tusee—finds self-empowerment despite the many efforts to silence her, many of her male characters are shown to be significantly disempowered as a result of contact with Euro-American assimilation forces, an illustration of the emasculating effects of "killing the Indian within." Zitkala-Ša's brother Dawee sets a kind of representational precedent in the early stories, which is twinned in later fictional pieces. Dawee returns from his Eastern education to try to help his tribe by fighting corruption in the local Indian Bureau, but he is fired from his position as a government clerk. Dawee is one of a number of disempowered Native men in *American Indian Stories*, men who are rendered unable to provide for or lead their families or communities as a result of assimilation efforts, an emasculation that is twinned in such characters as the "native preacher" in "The Great Spirit," the "Soft-Hearted Sioux," and Chief High Flier of "The Widespread Enigma of Blue Star Woman."

For example, "The Soft Hearted Sioux," is twinned with the autobiographical essay "The Great Spirit," depicting in this soft hearted Sioux a man as unsuccessful in converting his tribal members as the "native preacher" was in converting Zitkala-Ša. The soft hearted Sioux is a warrior's son who leaves the reservation for an education, and returns nine years later, "a stranger" (112) to convert his people to Christianity. Zitkala-Ša emphasizes his status as "stranger" to suggest that successful assimilation from the perspective of dominant culture aims not to make Native-American men part of that mainstream culture, but to cut them off from, and thus weaken, their tribal communities. Instead of becoming the brave huntsman and warrior his father hoped he would be, the Sioux explains, "At the mission school I learned it was wrong to kill. Nine winters I hunted for the soft heart of Christ, and prayed for the huntsmen who chased the buffalo on the plains" (112). The physicality of this metaphor for Christian spirituality foreshadows the story's later descriptions of starvation and bloodshed. The Sioux's education has left him unfit to provide for his now sick and helpless father, and the rest of the tribe abandons him and his family because they interpret his preaching and foreigner's dress to be traitorous (just as Zitkala-Ša's mother and tribe grew to view her as traitorous). The Sioux and his elderly parents starve, and the unskilled young hunter is unable to find food to save them. In this desperate situation, the son begins to change; just before he decides to kill a white rancher's cattle to save his father, he comments, "My neglected hair had grown long and fell upon my neck" (119). Zitkala-Ša's earlier shame over having her own hair cut off teaches non-Sioux readers that short hair can represent cowardice among the Sioux. The length of the son's hair becomes a telling twinned image strengthened by the story's placement within the collection.

By telling her stories in a way similar to recounting variants of a traditional cycle story, Zitkala-Ša affirms the oral tradition in which she was raised. In the shattering of her own family, as well as in the shattered families of her fictional pieces, Zitkala-Ša shows through communal characterization that the U.S. government's campaign of cultural genocide has recognized, and thus targeted, the healing power of intact generational connections, the disruption of which was a central tool in forced assimilation of Native children.

Asserting a Place for Chinese-American Identity: Sui Sin Far's *Mrs. Spring Fragrance and Other Writings*

In her 1909 autobiographical essay, "Leaves from the Mental Portfolio of an Eurasian," Sui Sin Far writes of the virulent anti-Chinese sentiment she experienced daily. In that essay, she shows that the Chinese were believed to be—as her employer described them—other than human. "I cannot reconcile myself to the thought that the Chinese are humans like ourselves," he comments to Sui Sin Far, whose Chinese ancestry is unknown to him; "They may have immortal souls, but their faces seem to be so utterly devoid of expression that I cannot help but doubt" (224). As Amy Ling notes, the Chinese immigrant was, in the imagination of mainstream American culture at the turn of the century, seen as "alien and unassimilable" ("Reading Her/stories" 69). Like, Sui Sin Far explores the psychological effects of American racism on its victims. Sui Sin Far uses intertextual twinning between and among her autobiographical and fictional stories in order to explore the consequences of American assimilation practices and contest prevailing monolithic definitions of American identity.

Functioning similarly to Zitkala-Ša's *American Indian Stories*, Sui Sin Far's *Mrs. Spring Fragrance* uses the short story form to celebrate of American cultural diversity through multifaceted characterization of Chinese-American ethnic identity. "What the short story and short story forms allow Sui Sin Far to do," Elizabeth Ammons explains, "is to present many different people's stories, with the cumulative effect in *Mrs. Spring Fragrance* of giving us a glimpse into a community bound together by shared traditions and problems but composed of individual lives, no one more important than the other" (*Conflicting Stories* 118-119).

Much like Zitkala-Ša, Sui Sin Far repeatedly portrays threatened families through variations on the story of intergenerational conflict resulting from assimilationist efforts. Many of her fictional stories center on a child's estrangement from his or her parents, which represents a distancing from Chinese cultural values. Very much evocative of Zitkala-Ša's own story of separation from her mother is Sui Sin Far's fictional "The Land of the Free," which is just one of her many stories about assimilation and the danger it poses to Chinese-American children and families. In "The Land," Sui Sin Far illustrates mainstream American society's willingness to shatter Chinese families in order to control definitions of who is an American and under what circumstances immigrants are to be permitted access to American rights and opportunities. In this case, the forced removal of a Chinese immigrant couple's infant, who is kept in an orphanage for ten months while the parents must battle an overwhelming and corrupt legal bureaucracy, illustrates the cost of Americanization. At the story's close, when the mother is finally reunited with her son, the child responds to her in fear, not recognizing his mother and instead clinging to the skirts of the white missionary woman in whose care he was kept during their separation. The baby's new allegiance can be read as an allegory of Americanization, the price of which is lost memory of one's cultural origins and a learned fear of the designated "Other."

Another connection between the two short story collections is the portrayal of children's suffering, found in Sui Sin Far's autobiography, "Leaves from the Mental Portfolio of an Eurasian," where she recounts childhood "battles" against racist children, and in a fictional tale of children and racism titled "Pat and Pan." Both stories illustrate the destructive nature of American racial categorization while showing that child-rearing is, in dominant U.S. culture, a process of indoctrinating children to accept racial hierarchy. "Pat and Pan" focuses on two young children, named in the title. Pat was born to a nameless white mother who was—for unstated reasons—a social outcast from the white community, and was taken in by the Lum Yooks, a loving Chinese couple (also social outcasts based on their race) who treated him "as their own" and "bestowed upon him equal love and care with the little daughter" Pan (164). This harmonious interracial family presents an image of an idealized national family, where the color line is no barrier to love and nurturing. But this tale ultimately ends in estrangement, suggesting Sui Sin Far's pessimism over most Americans' willingness to see past the color line or envision a united national family.

Anna Harrison, a white missionary woman, has alerted the white community to Pat's "unnatural" position as member of a Chinese family, and Mrs. Lum Yook knows "there are many tongues wagging because he lives under our roof" (164). Public opinion does, of course, win out in the end. The Lum Yooks are powerless to resist Pat's removal, and a white couple adopts the boy. Sui Sin Far frames "Pat and Pan" in such a way as to set up dramatic tension between the perspectives on family and community membership of Anna Harrison and of the Chinese adults and children whose lives she enters and changes drastically. As "Pat and Pan" opens, Harrison is in an urban Chinatown and spies the young white boy, Pat, and his Chinese sister, Pan, "[lying] there, in the entrance to the joss house, sound asleep in each other's arms" (160). Puzzled by the presence of a white boy so intimately positioned within this Chinatown setting, Harrison inquires about his identity, and an old Chinese vendor tells her that the boy is "of Lum Yook." "But he is white," asserts the puzzled woman, unable to reconcile the boy's race and his location within a Chinese family and community. The vendor answers, "Yes, him white; but all same, China boy" (160). Harrison "determines" to remove Pat from this setting in which he does not belong because "[f]or a white boy to grow up as a Chinese was unthinkable" (161).[5] What is "unthinkable" to Harrison is the fact that Americanness and Chineseness, categories she believes to be essentially different, are confused and blended in Pat's identity.

In this brief exchange, Sui Sin Far uses Harrison's character to evoke the perceived threat that Chinese immigrants represented in the imaginations of many turn-of-the-century white Americans. Often framed as an imminent invasion, Chinese immigration was frequently imaged as the "yellow peril" in mainstream media. Chinese immigrants became the target for U.S. racism, and fear of a Chinese invasion prompted race riots in California Chinatowns and the 1882 Chinese Exclusion Act. By contrasting the children's contentment in the Chinatown setting with Harrison's horror, Sui Sin Far creates a narrative tension between the children's loving sibling relationship—an idealized national "brotherhood"—and the socially constructed perspective of Harrison, who represents the viewpoint of "American civilization." To the not yet assimilated children, they are "naturally" brother and sister. Racialization, then, is what is unnatural in this story.

Also significant in the story's allegorical representation of American "family" relations on a national level is the adopted white boy's name, which, through twinned associations in popular discourse, takes on layered meaning in relation to the character of his Chinese sister. At the turn of the last century, popular print media and political cartoons depended on racial stereotypes to portray U.S. race relations and current legislative debates relating to civil rights and immigration controls. In their portrayal of Irish immigrants, such cartoons and editorials often used the label "Pat" to represent Irish men as they would use "John Chinaman" to represent Chinese men.[6] This stereotypical portrayal occurred at the same time that economic depression and unemployment rates escalated in the 1870s, spurring antagonism from white labor groups toward the Chinese that erupted into violent protest. The Irish were one of the groups most in competition with the Chinese for menial jobs, so the interracial conflict between Irish and Chinese was especially severe (Choy 112). Suggesting the labor competition that divided Irish and Chinese immigrants, Sui Sin Far evokes similar competition in the children's classroom. In response to Pan's academic success, Pat responds, "I hate you, Pan!" (163). Sui Sin Far's decision to give the adopted white boy a name used in reductive racial labeling expresses on the level of one shattered family, the human cost of enforced racial segregation. In his year within the white community, Pat's new family, teachers, and peers teach him the boundaries of American identity, boundaries which exclude the Chinese and their culture. When Pan meets her beloved brother a year later, Pat, in a group of white friends, turns on his sister with hate, shouting at her to get away from him, a scene that is twinned with Sui Sin Far's own memory of white children's racist slurs toward her. "Poor Pat!" laments Pan, "he Chinese no more!" (166).

Just as the separation between sister and brother represents division in the national family, so too do Sui Sin Far's stories of courtship and marriage represent the power dynamics determined by race and sex in America. Sui Sin Far employs allegorical self-representation, rendering her own story emblematic of such power relationships when she tells in "Leaves" the story of a white lieutenant who propositions her by explaining, "I came just because I had an idea that you might like to know me. I would like to know you. You look like such a nice little body. Say, wouldn't you like to go for a sail this lovely night? I will tell you all about the sweet little Chinese girls I met when we were at Hong Kong. They're not so shy!" (226). The Lieutenant associates Sui Sin Far with the Chinese prostitutes he encountered in Hong Kong and assumes her race and sex make her sexually available to him. It is perhaps because of such experiences that Sui Sin Far becomes a "very serious and sober minded spinster" (226), choosing sexual isolation that parallels her social isolation as a Eurasian woman.

In the short story "Its Wavering Image," Sui Sin Far offers a related analysis of sexual and racial politics, using courtship to present interracial relationships allegorically. The story tells of a romantic relationship between a Euro-American man named Mark Carson and a Eurasian woman named Pan, whose name recalls the young Chinese sister of "Pat and Pan." That Sui Sin Far chooses to twin the female characters' names between the two stories suggests some connections between the characters' situations, and indeed, while the childhood Pan suffers family fragmentation because of racial categorization, the adult Pan suffers personal, internal fragmentation when faced with those same unbending racial categories. Furthermore, the shared name contributes to communal characterization by alerting readers to the common systems of belief that cause both Pans to suffer. Carson's character illustrates the role of the mainstream gaze in constructing racial barriers and unequal power relations. Pan's biracial identity is threatening to Carson because she disturbs the racial categorization on which the stability of his own ideas about American identity rely; Pan "puzzles" Carson, who asks, "what was she? Chinese or white?" (61). His confusion is much like Anna Harrison's because he both identifies with her (in this case through desire) and resists her "difference." As for Pan's self-perception, "It was only after the coming of Mark Carson," the narrator tells us, "that the mystery of [Pan's] nature began to trouble her" (61). Her budding desire for Carson and his demand that she abandon her allegiance to the Chinese create of her identity a "wavering image" that she must actively bring back into focus.

His character functions emblematically, infusing the story's specific details of courtship with the national realities of unequal power relations between Euro-American men and women of color, and thereby reminding readers of the persistent patterns of sexual exploitation that result from those power disparities.[7] Because her proximity to other Chinese, her Chinatown surroundings, and her cultural practices mark Pan as Other, Carson hopes to remove her from association with the Chinese in order to locate his desire for her within the realm of the licensed and thereby legitimate it. His motivation is much the same as Anna Harrison's, a twinning by which Sui Sin Far emphasizes the pervasiveness of segregationist efforts by those in privileged positions. Carson responds to Pan's declaration of love for the Chinese people with disgust in attempt to reassert his control over the situation through language. The following dialogue ensues:

> "Pan," he cried, "you do not belong here. You are white—white."
> "No! No!" protested Pan.
> "You are," he asserted. "You have no right to be here." (63)

Insisting upon distinct, mutually exclusive racial categories, Carson demands of Pan, "you have got to decide what you will be—Chinese or white? You cannot be both" (63). Pan clearly will not be forced to give up her Chinese identity or community, despite her desire for Carson. Soon after, he betrays her trust by publishing a racist "exclusive" on Pan's community in the papers. Now, in "the clear passionless light of the afternoon" (64), Pan reads Carson's article, which "cruelly" and "ruthlessly spread before the ridiculing and uncomprehending foreigner" the sacred beliefs and traditions of her people (65). Readers are reminded here of Sui Sin Far's objections to stereotypical and uncomprehending portrayals of Chinese characters in fiction, objections she strengthens here by reversing mainstream definitions of "foreigners." In this passage, Pan compares her horror and shame for her unwitting role in this betrayal of her people to having "her own naked body and soul [...] exposed" (65), suggesting sexual as well as cultural violation.

Pan's story is further twinned with details of Sui Sin Far's autobiography. Like Sui Sin Far, Pan could pass as white and live free from the direct racism the Chinese suffer, but her sense of injustice over that racism and her allegiance to the Chinese is too strong to allow her to sacrifice honor for comfort. Sui Sin Far indicates in "Leaves" that because she, like Pan, can pass, she often hears first-hand racist comments from white speakers who, she comments, never dream "that I too am of the 'brown people' of the earth" (225). In "Its Wavering Image," Sui Sin Far creates Pan as a twinned version of her self; both author and fictional character eventually embrace the invisible ethnicity that marginalizes them. When Carson meets her again, two months later, Pan is dressed in traditional Chinese clothing. She declares to him, "I am a Chinese woman" (66). Not surprisingly, Carson believes Pan "was not herself tonight. She did not even *look* herself" (66, emphasis added). In "Leaves," Sui Sin Far declares to her similarly shocked boss and coworkers, "The Chinese may have no souls, no expression on their faces, be altogether beyond the pale of civilization, but whatever they are, I want you to understand that I am —I am a Chinese" (225).

Both Zitkala-Ša and Sui Sin Far can be said to practice what Lauren Berlant calls "Diva Citizenship": the act of publicly presenting "a different history, one that claimed the most intimate stories of subordinated people as information about *everyone's* citizenship" (221), thereby "calling on people *to change the social and institutional practices of citizenship to which they currently consent*" (223, emphasis added). The twinned incorporation of autobiography into short stories articulates that the personal is indeed political, that the individual's story is both representative and at the same time one of many in a composite portrait of communal characterization.

Notes

1 The two collections do differ, however. Zitkala-Ša's *American Indian Stories* was originally published as a compilation of autobiographical, fictional, and non-fiction selections, while Sui Sin Far's 1912 *Mrs. Spring Fragrance* did not originally include autobiographical or nonfiction essays, though the short stories it includes reveal numerous intertextual twinnings, as is the case in Zitkala-Ša's collection. However, at the same time that she wrote the fictional stories collected in *Mrs. Spring Fragrance*, Sui Sin Far was also publishing journalistic and autobiographical essays in the U.S. and Canada ("Leaves from the Mental Portfolio of an Eurasian," for example, was published in 1909). When in 1995 Amy Ling and Annette White-Parks published *Mrs. Spring Fragrance and Other Writings*, a collection of Sui Sin Far's fiction, journalistic, and autobiographical work, readers were offered an opportunity to consider connections not only among the short stories, but among this writer's entire oeuvre of resistance writing. So, we can consider intertextual twinnings among her fictional and non-fictional works as narrative patternings of oppositional representation across her entire project of resistance writing.

2 While Zitkala-Ša argues for citizenship as a necessary part of Native Americans' enfranchisement, there is, as Carol Batker explains, a paradoxical element to that stance: "Citizenship's legal emphasis on individualism was sometimes seen by Native Americas as a threat to tribal organization and to tribal status as separate nations. Moreover, in an article on the Black Hills Council, Zitkala-Ša's critique of the reservation system seems to

subordinate tribalism to Americanization and citizenship [...]. However, Zitkala Sa advocated citizenship not to oppose tribal organization, necessarily, but to protect tribal rights and treaties" (195).

3   For example, Paula Gunn Allen explains, "Traditional native novels are identified as 'cycles' by folklorists when they are referring to a number of stories that cluster around a more or less central theme and often feature particular characters and events" (*Spiderwoman's Granddaughters* 4).

4   Susag sees the character of Zitkala-Ša's mother as a covert way for Zitkala-Ša to communicate the values of Dakota people regarding children, focusing on displays of respect for the child and lessons of respect taught to the child (12).

5   In other stories, Sui Sin Far presents the opposite circumstance, when white missionaries or government workers take Chinese children away from their families to be raised by whites or where assimilation threatens to erase Chinese language and culture from children. See, for example, "In the Land of the Free" (93) and "The Wisdom of the New" (42).

6   See for example the entire collection of political cartoons relating to Chinese immigrants and immigration legislation in Philip Choy and Lorraine Dong, editors, *The Coming Man: Nineteenth Century American Perceptions of the Chinese*.

7   Sui Sin Far's use of twinning in "Its Wavering Image" illustrates both her incorporation of emblematic autobiography into her fiction and her linking of characters and circumstances across fictional pieces. It is, therefore, no surprise that we find a twin for Mark Carson in the character of James Carson from "The Story of One White Woman who Married a Chinese." Like his namesake, James Carson is also a selfish, manipulative, and racist white man of cruel nature. Furthermore, both men share the name of the western American "hero," Kit Carson, whose violent battles against the Navajo and Apache in the mid-nineteenth century represented in mainstream imagination the triumph of "civilization" over "savagery." By evoking the cultural myths of racial superiority and manifest destiny that Kit Carson embodies, Sui Sin Far critically examines the way European Americans define civilization in the U.S.

Works Cited

Allen, Paula Gunn. *Spiderwoman's Granddaughters: Traditional Tales and Contemporary Writing by Native American Women*. NY: Fawcett Columbine, 1989.

———. *The Sacred Hoop*. Boston, Beacon Press, 1992.

Ammons, Elizabeth and Annette White-Parks. Introduction. *Trickserism in Turn of the Century American Literature: A Multicultural Perspective*. Hanover: UP of New England, 1994.

Ammons, Elizabeth. *Conflicting Stories: American Women Writers at the Turn into the Twentieth Century*. NY: Oxford University Press, 1991.

———. "Men of Color, Women, and Uppity Art at the Turn of the Century." *American Realism and the Canon*. Ed. Tom Quirk and Gary Scharnhost. Newark: U Delaware P, 1994. 22-33.

Berkhofer, Robert F. Jr. *The White Man's Indian: Images of the American Indian from Culumbus to the Present*. NY: Alfred A Knopf, 1978.

Berlant, Lauren. "The Queen of America goes to Washington City: Harriet Jacobs, Frances Harper, Anita Hill." *American Literature* 65: 3 (1993 Sept.) 549-74.

Choy, Philip, Lorraine Dong, and Marlon Hom, ed. *The Coming Man: Nineteenth Century American Perceptions of the Chinese.* Seattle: University of Washington Press, 1995.

Fetterly, Judith and Marjorie Pryse, ed. *American Women Regionalists: 1850-1919.* NY: Norton, 1992.

Fisher, Dexter. Introduction. *American Indian Stories.* By Zitkala-Ša. Lincoln: U of Nebraska P, 1979.

———. "The Transformation of Tradition: A Study of Zitkala-Ša and Mourning Dove, Two Transitional American Indian Writers. *Critical Essays on Native American Literature.* Ed. Andrew Wiget. Boston: G.K. Hall & Co., 1985: 202-11.

———. "Zitkala-Ša: The Evolution of a Writer." *American Indian Quarterly* 5:3 (1979 August) 229-38.

Lanser, Susan Sniader. *Fictions of Authority: Women Writers and Narrative Voice.* Ithaca: Cornell University Press, 1992.

Ling, Amy. "Reading Her/stories Against His/stories in Early Chinese American Literature." *American Realism and the Canon.* Ed. Tom Quirk and Gary Scharnhorst. Newark: University Delaware Press, 1994. 54-67.

Prucha, Francis Paul. *American Indian Policy in Crisis: Chrstina Reformers and the Indian, 1865–1900.* Norman: U of Oklahoma P, 1976.

Sui Sin Far. *Mrs. Spring Fragrance and Other Writings.* Amy Ling and Annette White-Parks, eds. Urbana: U of Illinois P, 1995.

Trout, Lawanna, ed. *Native American Literature: An Anthology.* Chicago: NTC Contemporary Publishing, 1999.

White-Parks, Annette. "'We Wear The Mask': Sui Sin Far as One Example of Trickster Authorship." *Tricksterism in Turn-of-the-Century American Literature.* Ed Elizabeth Ammons and Annette White-Parks. Hanover: UP of New England, 1994.

Zitkala-Ša. *American Indian Stories.* Lincoln: University of Nebraska Press, 1979.

Laura's Unconscious Rejection of the Short Story in Katherine Anne Porter's "Flowering Judas"

Susana M. Jiménez-Placer
Universidade de Santiago de Compostela

One of the most prominent features of the short story is that it works partly through suggestion: the reader's imagination must go beyond the literal understanding of the words and the simple narrated facts in order to uncover an almost inexhaustible range of meanings which are often hidden behind an apparent simplicity. As other linguistic manifestations, the short story locates itself between what Hjelmslev called the *expression-substance* and the *content-substance*[1]; that is, it places itself within the realm of language understood as a playful, frolicsome form where rigid systematicity is being constantly overcome by the linguistic potentiality for the game. The short story, therefore, rests on the variety, ambiguity and flexibility of language, which thus become basic pillars in the construction of short fiction. Although this flexibility affects most linguistic expressions, the shortness that characterizes short fiction endows this aspect with special significance: if a single sentence may "generate multiple, often conflicting, meanings" (Johnson 46), then the short story takes clear advantage of this quality of language in order to enlarge its scope. Moreover, this essential linguistic multiplicity is usually complemented by the writer's resorting to symbols, which increases the fluidity of meanings required by this genre.

In short fiction, the use of language becomes thus a clear exponent of the existence of an unstable relationship between language itself and reality. In other words, most short stories are overt manifestations of the violation of what Derrida considers the basic theological goal of the *metaphysics of presence* and its *logocentrism*: the illusion of presence[2]. The main manifestation of this goal would be God's voice creating the universe. In Genesis, "everything that issues from the lips of God springs immediately in existence" (Barbeito 18), and as a consequence "everything is present to God immediately and simultaneously" (Barbeito 17). Thus presence and immediacy define God's discourse in the Bible and become the ultimate expression of the aim pursued by the *metaphysics of presence*. Therefore, this theological goal may be understood as an attempt to recover the language of presence and immediacy suitable for conversing with God by means of overcoming the linguistic diversity and arbitrariness which have filled the gap between words and reality since the loss of linguistic immediacy resulting from the human fall. In fact, the ambiguity and flexibility of language have been traditionally associated with the introduction of evil as part of the human nature after the fall: evil transformed human beings into contradictory creatures whose nature is a mixture of good and evil forces, and it opened a gap between the human language and reality, a space for the articulation of the linguistic game. Thus, the arbitrariness of language became the most clear expression of the complexity of the human nature.

In Katherine Anne Porter's "Flowering Judas" Laura's rejection of the human being as a sum of good and evil is reflected in her attitude concerning language, that is, in her blindness to its multiplicity, flexibility and arbitrariness. From this perspective her betrayal becomes double in this story: on the one hand she betrays herself as the human being that she as a character represents, and on the other hand, by means of depriving language of its symbolism, its density and multiplicity, Laura also betrays the essence of her own short story, reducing it to the status of a literal account of one of her evenings with Braggioni. This last betrayal is especially significant in a story such as "Flowering Judas" which has been described as one of the best examples of "Ezra Pound's definition of great literature as 'language charged with meaning to the utmost possible degree'" (Madden 123).

"Flowering Judas" is the story of an American woman, Laura, who is living in Mexico during the revolution. Every evening, when she comes home, she finds the revolutionist Braggioni there. One evening, while Braggioni is singing a song to her, the narrator gets into her mind in order to provide us with information about her role in the revolution, her job as an English teacher, and her visit to a church. We learn that Mexico represents for Laura an escape from her Catholic upbringing as well as the promise of revolutionary romance. But she does not feel at home in Mexico: the revolution does not come up to her expectations and she cannot be faithful either to her previous life or to her new revolutionary experience. The source of Laura's main problem in the story is to be found in her obsession with order and uniformity, which causes her unconscious rejection of the human being as a sum of good and evil, as a creature of both God and the devil. This rejection of the complexity of the human nature leads her to a complete denial of the human world as a temptation to evil without realizing that by means of doing so she is betraying her own humanity.

Moreover, for Laura this struggle against evil requires her denial of the linguistic arbitrariness and flexibility, which she interprets as vehicles of a devilish chaos. She insists on perceiving reality and language just on a fixed, literal level as if the rigidity of this approach were the only shelter against evil and corruption available to her. But she is mistaken: it is impossible to liberate language and the human being of evil because evil itself constitutes one of the essential elements in the nature of each of these terms. Furthermore, since we are considering that short fiction depends on the gap between words and reality opened by the presence of evil in the human language, Laura's denial of evil threatens the very essence of short fiction itself.

"Flowering Judas" is basically an expression of Katherine Anne Porter's disillusionment with the Mexican revolution. Her disappointment with the development of this war as shown in "Flowering Judas" may remind us of Milton's ideas concerning the failure of the seventeenth century English revolution as shown in *Paradise Lost*. Both the short story and the poem show how selfishness, narcissism and self-interest occupied a prominent position among the vices which contributed to the failure of the revolutionary movements[3]: self-interest led to division among the seventeenth century English revolutionists as well as among the twentieth century Mexican ones, which produced a generalized impression of chaos in both cases. But while in *Paradise Lost* the problem of language constitutes an essential part in Milton's "attempt to think *of the possibility of order, of establishing a new order*" (Barbeito 10, emphasis added), in "Flowering Judas" Katherine Anne Porter tries to reaffirm the unavoidable *humanity* of chaos by means of denouncing Laura's obsession with a dogmatic kind of order which finds its most evident manifestation in her attitude towards language.

Speech is one of the main attributes of the human being in both works. In "Flowering Judas" human beings are defined as "clay masks with the power of human speech" (CS 101)[4], and in *Paradise Lost* as well as in Genesis Adam is the clay figure that receives human life and speech from God (*Paradise Lost* VII: 505-15, VII: 524-26; Genesis 2:7, 2:19). In Milton's poem, the human speech constitutes also the main ingredient in the process of the devil's temptation. As we shall see later, when Satan tries to seduce Eve he resorts to his ability to manipulate words as his only weapon. The human speech gets thus infected with the devil's loquacity and becomes arbitrary, chaotic and unsuitable for *conversing* with God[5]: it becomes a corruption of God's gift and a sign of the human loss of His divine order.

In "Flowering Judas" Katherine Anne Porter blames Laura for the narrowness of her obsession with order and uniformity, and finds in this obsession the source of her denial of the complexity which the human speech *gained* as a consequence of the devil's temptation and which is essential in the short story. In fact, as we shall see later, this linguistic complexity constitutes one of the main vehicles of what Wright calls the "inner recalcitrance" of modern short fiction, the kind of "recalcitrance" that works "at the ground level of language" (Wright 121).

In Porter's story, the Mexican revolution is devoid of any real revolutionary activity and depends exclusively on the words spoken by its leaders. The revolutionists waste their time writing songs; prisoners are taken to jail for talking too much, and there they devote themselves to writing their memoirs and manifestoes: "During her leisure [Laura] goes to union meetings and listens to busy important voices quarreling over tactics, methods, internal politics" (CS 94), and then, "She smuggles letters from headquarters to men hiding from firing squads..." (CS 94). In Mexico, identity itself has been reduced to a set of boastful words, and waiting is the keyword in a revolution which seems to depend almost exclusively on the "equivocal phrases" (CS 94) that Laura repeats as a messenger; within this context, Braggioni is the perfect revolutionary leader who offers his comrades simply words in a "hypnotic voice" (CS 100) of which he takes good care.

Moreover, country has become a true Tower of Babel of foreign tongues and accents: English, Spanish, Polish, Roumanian.... The variety of languages that can be heard in Mexico emphasizes the chaotic atmosphere in "Flowering Judas," and suggests a parallelism with the biblical presentation of the *sinful* origin of the different human languages in Babel (Genesis 11: 1-9). Her contact with all these different languages could have helped Laura realize that "the relation between the signifier and the signified in any given sign is arbitrary (there is no natural resemblance between sound and idea)" (Johnson 41), but her obsession with order will not allow her to assume this arbitrariness as one of the fundamental aspects of the human speech. The biblical parallelism may even suggest that Laura understands the existence of different languages as the chaotic consequence of the human evil in Babel, and accordingly she interprets this multiplicity as a curse, a fault that she must try to overcome. In this sense the narrator's use of language subtly points out the futility of Laura's attempt:

> If the prisoners confuse night and day, and complain, "Dear little Laura, time doesn't pass in this infernal hole and I won't know when it is time to sleep unless I have a

reminder," she brings them their favorite narcotics, and says in a tone that does not wound them with pity, *"Tonight will really be night for you,"* and though her *Spanish amuses them*, they find her comforting, useful. (CS 94, emphasis added)

Laura's words are written in English and in direct speech. We as readers are thus led to think that we are reading an exact transcription of the words that she has actually uttered, only to discover just after having read them that she was speaking in Spanish, not in English. The narrator is offering us not only a transcription but also a translation of her words: she is supposed to have spoken in Spanish but this is English, not Spanish. What the narrator seems to be suggesting is that we as readers can read the words in English but assuming that they are in Spanish, that is, assuming that they are in fact different words from the ones printed on the page. The narrator is thus forcing us not only to acknowledge but also to experience by ourselves in our own reading activity the arbitrariness and flexibility of the linguistic sign as manifested in the existence of different languages, the same arbitrariness and flexibility that Laura condemns as synonymous with sin and corruption.

But this story goes even further: it illustrates how this kind of arbitrariness is unavoidable even within the scope of one single language, and how it is this quality itself that allows the messages that Laura repeats to be "disguised in equivocal phrases" (CS 94). In "Flowering Judas" this aspect finds its most evident expression in the messages of love written by the Indian children of Xochimilco who are learning English with Laura as their teacher. When these Indian children write messages of love on the blackboard, they do not write the words properly: in their messages the word "love" becomes "lov" and "teacher" "ticher" (CS 95). But in spite of these peculiar, non-normative spellings we as readers can still identify this language as English and understand the children's message. As in the previous case, the story itself allows us to experience the flexibility of language that makes possible that "love" can be "lov". But for Laura this is just a new ingredient in the surrounding chaos which she is struggling to overcome. Ironically, her own story depends on the fact that words are not so fixed as she thinks, not even within the scope of her own perfectly correct English language.

Laura lives within this revolutionary context where human words and human tongues have become representative of the disorder of the surrounding reality. For her the essence of this chaos finds its most clear expression in the prominence of words in the revolution: while she listens to Braggioni, Laura can perceive the complete emptiness of his revolutionary discourse, that is, she can perceive the excessive distance that separates words and reality in the context of the Mexican revolution, and her direct reaction is her condemnation of the resulting gap and her consequent attempt to overcome this distance which contains the flexibility, multiplicity and diversity of language as well as the essential symbolic function (Kristeva 136) which gives language what Derrida calls its supplementary character. Ignoring the existence of the "equivocal phrases," which are "equivocal" thanks to the linguistic flexibility, Laura decides to search in language for a source of order and control, a shelter that can protect her from the threat of complete chaos: "she sits in her deep chair with an open book on her knees, resting her eyes on the consoling rigidity of the printed page" (CS 91). As this passage announces, Laura does not realize that the complete erasure of the linguistic flexibility can only cause the destruction of real human speech through its reduction to its immediate expression-substance, as we shall analyze later. Language becomes thus for Laura a potential "overarching structure of order and stability," a structure that Robert Brinkmeyer considers unattainable through the knowledge of oneself in Katherine Anne Porter's fiction (Brinkmeyer 6). With her attitude Laura seems to be forgetting that the self is "itself a disorder and confusion of forces and identities that resist clarity and stability" (Brinkmeyer 6), a notion that according to Leitch is essential in the modern short story because it contributes to what he calls its "debunking rhythm": "these stories commonly debunk a particular subject: the concept of a public identity, a self that acts in such a knowable, deliberate way as to assert a stable, discrete identity" (Leitch 133-134). From this perspective, Laura's obsession with order would be just an expression of her faith in the possibility of having "a stable and discrete personal identity," a faith which is at odds with the "debunking rhythm" of modern short fiction.

It is, therefore, within the realm of language that Laura searches in vain for the order and uniformity which she cannot find anywhere else. There she discovers the word which, according to her, prevents her from being led into the chaos of evil, the word which constitutes the "very cells of her flesh," the "one holy talismanic word" from which she "draws her strength": "No. No. No" (CS 97). Laura finds in this word the essence of her order and stability. Thus, her "no" becomes a manifestation of her attempt to suppress the evil side, that is, the element of chaos—in the human being and the human language. By means of her constant repetition of the word "no" she is symbolically reversing the scene of Eve's fall: she is a new Eve resisting the temptation of the snake which brings evil and chaos to the human nature as well as to the human language. According to this interpretation, her "no" would represent a symbolical attempt to recover the divine order that characterized the relationship between words and reality as well as between God and the human being before the fall.

But in "Flowering Judas" Katherine Anne Porter condemns this attempt and implicitly proposes a modern reading of the biblical episode of the human fall, more in accordance with her own ideas about the human being. All along her career Katherine Anne Porter put special emphasis on the idea that human beings had to be first of all human[6], and for her a human being is a sum of conflicting forces, a mixture of good and evil. In other words, for Porter a human being is the complex product of Eve's acceptance of the forbidden fruit and of the resulting human fall. When Laura symbolically says "no" to the devil's temptation rejecting the fruit of the tree of knowledge, she is saying "no" to what Katherine Anne Porter considered to be one of the essential aspects in the human nature: the knowledge of good and evil. Therefore, by means of rejecting evil Laura is unconsciously betraying humanity in general and herself as a human being.

In *Paradise Lost* Satan establishes a direct link between the forbidden fruit and the human speech: according to the Satanic snake, *its* speech is one of the immediate consequences of *its* having eaten the fruit of the tree of knowledge (*Paradise Lost* IX:595-601). Speech was thus charged with the stain of Satanic evil which manifests itself in the distance which had separated words from reality since the fall. The beguiling and seducing words which Satan himself addresses to Eve to tempt her to constitute an example of the rhetorical use of the linguistic diversity which fills this gap opened between words and reality by the presence of evil[7]. In this poem, Satan's fall and his use of words function as an anticipation of the human fall and its consequences for human speech: in fact, after the fall, Adam reacts to God's reprimand after the fall with a loquacity more proper to the devil's discourse than to the divine conversation with God (*Paradise Lost*, X: 124-144) [8].

In *Paradise Lost* the problem of the human speech is therefore intimately related to the fall: the introduction of evil in human nature is directly linked to the discovery of the rhetorical possibilities which mediate between the human words and reality as a consequence of the loss of the divine order after the fall. In other words, the incorporation of evil in human nature and language marks the origin of the linguistic distance that Laura tries to overcome. From this perspective Laura's "no" would imply a denial of the devil's use of the diversity of language. Her "no" would mean the rejection of the possibilities offered by this new linguistic flexibility taught by Satan and symbolically incorporated to human nature and speech by means of eating the forbidden fruit.

In fact, in "Flowering Judas" Laura's obsession with order, control and uniformity limits even her understanding of the word "no." She can only accept one fixed interpretation of this word—for her "no" means always a denial of evil—and is blind to any other possible connotations of this same term. She cannot realize that even her "holy talismanic word" can be subject to multiple interpretations, as the narrator seems to suggest when he repeats the word "no" three times in the text (CS 97) reminding us of St. Peter's denial of Christ in the Gospel (Luke 22: 34, 61-62). Laura's "no" may imply the rejection of Satan's evil in Eden, but it may also imply a denial of Christ's goodness as shown in the Gospel. Laura ignores this second possible implication: she can only understand her "no" as that of a pure, innocent Eve living in an Edenic paradise, but she is actually living in a revolutionary chaos, and ironically her role in this revolution is closer to St. Peter's than to Eve's. If Braggioni represents a distorted image of Christ as a "professional lover of humanity" (CS 98),[9] then Laura may well be a distorted image of Saint Peter, the apostle who repeats the Lord's—Braggioni's—words all over the village.

The presentation of Braggioni as a distorted Christ proves again the active role of the narrator in this story: he is constantly undermining Laura's conceptions by means of his word choice which usually serves as a counterpart to Laura's attempt to overcome linguistic diversity: "This is her private *heresy*, for in her special group the machine is *sacred*, and will be the *salvation* of the workers" (CS 92, emphasis added). By means of his constant use of religious terms to refer to the revolution the narrator is not only suggesting Laura's own contradictory nature, but he is also subtly underlining the flexibility of language. He is proving that even those words with a primary religious meaning, and thus primarily related to the church, can be used to describe a revolution which is, at least at first sight, at odds with the Catholic ritual. In this sense the narrator's words are also especially meaningful when he describes Laura's appearance while Braggioni is singing to her. According to him, Laura "wears the uniform of an idea": the "idea" is socialism, but the "uniform" is that of a nun. Revolutionary principles dressed in a Catholic attire: this is the image suggested by the narrator's words in order to unveil Laura's basic tension in the story. In his words Laura becomes the perfect embodiment of what she is trying to repress: the uniform that she wears is the most precise evidence of her own lack of uniformity and order, that is, it is the expression of her failure to overcome chaos. Moreover, the "fullness of her breasts, like a nursing mother's" is obviously at odds with her "notorious virginity" (CS 97).[10] Thus, through his choice of words the narrator emphasizes Laura's inner tension showing how her obsession with order is a direct manifestation of her betrayal of herself as a complex, contradictory human being. At the same time, the narrator's words are an evident manifestation of the same linguistic flexibility and diversity which Laura tries to ignore when she reduces language to a rigid system of order. Finally, the narrator's use of language in "Flowering Judas" shows how the story itself subtly rebels against Laura's attitude and conceptions undermining her search for order and suggesting its destructive consequences.

Laura hoped she would find in Mexico an Edenic paradise inhabited by pure Adams and Eves, but what she finds there is a *lost paradise* exclusively inhabited by "clay masks with the power of human speech," that is, the kind of speech that has been already infected with Satan's evil. Mexico is a world crowded with human beings, who are fallen Adams and Eves made of clay not as a sign of creation but as the seal of death on them. The "immaculate voices" of the Indian children who bring flowers to her constitute the only expression of purity that she can find in Mexico: "When she appears in the classroom they crowd about her with smiles on their wise, innocent, clay-colored faces, crying, 'Good morning, my titcher!' in immaculate voices, and they make of her desk a fresh garden of flowers every day" (CS 93-94). The children's flowers represent an Edenic world of innocent love and womanhood. They are symbols of love, but Laura cannot accept this symbolical implication because it would force her to go beyond the limits of her strict order. Any process of symbolization means the establishment of a link between the symbolizing and the symbolized entities, but the presence of such a link presupposes the existence of a distance between both terms—the symbolizing and the symbolized—the same distance which separates words from reality, and which Laura interprets as the source of chaos in language because it is the space of linguistic diversity. Owing to her obsession with order and her consequent struggle against the ambiguity and deviation introduced by symbolism Laura can only understand the *proper meaning* of an object in reality; for her, language and images are never "charged with meaning to the utmost possible degree." According to her literal approach to reality a flower is just a flower, an object devoid of any symbolical connotations. The logical consequence of this attitude is her inability to understand either the symbolical meaning of the flowers which the Indian children bring to her desk, or the symbolical implications of the flower which she throws to the "brown, shock-haired youth [who] stood in her patio one night and sang like a lost soul for two hours" (CS 96). And it is also because of this literal approach to reality that when she visits the church she perceives the male-saint there just as a material object, a "battered doll-shape" with "lace-trimmed drawers" which "hang limply around his ankles below the hieratic dignity of his velvet robe" (CS 92). Similarly, when the bell tolls at night before her final dream, she finds it difficult to understand its symbolical meaning: "The tolling of the midnight bell is a signal, but what does it mean?" (CS 101).

When we meet the children for the second time in the story they are drawing flowers and writing messages of love on the blackboard. Laura can only recognize the literal reference in reality of the drawn flowers but she is still unable to understand their deeper symbolic meaning:

> Next morning the children made a celebration and spent their playtime writing on the blackboard, "We lov ar ticher", and with tinted chalks they drew wreaths of flowers around the words. The young hero wrote her a letter: "I am a very foolish, wasteful, impulsive man. I should have first said I love you, and then you would not have run away. But you shall see me again." Laura thought, "I must send him a box of colored crayons," but she was trying to forgive herself for having spurred her horse at the wrong moment. (CS 95-96)

In addition to her inability to understand the symbolical meaning of the drawn flowers, Laura ignores the content of the written messages and gives no sign of recognition of the innocent love that they convey. As this passage suggests, in Laura's mind both the drawn flowers and the written words become just chalk—or crayon—devoid of any real meaning. Her reaction to her suitor's letter makes this clear. When Laura reads this letter and thinks "I must send him a box of colored crayons," she is establishing a parallelism between the children's words and flowers on the blackboard and her suitor's declaration of love, and she is reducing both at the same time to chalk and crayon respectively. As we have already observed, Laura's "no" may be symbolically interpreted as an attempt to deny the temptation of evil and to recover the relationship of presence and immediacy between language and reality as the utmost expression of the order lost in the human fall. In other words, her "no" is an expression of her rebellion against the distance required in any process of symbolization. The impossibility of achieving this immediacy within the realm of articulate speech finds expression in the reductive consequences of Laura's attitude as shown in this passage: the only presence and immediacy possible in articulate human language is that which reduces the word "love" to its *present and immediate* material of expression: crayon or chalk. When the distance required by any process of symbolization is destroyed, everything becomes just an object in reality, even words: language would cease being a form in Hjelmslev's terms to become its material of expression. Only then would language be the fixed, rigid structure of order that Laura is searching for on the "printed page" on which she rests her eyes during Braggoni's courtship.

The narrator's use of language and his exploitation of its flexibility in "Flowering Judas" is a manifestation of the story's rebellion against Laura's obsession with order and uniformity. But the story also rebels against Laura concerning the question of symbols: "Flowering Judas" is an overt exhibition of symbols and symbolical patterns which the reader has to be able to discern in order to understand the story and recognize its literary greatness. The story seems to be thus rebelling against Laura because, as we suggested above, her attitude threatens all the features on which the essential "inner recalcitrance" of short fiction relies.

In "Recalcitrance in the Short Story," Wright distinguishes two forces at work in fiction, "the force of a shaping form and the resistance of the shaped material," and he calls this resistance "recalcitrance": "formal recalcitrance is simply the resistance offered by the materials to that form as it tries to shape them" (Wright 115, 116). In the more specific case of the short story, he distinguishes two varieties of recalcitrance, "inner recalcitrance" and "final recalcitrance." "Inner recalcitrance" depends on the "intensity of detail that shortness confers," which means that "words and images" gain special prominence in the short story (Wright 120–21). In fact, the "intensity of detail" of short fiction requires the recognition of the multiple, diverse and even contradictory symbolical burden of words and images, which is precisely what Laura condemns. For her the resistance that this "inner recalcitrance" offers to the form that tries to unify and shape the story would be another expression of the forces of disorder, diversity and deviation that she is trying to overcome. But Laura herself cannot help being the bearer of her own "inner resistance" as her final dream suggests.

Laura's attitude concerning language and symbols opens a new range of possible interpretations of her final dream. Laura's thoughts before her dream summarize her mental condition that night: "1-2-3-4-5—it is monstrous to confuse love with revolution, night with day, life with death—ah, Eugenio!" (CS 101). She would like to draw a clear line separating the terms "love" and "revolution," "night" and "day," "life" and "death" in order to define them without any possible confusion; but the multiplicity of meanings, images and symbols of her dream deprive her of the satisfaction of this wish.

Her dream is organized around distortions, inversions, and symbols: it represents the final outburst of symbolism and of the diversity, ambiguity and flexibility which it originates in the story. But it happens inside Laura's mind and she seems unable to apprehend this sudden wealth of symbolical implications and distorted meanings. For her the flowers in her dream are just flowers, the tree is just a tree, and she eats the flowers just because they satisfy her thirst and hunger. In spite of her blindness, the description of her eating the flowers of the Judas tree is an evident reference to the Holy Communion in the story:

> Then eat these flowers, poor prisoner, said Eugenio in a voice of pity, take and eat: and from the Judas tree he stripped the warm bleeding flowers, and held them to her

lips. She saw that his hand was fleshless, a cluster of small white petrified branches, and his eye sockets were without light, but she ate the flowers greedily for they satisfied both hunger and thirst. Murderer! said Eugenio, and Cannibal! This is my body and my blood. Laura cried No! And at the sound of her own voice, she awoke trembling, and was afraid to sleep again. (CS 102)

The basic religious meaning of the Holy Communion is one of spiritual redemption: the return to a state of bliss through communion with Christ. This transcendental meaning is achieved through the performance of a religious ritual that literally consists in eating bread—flowers in Laura's dream—and drinking wine as symbols of the elements mentioned in the sacrament, Christ's body and blood. Laura's dream shows how, in accordance with her general inability to discern symbolical implications, when she eats the flowers of her dream she thinks that she is just eating flowers, which suggests her betrayal of the sacrament of the Holy Communion. For her, the ritual would consist simply in eating bread—here flowers—and drinking wine devoid of any symbolical, spiritual meaning.

But depriving the Holy Communion of its symbolism may have another reading, as Eugenio's words point out when he reminds Laura that her attitude transforms the religious sacrament into an act of cannibalism: "Murderer! said Eugenio, and cannibal! This is my body and my blood." Taking into account the general context of the story, Laura's cannibalism can be interpreted as a direct consequence of her demand of linguistic immediacy and order, which forces her to ignore every form of symbolism even in language: deprived of its symbolical distance, the words of the Christian ritual would transform it into something similar to a cannibalistic blood sacrifice, as the reference to T.S. Eliot's "Gerontion" in the title of the story seems to confirm.

Laura's dream makes thus evident that her rejection of symbolism and her denial of the diversity of language as manifestations of her obsession with order and of her rejection of evil can only lead her to the cannibalistic betrayal of Eugenio and what he represents in the story: the revolution, Christ and the human being as a complex being. This betrayal becomes a self-betrayal as soon as we realize that these three terms associated to Eugenio contain Laura's own inner tension in the story. Thus, her final dream tries to teach her that all her attempts to get rid of evil and of the complexity which it brings to the human nature and the human language are treacherous and highly self-destructive. From this perspective, we can consider that Laura's dream contains the "debunking" potentiality of the story in the sense Leitch gives to this word, since as a consequence of this final experience Laura should be moving from an illusion of personal wholeness, order and self-knowledge to the recognition of this illusion as such (Leitch 134). This epiphanic moment in Laura's development should imply her acknowledgement of the unsolved tensions and contradictions that affect her as a human being, that is, as a sum of good and evil. Her use of the word "no" in her dream becomes now significant.

At the beginning of her dream Laura repeats the word "no" three times to Eugenio, and becomes the embodiment of Saint Peter denying Eugenio/Christ (CS 102). But in her dream Eugenio is also identified with the tree representing Judas. Laura is again confronted with the multiplicity of her own "holy talismanic word" itself: if she wants to say "no" to Eugenio/Judas she must also say "no" to Eugenio/Christ. Each time she says "no" she is rejecting both Christ and Judas, the betrayed and the betrayer, good and evil. In other words, she is rejecting humanity as a sum of good and evil forces.

The last "no," the fourth "no," has been understood by the critics either as Laura's reaffirmation of her attitude of denial, which would imply her rejection of the final dream of self-awareness (Madden 132), or as "a denial of her previous denials" (Lavers 81). In other words, Laura's "no" has been interpreted either as a negation of the epiphanic moment represented by her dream or as a reaffirmation of this same epiphanic experience which, as we have just suggested, would mean her recognition of the human complexity and of the resulting futility of her attempt to achieve a perfect order.

Along this essay we have been trying to prove that Laura's obsession with order finds one of its most evident expressions in her attempt to overcome the distance originated by any process of symbolization, the space of diversity and flexibility. More concretely, we have suggested that her blindness to the possible connotations of the word "no" gives proof of the reductive consequences of her attitude. At the end of the story the last "no" is there to remind us that Laura's potential epiphanic moment should also involve her recognition of the multiple implications and diverse meanings that even her "holy talismanic word" may have.

As we have just suggested, the last "no" contains a contradiction because it is both a negation and a reaffirmation of Laura's epiphanic experience, and we consider that any critical attempt to solve this contradiction represents a failure to understand the deep implications of this story. In other words, we consider that if we persist in searching for a fixed meaning for this word, we will be for ever reenacting Laura's fault. From our point of view the last "no" is there to prevent any certainty about Laura's experience; it is there to "[cut] off our expectations for clarification" (Wright 122), which makes this short word the main expression of what Wright calls "final recalcitrance":

> Final recalcitrance is an obstacle to artistic comprehension caused by the seemingly premature placing of the end, an effect of incompleteness requiring the reader to look

back, recalculate, and reconsider, so as to satisfy the expectation of wholeness that he has brought to the story. (Wright 121)

Wright distinguishes five varieties of "final recalcitrance" and mentions "Flowering Judas" as an example of the third type, "stories of unexplained juxtaposition," because according to him "the dream in 'Flowering Judas' confronts a juxtaposition of diverse problems" (Wright 126). My view differs slightly from his because I have chosen to concentrate on the last "no" as bearer of the "final recalcitrance" of the story. From my perspective this word enhances the lack of closure and the inconclusiveness that critics have praised in "Flowering Judas," because it is not until this word is pronounced by Laura that we are forced to question the significance of her epiphanic dream. Laura's "no" is the ending that "aggravates [recalcitrance], presenting a new challenge to the reader that can only be resolved by reflection after the reading" (Wright 121).

If I am trying to put special emphasis on the resistance offered by the word "no" it is not because I have any serious objection to Wright's classification of "Flowering Judas" within the third variety of resistance he mentions. In fact, "Flowering Judas" is a story of "unexplained juxtaposition" where "the reader is confronted with an array of disparate materials and no explanation of what unites them" (Wright 125). I focus attention on the word "no" because I suggest that the "final recalcitrance" in "Flowering Judas" happens on a linguistic level and is thus inextricably bound to its "inner recalcitrance." In other words, the final resistance contained in the word "no" depends on the fact that this same term is also a bearer of inner resistance and it has been so all along the story. It is the presence of this inner kind of resistance in the shape of the contradiction which the word "no" contains that carries the final resistance of the story, the final obstacle for its understanding. The word "no" is now "charged with meaning to the utmost possible degree," which means that it is charged with "inner resistance," and it is precisely the variety and diversity of its meanings and implications that destroy any possibility of clarification at the end of the story and makes it inconclusive. Summarizing, "no" contains the final recalcitrance of the story because it bears the kind of linguistic resistance which is characteristic of "inner recalcitrance." This is the reason why the only thing that we can *know for certain* at the end of the story is that with her last "no" Laura may be opening herself to a new dimension of herself and of her "holy talismanic word." Or not.

Notes

1. Hjelmslev understood language essentially as a form; language was for him the combination—or play—of the expression-form and the content-form. "And by virtue of the content-form and the expression-form, and only by virtue of them, exist respectively the content-substance and the expression-substance, which appear by the form's being projected on to the purport, just as an open net casts its shadow down on an individual surface" (Hjelmslev 57).

2. According to Derrida, the human voice has traditionally been the main vehicle of the human illusion of self-presence (see "la fin du livre et le commencement de l'écriture"; "linguistique et grammatologie" in *De la Grammatologie*).

3. Leon Gottfried offers us an analysis of the revolutionist Braggioni in "Flowering Judas" in relation to Milton's Satan emphasizing the role of self-love in their characterization: "Of these, pride or excessive love of self, the sin of Lucifer, is primary [in Braggioni]. Braggioni is vain and sensitive because of the 'vast cureless wound of his self-esteem.' Like Milton's Satan, he is an effective leader because he 'loves himself with such tenderness and amplitude and eternal charity that his followers [...] warm themselves in the reflected glow' and convince themselves of his nobility" (Gottfried 109).

4. I use the abbreviation CS for *The Collected Stories of Katherine Anne Porter*.

5. Manuel Barbeito considers that the term "converse" is "Milton's favorite expression for the ideal relationship between creatures, not only linguistic, but social or sexual too. That is why it is applied to the perfect linguistic exchange which takes place in God's full presence" (Barbeito 19). According to him Adam's obedience and listening to Eve after her fall "involves, contrary to conversing, a diverting from the ways of God, the loss of this Guide" (Barbeito 22).

6. According to her own words to James Ruoff, "You may live in an attic, and you'll probably have fine company if you do, but first you have to become a human being" (Ruoff 65).

7. According to Barbeito, although in *Paradise Lost* Adam's knowledge is defined as "sudden", i.e., "immediate, without process or any necessity of discursive reasoning" (Barbeito 18), immediacy and presence are not complete in human speech even before the fall: they pertain only to God. In human discourse "the distance is inscribed between the immediacy and suddenness of the divine, on the one hand, and process and mediation of the human, on the other" (Barbeito 25). For the sake of our analysis we may consider that after the fall, "the immediacy and suddenness of the divine" were utterly lost in human speech, and as a consequence the "process and mediation of the human" gained more relevance in language.

8. Barbeito notes, "This loquacity of Adam's shows a corruption of the Word, as a result of the fall, at two levels: first, in his self-deceptive exculpatory argument; and second, in his parody of the words of his creator" (13-14).

9. Most critics have acknowledged this ironical presentation of Braggioni as a Christ-like figure in this story: see, for instance, West 92; Gottfried 109; Madden 129; Unrue 140.

10. Christian imagery is so outstanding in this story that we may also see here an allusion to Mary, mother of Christ and Virgin.

Works Cited

Barbeito, Manuel. "Introduction." *Paradise Lost: The Word, the World, the Words*. Ed. Manuel Barbeito. Santiago de Compostela: Universidade de Santiago de Compostela, 1991: 5-36.

Brinkmeyer, Robert. *Katherine Anne Porter's Artistic Development*. Baton Rouge: Louisiana State UP, 1993.

Derrida, Jacques. *De la Grammatologie*. Paris: Lés Éditions de Minuit, 1963.

Gottfried, Leon. "Death's Other Kingdom: Dantesque and Theological Symbolism in 'Flowering Judas.'" *"Flowering Judas."* Ed. Virginia Spencer Carr. New Brunswick: Rutgers UP, 1993: 99-120.

Hjelmslev, Louis. *Prolegomena to a Theory of Language*. Madison: U of Wisconsin P, 1961.

Johnson, Barbara. "Writing." *Critical Terms for Literary Study*. Ed. Frank Lentricchia & Thomas MacLaughlin. Chicago: U of Chicago P, 1990.

Kristeva, Julia. *Desire in Language: A Semiotic Approach to Literature and Art*. Trans. Thomas Gora, Alice Jardine, & Leon S. Roudiez. Ed. Leon S. Roudiez. NY: Columbia UP, 1980.

Lavers, Norman. "'Flowering Judas' and the failure of Amour Courtois." *Studies in Short Fiction* 28 (1991): 77-82.

Leitch, Thomas M. "The Debunking Rhythm of the American Short Story." *Short Story Theory at a Crossroads*. Ed. Susan Lohafer & Jo Ellyn Clarey. Baton Rouge: Louisiana State UP, 1989.

MacLaughlin, Thomas. "Figurative Language." *Critical Terms for Literary Study*. Ed. Frank Lentricchia & Thomas MacLaughlin. Chicago: U of Chicago P, 1990.

Madden, David. "The Charged Image in Katherine Anne Porter's 'Flowering Judas.'" *"Flowering Judas."* Ed. Virginia Spencer Carr. New Brunswick: Rutgers UP, 1993: 121-135.

Milton, John. *Paradise Lost & Paradise Regained*. Ed. Christopher Ricks. NY: New American Library, 1982.

Porter, Katherine Anne. *The Collected Stories*. NY: Harcourt Brace & Company, 1979.

———. *"Flowering Judas."* Ed. Virginia Spencer Carr. New Jersey: Rutgers UP, 1993.

Ruoff, James. "Katherine Anne Porter Comes to Kansas." *Katherine Anne Porter: Conversations*. Ed. Joan Givner. Jackson: UP of Mississippi, 1987: 61-68.

Unrue, Darlene Harbour. "Revolution and the Female Principle in 'Flowering Judas.'" *"Flowering Judas."* Ed. Virginia Spencer Carr. New Brunswick: Rutgers UP, 1993: 137-152.

West, Ray B. "Katherine Anne Porter: Symbol and Theme in 'Flowering Judas.'" *"Flowering Judas."* Ed. Virginia Spencer Carr. New Brunswick: Rutgers UP, 1993: 89-97.

Wright, Austin M. "Recalcitrance in the Short Story." *Short Story Theory at a Crossroads*. Ed. Susan Lohafer & Jo Ellyn Clarey. Baton Rouge: Louisiana State UP, 1989.

"Beyond Human Reach": Silence and Contiguity in Katherine Anne Porter's "Holiday" and "He"

Rachel Lister

Durham University

In 1963, Katherine Anne Porter declared: "I simply don't believe in style. The style is you [...] a cultivated style would be like a mask [...] your style is an emanation from your own being" (Plimpton 44-5). Porter's description echoes Roland Barthes's observation that style "has its roots in the depths of the author's personal and secret mythology." Barthes argues that whilst style is a "reflex," writing itself evolves directly from the author's experience of discourse. It is "an act of historical solidarity, full of the recollection of previous usage, never innocent [...]. Writing as Freedom is mere moment" (Barthes 10, 14, 17).

If we accept Barthes's distinction between style and writing, we may access Porter's écriture through her engagement with her predecessors and contemporaries. In *The Days Before*, her analysis of other short story writers illuminates the founding principles of her aesthetics: lucidity, objectivity and concision. Praise for contemporaries such as Katherine Mansfield and Eudora Welty centers on authorial reserve: Mansfield "airs no theories, but simply presents to the reader a situation, a place, and a character, and there it is" (Porter, *Days* 35). Affinities with Willa Cather arise from shared principles of formal compression. In "The Art of Fiction," Cather reveals her strategy of "finding what conventions of form and detail one can do without and yet preserving the spirit of the whole—so that all one has suppressed [...] is there to the reader's consciousness as much as if it were in type on the page" (102). For Cather and Porter, compression fosters repletion and absence betokens presence.

Porter's manipulation of the narrative voices in her stories operates in conjunction with her poetics of silence.[1] The notion of the mediating 'narrator' figure continues to furnish critics with definitional problems. Porter's cast of narrative voices is deceptively large. We might attach various shades of identity to the narrating agent but it is generally difficult to personalize the voice. For the purposes of this essay, I will refer to the transmitting source of the story as the 'narrative voice' unless it is clearly personalized. I will use the term as a metonymy for the narrating agent and consider how this presence changes as her writing develops. In "Noon Wine" and "María Concepción," the absence of narratorial comment creates a remoteness that initially divorces the reader from the text. The effacement of the narratorial presence infers correlatively the erasure of "the inscribed audience" (Suleiman 15). When the author withdraws the presence of both the narrator and the "inscribed audience," the text declares itself as silent. Paradoxically, it is this silence which ultimately entices the reader to these stories; the charged uncertainty which energizes these narratives emanates from the seemingly impenetrable atmosphere. Silence engages the reader in a continual dialectic of enlightenment and preclusion, thus generating new forms and levels of text/reader communication.

Wolfgang Iser's phenomenological codification of the reading process posits a similar form of dynamic between text and reader. He argues that textual meaning evolves from the process of interaction between the "aesthetic pole"—"the realization accomplished by the reader"—and the "artistic pole"—the author's text (*Act* 21). In contrast to the New Critical emphasis on the self-sufficiency of the text, Iser focuses attention on the role of the reader; he advances the notion of reading as an active, experiential process, in which meaning remains provisional and contingent. Blanks and silences perform an essential function in the act of interpretation and the preservation of this contingency: "Communication in literature, then, is a process set in motion and regulated, not by a given code, but by a mutually restrictive and magnifying interaction between the explicit and the implicit, between revelation and concealment [...] the gaps function as a kind of pivot on which the whole text/reader relationship revolves" (*Prospecting* 68).

Recent studies of Iser's formulation have illuminated the inconsistencies in his argument. Elizabeth Freund argues that his "seemingly fair distribution of authority between two centres" is "difficult to maintain" (147). Iser claims that, "the literary text makes no real objective demands on the reader," yet he also states that, for communication between text and reader to be "successful," the text must "control" the reader's activity in some way (*Prospecting* 29; *Act* 167); the methodology and level of this control defies classification; it cannot be understood as "a tangible entity occurring independently of the process of communication. Although exercised *by* the text, it is not *in* the text" (*Act* 168; Iser's emphasis).

Whilst many unanswered questions remain concerning the precise locus of interpretative authority and agency in the text/reader relationship, Iser's formulations offer a fertile line of inquiry for a reading of Porter's silences. Although the basis for his theories is the novel, I would suggest that his centralization of blanks and negations in the interpretative process is particularly applicable to the elliptical modern short story: a form that, Mary Rohrberger argues, maneuvers the reader into the position of "co-creator" of the text (106). For Chekhov, it was the short story's requisite incompleteness that distinguished the form from the novel: "Long detailed works have their own peculiar aims, which require a most careful execution [...]. But in a short story, it is better to say not enough than to say too much" (197).

Dominant metaphors for the short story form emphasize its ineffability and ambivalence: Suzanne C. Ferguson and Eudora Welty designate "mystery" as the key component of the short story;[2] Valerie Shaw illuminates how the form often deals with the "borderline" between antithetical states such as the "known and the unknown" (192); Julio Cortázar locates the power of the form in its paradoxical dynamics: the short story "cuts off a fragment of reality" in such a way that it "acts like an explosion," opening up a "more ample reality" (246). There are striking similarities between these characteristics and the dualistic mechanics of silence; as an ontologically dialectical symbol, silence frustrates fixed definition: it may signify "plenum" or "void" (Hassan 15, 13); it may serve as a vehicle for openness and containment; it resists interpretative closure, whilst unfurling a welter of possibilities. The following readings of "He" and "Holiday" will examine how Porter exploits the elliptical form of the modern short story to preserve the duality of the reader's interpretive experience (169).

In "He," Porter engages the reader in this kind of process through her negotiation of the narrative voice. We can trace the original conception of voice as a form of poetic back to distinctions formulated in Plato's *Republic* (91-2). He distinguishes between representational modes, contrasting diegesis, where the poet identifies himself as the teller of the tale and does not attempt to suggest otherwise, with instances where he strives for the illusion that he is not speaking, and that character and action are merely shown: the mimetic mode. Narratologists have queried this dichotomy; they argue that pure mimesis is always illusory, and that, however effaced the narrator's presence is, the reader is always aware of it.[3] Thus it is more productive to consider these modes as "representing a continuum with minimal narrator coloring at one end, and maximal narrator coloring at the other" (Hawthorn 43).

Critics generally place Porter towards the mimetic end of the representational scale.[4] Her mandate of authorial reserve certainly appears to validate this position. The narrative voice in "He" oscillates between narratorial stances, sliding across the mimetic/diegetic continuum. Although Mrs. Whipple's consciousness is the ostensible locus of focalization, the narrative voice repeatedly claims autonomy in the story's discursive hierarchy. At times we are offered a direct representation of Mrs. Whipple's words and at others the narrator ventriloquises for her, reworking her words, both *showing* her internal states and *telling* us what occurred there.

The narrative opens with free indirect discourse and confronts the reader with a conflation of voices. The multiple functions and effects of free indirect discourse have been the subject of much narratological debate.[5] It is generally accepted that it operates through an intermingling of mimesis and diegesis, creating either an "ironic distancing" between reader and character or eliciting an "empathetic response" from the reader (Stanzel 808). Free indirect discourse in "He" functions primarily as an instrument of irony; the narrative voice's framing of Mrs. Whipple's speech is a verbal nudge to the reader.[6] It slips effortlessly into Mrs. Whipple's idiom within the confines of a sentence— the phrases "anyhow" and "for good measure" exude colloquial resonance (57)—and yet deploys repetition and qualification to cast a subversive gloss over her declarations: "Mrs Whipple was all for taking what was sent and calling it good, anyhow when the neighbours were in earshot" (57).

The reader learns quickly that reiteration is the fundamental principle of Mrs. Whipple's discourse; in the first paragraph we hear three times that "Life was very hard for the Whipples" (57). Walter Ong draws parallels between mimetic representation and the psychology of orality; Mrs. Whipple's verbal smokescreen is mimetic as it emerges from "pre-existent, imitable, formulary elements" (284). The reiterative process of imitation becomes, for Mrs. Whipple, an "overwhelming and preemptive state of mind" (283). It is interesting that Ong contrasts these mimetic oral practices with ironic discourses, which he associates primarily with writing. Ong observes how the more sophisticated forms of irony work in opposition to the participatory functions of orality, generating "deliberately unresolved ambiguity" (290). In "He," Porter dramatizes this tension between imitative and subversive strategies, placing the reader at the center of a discursive dialectic.

Porter's narrative voice informs us that "Whenever (Mrs Whipple) was thinking, her lips moved, making words," signaling her protagonist's urgent need to silence unsettling, aberrant thought with carefully scripted rhetoric

(60). According to the tenets of existentialist thought, "Verbosity [...] blocks the way to an understanding of Being" (Grimsley 56). The verb "making" and the precise delineation of the movement of Mrs. Whipple's lips illuminate the physicality of the Word and reveal how her manufactured speech acts as a barrier, impeding the free play of consciousness. As readers we must learn to read the gaps in Mrs. Whipple's rhetoric of denial. It is the blanks that permeate her dialogue—the refusal to acknowledge His subjectivity is the most prevalent example—that "initiate structured operations" in the reader (Iser, *Act* 25). Her vocalizations do not form an autonomous, independent text. Moments of near-contiguity between the reader and Mrs. Whipple are displaced by complicit interpretative acts between the reader and the narrative voice as they converge in their quest to fill in the gaps. The narrative voice represents Mrs. Whipple's reaction to the slaughtered pig with language that recalls her response to her son. Although she "felt badly" about it, (one of Mrs. Whipple's preponderant phrases), "the sight of the pig scraped pink and naked made her sick. He was too fat and soft and pitiful-looking" (60). This description revives images of Him that are scattered throughout the text—"Rolls of fat covered Him like an overcoat," "He blubbered and rolled"—and Mrs. Whipple's conflicted response: after boxing His ears, her knees start to tremble with anger and remorse (58, 65, 61).

Porter's use of the image here signals her assimilation of another Modernist poetic. Ezra Pound presents the "image" as "the word beyond formulated language." He argues that it signified "the furthest possible remove from rhetoric," which, for him, is merely "the art of dressing up [...] matter so as to fool the audience for the time being" (Pound 466). Writing within the confines of the short story form, Porter uses the image both as a powerful counter-discourse to Mrs. Whipple's scripted rhetoric and another method of silent reader-orientation.

As an unwritten text, He creates the most indeterminate ellipsis in the story; unable to tell, He can only show his emotional energy to the reader. In the midst of rhetorical and narratorial manipulation, His silences grow all the more resonant. He epitomizes the "tension and pull of the unspoken and unseen," embodying the silence that infiltrates the gaps of Mrs. Whipple's language (Auchard 10). Whilst she refuses to read His silence as a valid mode of discourse, for the reader it constitutes a powerful presence, tacitly soliciting our imaginative faculties. We might speculate about His subjectivity only to the extent that it is manifested in His external behavior. Porter counters this indirection by conjuring His emotional responses in straightforward language—"He gave a great jolting breath," "He blinked and blinked and rubbed His head" (60, 61)—and by liberating His mode of communication from the narratorial gloss that binds the other discourses. His absence from the dinner table and His "great jolting breath" as He slaughters the pig, signal an affective sensibility superior to that of His family. His tears in the closing scene finally authenticate His silence as a genuine mode of knowing.

The narrative voice's qualifying tactics reveal Mrs. Whipple's clamorous reiterations of parental devotion to be a strategy designed to elude suppressed intimations of guilt. Situated amongst the varied members of her audience—the reader, the community, the narrator—is her conscience. At the end of the story, His spontaneous outburst of sorrow ruptures her surface discourse and her strategy implodes. The narrative voice registers this transition by shifting into a free indirect form that comprises the closest mimesis of Mrs. Whipple's mind in the story; the ironic voice dissipates and Mrs. Whipple's submerged dialogue of self-interrogation is fully exposed: "Maybe He remembered that time she boxed His ears; maybe He had been scared that day with the bull; maybe He had slept cold and couldn't tell her about it [...]" (67). This time repetition signals the frantic gesturing of a consciousness racked by deep conflict.[7] This final penetration gestures towards the Modernist stream-of-consciousness technique; the turbulence of Mrs. Whipple's inner voice finds its syntactical equivalent in the hurried prose. Earlier representations have framed Mrs. Whipple as an object of the reader's and the narrator's speculation. In this single sentence she gravitates towards fully-fledged subjecthood.

The shift from a near-diegetic to a near-mimetic perspective prompts the reader to query the autonomy of the narrative voice. We have revealed how Porter manipulates the voice to reveal the hiatus between its discernment and Mrs. Whipple's myopia; this gap implicates the reader in a collusive "between-the-lines dialogue" with the narrative voice (Gibson 3). In the final scene, the ironic inflection dissolves, exposing the extent of narratorial control in the text/reader relationship; paradoxically, the quasi-absence of the 'diegetic' narrative voice alerts us to its presence. As readers we sense that, by relying upon the voice as an arbiter of truth, we have restricted ourselves to a circumscribed, liminal position. The narrative voice has set us up as "mock readers" (Gibson 1). This distance incites the reader to scrutinize the narrative voice's method of manipulation. He discovers that, ironically, the voice shares discursive strategies with Mrs. Whipple; it negotiates its discourse through gaps that preclude the reader.

By examining a further possible narratorial stance, we can reveal how the narrative voice polices the reader's knowledge: the stance of the representative communal onlooker.[8] There are moments in "He" when narrative and communal discourses converge; the voice preserves the collective silence that denies His agency and marginalizes Him from His environment and the reader. At times it assumes a communal vernacular, even whilst divorcing itself from the stigma of neighborhood gossip: after intimating the neighbors' true feelings that He would be better off dead, the narrative voice adds with conspiratorial outrage: "This behind the Whipples' backs" (57).

These subtle variations in perspective from godlike omniscience to communal partiality make it difficult for the reader to locate any defined moral stance towards Mrs. Whipple. Whilst readers might be lured by highly sentimental or moralistic interpretations of "He," Porter's negotiation of the narrative's silent spaces disables either of these responses.[9] The neighbor's apprehensive backward glance serves as a paradigm for the reader's position at the end of the story. The climax presents the reader with unfamiliar territory, as the guiding force of the narrative voice recedes. Having retained his detachment by engaging in ironic speculation with the narrator, the reader is suddenly exiled to the position of silent onlooker; like the neighbor, he is unable to fix his gaze knowingly on any of the characters. The impact of the final sentence demonstrates Porter's acclaimed aptitude for condensing a welter of implications within the bounds of the "succinct summarizing sentence" (Heilman 226). More specifically, it exemplifies the retroactive dynamism of her final sentences; the retreat of the narrative voice from its ironic standpoint and the hushed aura that envelops the climax impel us towards the "post-reading reflective process," through which we will re-interrogate the text (Iser *Act* 123). In "He" Porter engages the reader in a constant search for a clear, untrammeled line of communication and reveals the limits of language as a representative mode: a theme that would dominate her later stories.

Fifteen years after writing "He," Porter remained fascinated by the mechanics of silence. In "Holiday," she exploits fully the communicative boundaries of the limited point of view; she deploys a retrospective first-person 'witness-narrator,' imposing restrictions on the reader's perspective. As Norman Friedman observes, "The reader has available to him only the thoughts [...] of the witness-narrator; he therefore views the story from what may be called the wandering periphery" (1174).

The illusion of immediacy and intimacy that a personalized narrative voice usually provides is offset by the narrator's announcement that her focalization is retrospective. The narrator's scornful appraisal of her former cognitive deficiencies illuminates the gap between experience and narration; she dismisses her youthful philosophies as "nonsense" (443). By emphasizing this hiatus, the narrator sets up readerly expectations of a trajectory from innocence to experience. Having acquired a more stable view of the world, she will construct a more coherent interpretation of her adventure.

Dorrit Cohn observes that the "special restraints and freedoms of first-person retrospection result in tensions and ambiguities" (145). These tensions underpin the opening paragraph of "Holiday," when, having set up a narrative of ignorance yielding to knowledge, the narrator attempts to negate her own centrality to that narrative. She deflects the reader's interest away from her own "troubles," prohibiting his entry into her silent psychological spaces (443). She establishes the principles of restraint and retreat which inform her narrative. By demarcating the locus and the formal parameters of her story, she attempts to dictate the boundaries of the reader's knowledge. However, her insistent silence on her past alerts us to the centrality of gaps in a narrative that is riddled with what Roman Ingarden defines as "places of indeterminacy" (50); this silence is the first of a series of omissions that transports the reader away from his explicit role as passive recipient and towards the position of "co-creator."

Silence is a ubiquitous presence in "Holiday," but the "most constitutive blanks" inhere in the narrative voice itself (Iser, *Act* 167). The narrator employs a variety of strategies to construct her own poetics of silence, inscribing the reader in a nexus of felt omissions. Despite her opening gesture of asceticism, her silences dictate the orientation of the story, turning it into a narrative of indirection and illusion.

"Holiday" confronts the reader with two forms of blank: those that operate as encoded instructions to activate the reader's collaboration, and those more indeterminate spaces that signal the narrator's subconscious will towards suppression; the tension between these modes of concealment makes it difficult to ascertain the level of conscious reader-manipulation. The communication between narrator and reader involves the kind of process described by Iser: it is a "mutually restrictive and magnifying interaction between revelation and concealment." The selectivity of the narrator's accounts and her ambivalence towards the act of narration itself impel the reader to assume the responsibilities of a surrogate narrator. To a certain degree, the narrator's silences release us from the limits of first-person narration.

In some cases, the narrator creates gaps purposefully as a strategy of displacement and evasion; they are an index of her disinclination towards explicit judgment. When a recalled incident invites interpretation rather than reportage, the narrator refuses to register this transition; she wants to create the impression of showing rather than telling and therefore creates an ellipsis that the reader must fill in order to, in Ingarden's terminology, "concretise" her buried impressions (Ingarden 51). When Father Müller claims his affinity with Marxist ideologies, we sense the narrator's unease at the contradiction between Communist abstractions and the Müllers' hierarchical labor structure. She elucidates the paradox but refuses to explore its implications, leaving the reader with a literal blank space in which to question Father Müller's politics. We must reach beyond the façade of reportage and interpret for ourselves.

At other moments, the narrator constructs a surface discourse to obfuscate troubling inconsistencies; her discourse on silence is an effective example. When she arrives at the farm, she codifies silence as a medium of self-renewal. It opens the door to a return to the ontological self: "I loved that silence which means freedom from the constant pressure of other minds [...] that freedom to fold up in quiet and go back to my own centre, to find out again [...] what creature it is that rules me finally" (449). These transcendental cadences emanate from the landscape that surrounds her—"the flower clusters shivered in a soundless dance of delicately woven light" (456)—and the "almost mystical inertia" of the cyclic rituals performed by the Müllers (455). These connotations extend to the narrator's reception of Ottilie, whose silence transfixes her, awakening her interpretive capacities: "She drifted into my mind like a bit of weed [...] floating but fixed, refusing to be carried away" (464). Situated in the midst of a cacophony of interchangeable voices, Ottilie's silence defines her as "the only individual in the house" (454); for the narrator, she confirms the primacy of silence amongst discursive performances.

These positive associations run counter to the more duplicitous silences that the narrator tries to mask. The Müllers' occlusion of Ottilie illuminates the other side of silence; although "Holiday" is, ostensibly, *about* them, the exclusion of Ottilie alienates the reader. The narrator disguises their silence, framing it as "simple forgetfulness" and "pure self-defence" (464). Her only form of indictment is indirect; like the narrative voice in "He," she resorts to imagistic glosses as a means of revealing and concealing. She juxtaposes animal imagery with Ottilie's appearances to infer her status in the Müller hierarchy. She confuses the howling of the dog with Ottilie's cry of protestation; the image of Kuno caught in a trap prefigures the description of Ottilie, excluded from her mother's funeral and confined to the kitchen.

Therefore the narrator actively incites the reader to recognize Ottilie's buried narrative as the "second story" of "Holiday." Armine Kotin Mortimer highlights how the tacit presence of "second stories" within the short story form enables the reader to achieve new levels of agency in the text/reader dynamic (276): "The second-story reader is a special case of 'the reader in the text' [...]. His stage directions are often directly encoded in the text, in the form of a created model, an obvious guide" (296). Mortimer claims that, in some narratives, the second-story construction "does not leave the outcome up in the air; quite to the contrary, it often brings closure to the first" (277). In

"Holiday," Porter develops this process further. She exploits the presence of the embedded narrative to alert the reader to further places of indeterminacy, without offering closure. There are, however, clues within the "obvious" second story that point towards other suppressed stories, such as the narrator's silent past. The narrator's representations of Ottilie are carefully staged. She manages our contact with Ottilie as scrupulously as she controls our access to her consciousness: she follows each of Ottilie's appearances at the dinner table with ellipses, severing the lines of communication with the reader, and conjures the mute servant's appearance in vocabulary that preserves her aura of indeterminacy. Although she writes with the benefit of retrospection, she employs modalities in her representations: "Her muteness *seemed* nearly absolute"; her face is covered in "patternless blackened seams *as if* the perishable flesh has been wrung in a hard cruel fist" (458, emphasis added). Boris Uspensky classifies modalities in narrative discourse as "words of estrangement," that signal the "remote position of the observer" (85-6); they enable the narrator to monitor the gap that separates Ottilie from the reader.

By viewing the narrator's nebulous renderings of Ottilie as a conscious strategy, we bring to the fore hitherto concealed possibilities: to what extent does Ottilie function as the narrator's silent double? As a mute text, she offers the narrator a blank space upon which she might project her own anxieties and fantasies. The constant references to Ottilie's spectral qualities sustain this reading: she is a "perpetual ghost" that confounds the narrator's sense of reality; when Ottilie enters the room, the narrator writes that, "nothing could make her seem real" (472, 462). In his psychoanalytic codification of reading, Norman Holland suggests that "interpretation is a function of identity"; as we read, "We work out through the text our own characteristic patterns of desire and adaptation," using the text to "replicate ourselves" (123, 124). If we apply Holland's theory to the narrator's retrospective 'reading' of Ottilie, the gap between reader and narrator widens; we must question how far the narrator's rendition is a function of her psychic state and a subconscious act of self-duplication.

The reader gains particular agency in "Holiday" when the gaps signify a subconscious form of negation rather than a conscious strategy of evasion. In contrast to her habitual economy, Porter designates a large amount of textual space in "Holiday" to descriptions of physical surroundings, in which the narrator seems to retreat and teleological progression is suspended. These prolonged evocations illuminate further levels of denial; the descriptions reveal the narrator's unacknowledged shift from naïve exultation to uneasy ambivalence towards the Müllers. Immediately after the narrator has attempted to "reason out" their neglect of Ottilie, a storm hits the farm (464).

Images of potential destruction—the striking of the cloudburst upon the house—portend the possible collapse of the family's rigid ideologies and form a correlative to the narrator's burgeoning unease. It is fitting that, whilst under violent attack, the "house stood to its foundations." The narrator knows that the Müllers' lifestyle will "arrange itself again in another order, yet it would be the same," just as, in the final scene, she recognizes that Ottilie's reprieve from servitude is temporary (464).

The narrator's strategy of illusion reaches its climax in the closing vignette, as she formulates an ending that veils the ineluctable contradictions at the heart of her story. While recognizing that the central gap between herself and Ottilie will never be bridged, she claims that they have achieved an unprecedented level of contiguity. The binary oppositions that underpin the Müller regime seem to collapse when the narrator claims that, paradoxically, it is Ottilie's very inaccessibility that conduces this proximity: "she was beyond my reach [...] and yet, had I not come nearer to her than I had to anyone else in my attempt to deny and bridge the distance between us [...]" (472).

George Core reads "Holiday" as a dramatization of the narrator's impulse to return to a prelapsarian world and recover the Empsonian pastoral ideal. The narrator and Ottilie seem to step momentarily beyond the discursive barriers of the Müller world; we might conclude that the narrator has accomplished a transitory retrieval of prelinguistic innocence. This alluring interpretation is, however, deceptively neat. If we approach "Holiday" as a narrative of illusion, we must read the ending as a kind of fantastical resolution and a final paradigm for the narrator's method of displacement. Through her simulated epiphany, the narrator has constructed her own fiction of universality and identity. Undercutting this fiction and the buoyant atmosphere—the image of the "jovial antics" of the wheels is a more obvious correlative here (472)—are the silences that the narrator has acknowledged only indirectly. The selectivity of the narrator's account must be brought to bear on the ending. As Iser affirms, "The new moment is not isolated, but stands out against the old" (Iser, *Act* 114).

In "He" and "Holiday," Porter denies the reader the ultimate act of "concretization." Both stories "initiate performances of meaning rather than formulating definitive meanings themselves" (Iser, *Act* 26-7). By reading the silences of Porter's stories, we are alerted to the illusory nature of all narrative constructs.

Notes

1. Janis P. Stout offers illuminating readings of Porter's manipulation of silence in "Noon Wine" and the Miranda stories; see "Katherine Anne Porter's Reticent Style" in *Strategies of Reticence*. In particular, Stout explores how heroines Miranda and Laura use "reticence" as a "strategy for asserting self-will in the face of a powerful and threatening male hegemony" (185). My reading will examine primarily the function of silence in Porter's narrative discourse.
2. Welty writes: "Every good story has mystery—not the puzzle kind—but the mystery of allurement" (56) in "The Reading and Writing of Short Stories," *Atlantic Monthly* February (1949). Suzanne Ferguson observes how the "moral" of the modern short story is a "hardly won proposition, whose validity remains conditional and implicit, unconfirmed by the authorial voice, giving the story both "unity of effect" and a certain vagueness or mystery" (228).
3. In *Narrative Discourse*, Gérard Genette claims that, "mimesis in words can only be mimesis of words" (164).
4. Janis P. Stout writes that "Porter shows us things, and if we are perspicacious we will find them uncomfortable; but she does not *make* us uncomfortable" (22).
5. See Manfred Jahn, 446.
6. Both Bruce W. Jorgensen and Debra A. Moddelmog characterise the narrative voice in "He" as ironic.
7. My reading differs from Debra A. Moddelmog's here; Moddelmog argues that the final scene "reaffirms Mrs Whipple's callousness" (124).
8. Southern modernists Eudora Welty and William Faulkner deploy this kind of narrator to achieve a choric effect in their narratives. See "Petrified Man" by Welty and Faulkner's "A Rose for Emily." Unlike the voices in these stories, the narrative voice in "He" attempts to distance itself from the communal discourse by exposing the neighbors' gossip to the reader; it reveals how the community casts aspersions on the Whipple lineage, framing Him as a punishment for the "sins of the fathers" (57). This suggests that it is perhaps education or worldly experience that separates the narrative voice from the community.
9. Bruce W. Jorgensen writes that his students either "excessively pitied Mrs Whipple, or they excessively, moralistically condemned her" (108).

Works Cited

Auchard, John. *Silence in Henry James: the Heritage of Symbolism and Decadence*. University Park: Penn State UP, 1986.

Barthes, Roland. *Writing Degree Zero*. Ed. Annette Lavers and Colin Smith. NY: Hill, 1968.

Cather, Willa. *On Writing*. NY: Knopf, 1953.

Chekhov, Anton. "To I.L. Shcheglov." 22 January 1888. *The New Short Story Theories*. Ed. Charles May. Athens, OH: Ohio UP, 1994. 197-8.

Cohn, Dorrit. *Transparent Minds: Narrative Modes for Presenting Consciousness in Fiction*. 1978. Princeton, NJ: Princeton UP, 1983.

Core, George. "'Holiday': A Version of Pastoral." *Katherine Anne Porter: A Collection of Critical Essays*. Ed. Robert Penn Warren. Englewood Cliffs, NJ: Spectrum-Prentice, 1979. 117-25.

Cortázar, Julio. "Some Aspects of the Short Story." Trans. Aden W. Hayes. *The New Short Story Theories*. Ed. Charles May. Athens, OH: Ohio UP, 1994. 245-55.

Faulkner, William. "A Rose for Emily." 1951. *Collected Stories*. London:Vintage,1995. 119-30.

Ferguson, Suzanne C. "Defining the Short Story: Impressionism and Form." *The New Short Story Theories*. Ed. Charles May. Athens, OH: Ohio UP, 1994. 218-29.

Freund, Elizabeth. *The Return of the Reader: Reader-Response Criticism*. London: Methuen, 1987.

Friedman, Norman. "Point of View in Fiction." *PMLA* 70 (1995): 1160-84.

Genette, Gérard. *Figures of Literary Discourse*. Trans. Alan Sheridan. Oxford: Blackwell, 1982.

———. *Narrative Discourse: An Essay in Method*. Trans. Jane E. Lewin. 1980. Ithaca, NY: Cornell UP, 1983.

Gibson, Walker. "Authors, Speakers, Readers, and Mock Readers." *Reader-Response Criticism: From Formalism to Post-Structuralism*. Ed. Jane Thompkins. Baltimore: Johns Hopkins UP, 1980. 1-6.

Grimsley, Ronald. *Existentialist Thought*. 1955. Cardiff: U of Wales P, 1967.

Hassan, Ihab. *The Dismemberment of Orpheus: Toward a Postmodern Literature*. NY: 1971.

Hawthorn, Jeremy. *A Concise Glossary of Contemporary Literary Theory*. London: Arnold-Hodder, 1992.

Heilman, Robert. "Ship of Fools: Notes on Style." *Critical Essays on Katherine Anne Porter*. Ed. Danielle Unrue. NY: Hall, 1997. 222-32.

Holland, Norman, N. "Unity Identity Text Self." *Reader-Response Criticism: From Formalism to Post-Structuralism*. Ed. Jane Thompkins. Baltimore: Johns Hopkins UP, 1980. 118-33.

Ingarden, Roman. *The Cognition of the Literary Work of Art*. Trans. Ruth Ann Crowley and Kevin R. Olson. 1968. Evanston: Northwestern UP, 1973.

———. *The Literary Work of Art*. Trans. George G. Grabowicz. 1973. Evanston: Northwestern UP, 1980.

Ingram, Forrest L. *Representative Short Story Cycles of the Twentieth Century: Studies in a Literary Genre*. Paris: Mouton, 1971.

Iser, Wolfgang. *The Act of Reading: a Theory of Aesthetic Response*. 1978. Baltimore: Johns Hopkins UP, 1987.

———. *The Implied Reader: Patterns of Communication in Prose Fiction from Bunyan to Beckett*. 1974. Baltimore: Johns Hopkins UP, 1987.

———. "Indeterminacy and the Reader's Response in Prose Fiction." *Prospecting: From Reader Response to Literary Anthropology*. Baltimore: Johns Hopkins UP, 1989. 3-30.

———. "Interaction Between Text and Reader." *Prospecting: From Reader Response to Literary Anthropology*. Baltimore: Johns Hopkins UP, 1989. 31-41.

Jahn, Manfred. "Frames, Preferences, and the Reading of Third-Person Narratives: Toward a Cognitive Narratology." *Poetics Today* 18 (1997): 441-68.

Jorgensen, Bruce, W. "'The Other Side of Silence': Katherine Anne Porter's "He" as Tragedy." *Katherine Anne Porter*. Ed. Harold Bloom. NY: Chelsea, 1986. 107-15. 1998.

May, Charles E., ed. *The New Short Story Theories*. Athens, OH: Ohio UP, 1994.

Moddelmog, Debra, A. "Narrative Irony and Hidden Motivations in Katherine Anne Porter's 'He.'" *Katherine Anne Porter*. Ed. Harold Bloom. NY: Chelsea, 1986. 117-25.

Mortimer, Armine Kotin. "Second Stories." *Short Story Theory at a Crossroads*. Ed. Susan Lohafer and Jo Ellyn Clarey. Baton Rouge: Louisiana State UP, 1989. 276-98.

Ong, Walter J. *Interfaces of the Word: Studies in the Evolution of Consciousness and Literature*. Ithaca, NY: Cornell UP, 1977.

Plato. *The Republic*. Trans. Desmond Lee. 2nd ed. 1955. London: Penguin, 1987.

Porter, Katherine Anne. *The Days Before*. 1926. London: Secker, 1953.

———. "He." *The Collected Stories*. 1964. London: Virago, 1985. 57-67.

———. "Holiday." *The Collected Stories*. 1964. London: Virago, 1985. 443-73.

———. Interview with Barbara Thompson. *Women Writers at Work: The Paris Review Interviews*. Ed. George Plimpton. London: Harvill, 1999. 27-50.

———. "María Concepción." *The Collected Stories*. 1964. London: Virago, 1985. 9-28.

———. "Noon Wine." *The Collected Stories*. 1964. London: Virago, 1985. 247-96.

Pound, Ezra. "Voriticism." *The Fortnightly Review*. XCVI (1914): 461-71.

Rohrberger, Mary. *Hawthorne and the Modern Short Story: A Study in Genre*. Mouton: The Hague, 1966.

Shaw, Valerie. *The Short Story: A Critical Introduction*. London: Longman, 1985.

Stanzel, Franz. "A Low-Structuralist at Bay? Further Thoughts on a Theory of Narrative." *Poetics Today* 11 (1990): 804-16.

Stout, Janis P. *Strategies of Reticence: Silence and Meaning in Jane Austen, Willa Cather, Katherine Anne Porter and Joan Didion*. Charlottesville: UP of Virginia, 1990.

Suleiman, Susan R. "Introduction: Varieties of Audience-Oriented Criticism." *The Reader in the Text: Essays on Audience and Interpretation*. Ed. Suleiman and Inge Crosman. Princeton: Princeton UP, 1980. 3-45.

Uspensky, Boris. *A Poetics of Composition : The Structure of the Artistic Text and Typology of a Compositional Form*. Trans. Valentina Zavarin and Susan Wittig. 1973. Berkeley : U of California P, 1983.

Welty, Eudora. "Petrified Man." *Collected Stories of Eudora Welty*. London: Penguin, 1983. 17-28.

———. *The Eye of the Story: Selected Essays and Reviews*. 1979. London: Virago, 1987.

Flannery O'Connor's "The Temple of the Holy Ghost" and "Parker's Back" as Dermatology/Theology

Sue Brannan Walker
University of South Alabama

> In the future let no one make trouble for me,
> for I bear the marks of Jesus branded on my body.
> *Paul's Letter to the Galatians 6:17*

> I think you can tell a lot about a person just by reading their skin.
> *Charlie Cartwright, tattoo artist*

> Imagine God as tailor. His shelves are lined with rolls of skin, each with its subtleties of texture and hue. Six days a week He cuts lengths with which to wrap those small piles of flesh and bone into the clever parcels we call babies. [...] He uses the occasional handicraft, a remnant of yard goods, the last of an otherwise perfect bolt, dusty, soiled, perhaps a bit too small or too large, one whose woof is warped or that is cut on the bias. I have received many such people in my examination room. Like imperfect postage stamps, they are the collector's items of the human race.
> *Richard Selzer*, Mortal Lessons

Skin, as an anastomosis of the medical body, the religious body, and the textual body in Flannery O'Connor's "The Temple of the Holy Ghost" and "Parker's Back," reveals a preoccupation with the body and the soul, with the internal and the external, with mortality and immortality, with sickness and death. As Marc Lappé points out in *The Body's Edge: Our Cultural Obsession with Skin*, the derma "transcends its function as an elastic membrane that bends and stretches with our bodily movements. It is the membrane that separates the living from the nonliving; [...] it is an invaluable asset for psychic as well as physical well-being" (217). Psychoanalyst Didier Anzieu, author of

The Skin Ego and *A Skin for Thought* speaks of the function of the skin in conjunction with the mind as the "skin-ego," and says that it "provides one of the frameworks for, or one of the processes of, thought" (*Skin Ego* 230). According to Anzieu, "the spoken word, and even more the written word, has the power to function as a skin"[1] (*Skin Ego* 131). Anzieu explains that

> the psychoanalytic perspective differs fundamentally from psycho-physiological or psycho-sociological perspectives, in that it takes into account the existence and permanent importance of individual phantasy, conscious, pre-conscious and unconscious, and the role of that phantasy both as a bridge and as an intermediary screen between the psyche and the body, the world, and other psyches. The Skin Ego is a reality of the order of phantasy: it figures in phantasies, dreams, everyday speech, posture and disturbances of thought; and it provides the imaginary space on which phantasies, dreams, thinking and every form of psychopathological organization are constituted. (*Skin Ego* 4)

He further asserts that "after an intense emotional upset [...] words provide for a reconstitution of the psychical envelope, a symbolic skin" (*Skin Ego* 231).

I shall read "Parker's Back" against the earlier 1954 "The Temple of the Holy Ghost" to perform a diagnostic of the stories' skin—the etchings on parchment—the body that is text, that is marked by proscriptions, inscriptions, and prescriptions. Although the body, for Christians, as well as for Roman Catholics, has been and often is problematic, Flannery O'Connor in "Some Aspects of the Grotesque in Southern Fiction," sees it as central to her mission in conveying the "ills and mysteries of life" (CW[2] 815). Speaking specifically of the body in relation to the act of writing itself, she says, in "The Fiction Writer And His Country," that "[t]he country that the writer is concerned with [...] is [...] the region that most immediately envelops him, or simply the country, with its body of manners, that he knows well enough to employ" (CW 802). That which surrounds the body is, of course, the skin, and this is the physical terrain that O'Connor comes to know through the lupus rash inflicting her skin. Regarding the stories she has written, she says that they are about people "who are afflicted in both mind and body" (CW 804). "When we talk about the writer's country," she says, "we are liable to forget that no matter what particular country it is, it is inside as well as outside him. Art requires a delicate adjustment of the outer and inner worlds [...]. The writer's value is lost, both to himself and to his country, as soon as he ceases to see that country as a part of himself" (CW 806). The country is, at once, the self and the South, and, in "The Catholic Novelist in the Protestant South," O'Connor notes that "[i]t takes a story of mythic dimensions; one which belongs to everybody; one in which everybody is able to recognize the hand of God and imagine its descent upon himself" (CW 858-859). O'Connor believes that it is her mission as a novelist to measure herself against religious truth and to accept God's will. Although Flannery O'Connor does not mention medicine in her explanations regarding the country of the writer, Michel Foucault, in *The Birth of the Clinic: An Archaeology of Medical Perception* links body, medicine and the soul. "[T]he myth of a nationalized medical profession," he says, concerns the fact that it is "organized like the clergy" (32). Doctors, he feels, are "priests of the body" (32).

The linkage that exists between mind and body is further explained by Jeanne Campbell Reesman, in "Women, Language and the Grotesque in Flannery O'Connor and Eudora Welty." She says that in Flannery O'Connor's work, "the body's margins (mouth, genitals, breasts, phallus, nose, and potbelly) take on special grotesque meaning" and she mentions, by way of example, the characters of "Good Country People": Joy-Hulga's artificial leg, Mrs. Freeman's truck-like face, and the way that Mrs. Hopewell talked her head off. These, she says, exhibit the author's "self-hatred of the female body" (47). Without going as far as Reesman in claiming that O'Connor's work signifies hatred, her work certainly exhibits angst over a body that betrays itself. O'Connor's stories are manifestations of that betrayal, and as Peter Brooks, in *Body Work: Objects of Desire in Modern Narrative*, shows, the text represents the body as the body represents the text (6). He comments that

> [t]he surface of the body, the skin, [...] provides the ground for the articulation of orifices, erotogenic rims, cuts on the body's surface, loci of exchange between the inside and the outside, points of conversion of the outside into the body, and of the inside out of the body. These are sites not only for the reception and transmission of information but also for bodily secretions, [...] ongoing processes of sensory stimulation which require some form of signification and sociocultural and psychical representation. (36)

Marks on the body's surface—as print on the page and tattoos on skin— are features of the surface "landscape" that reveal pocks, scars, and deformities, all part of regions and zones–even erogenous zones. In "The Temple of the Holy Ghost," Sister Perpetua issues an edict concerning what a woman ought to say should "a man behave in an ungentlemanly manner [...] in the back of an automobile"–i.e. 'Stop sir! I am a Temple of the Holy Ghost?'" (199). The body, while it is the subject of sin, is not to be subjected to sin that manifests itself not only in acts, but in what is seen. Sinfulness is an aspect of the gaze, and the freak who is both a man and a woman in "The Temple of the Holy Ghost," tells the onlookers:

> I'm going to show you this and if you laugh, God may strike you the same way [...]. God made me thisaway and if you laugh He may strike you the same way. This is the way He wanted me to be and I ain't disputing His way. I'm showing you because I got

to make the best of it. [...] I never done it to myself nor had a thing to do with it but I'm making the best of it. I don't dispute hit. (CW 206)

The hermaphrodite's sermon appends a dire warning: "If anybody desecrates the temple of God, God will bring him to ruin" (CW 207). The freak states that he, Temples One and Two, are holy and part of God's intentional plan for them. This raises a question regarding the hermaphrodite's message. If he is a mouthpiece of the Holy Spirit, is his sermon to be believed? Is his message one of redemption in which both the sinner and the freak are to be accepted as part of an inexplicable grand design? And what about the deity? Does the story imply, even if Flannery O'Connor does not, that God is, indeed, vengeful and inflicts punishment on those who act contrary to His will? If this is probable, what additional questions may be raised about those who suffer a terminal illness? Perhaps the story brings to light unconscious issues, especially when Flannery O'Connor's unstinting faith is set beside her comments that she "does not lead a holy life" and that "her virtues are as timid as her vices" (Buchanan 138). She says, in a 20 July 1955 letter to "A" (recently identified as Elizabeth Hester) that she thinks that "the Church is the only thing that is going to make the terrible world we are coming to endurable; the only thing that makes the Church endurable is that it is somehow the body of Christ and that on this we are fed" (CW 942). On the other hand, on 4 August 1962, she writes "A" a somewhat lengthy commentary on freaks:

> Last Saturday two of the Sisters came down [to Milledgeville] and brought the L—— family, all except —— —— who has had a couple of tumors removed already and couldn't take any more riding. The father is dying of cancer and looked it. They brought Mary Ann very close. The mother has huge black eyes and the father has an over-large elongated head, the face covered with warts. I was much impressed with them. You hear of The Poor, but you seldom see them. I don't mean just poor folks, I mean people whose vocation it is to be poor and to have God touch them in just that way.
> Odd about "The Temple of the Holy Ghost." Nobody notices it. It is never anthologized, never commented upon. A few nuns have mentioned it with pleasure, but nobody else besides you. (CW 1172)

The story *is* comment, and it brings pleasure to a few nuns. Like the skin of the onion that the narrator mentions in "Parker's Back," what is revealed when a few layers of skin are peeled away from its outer casing? In order to understand the complexity of meaning in O'Connor's stories, it is necessary to examine what lies beneath the surface, to inspect the epidermis in order to see what can be known about the body's struggle with the immune system, the struggle with the self, i.e., the skin ego. In "Some Aspects of the Grotesque in Southern Fiction":

> O'Connor explains that a writer has to descend far enough into himself to reach those underground springs that give life to his work. This descent into himself will, at the same time, be a descent into his region. It will be a descent through the darkness of the familiar into a world where, like the blind man cured in the gospels, he sees as if they were trees, but walking. This is the beginning of vision, and I feel it is a vision which we in the South must at least try to understand if we want to participate in the continuance of a vital Southern literature. (CW 821)

In spite of recognizing the need to "descend through the darkness of the familiar," O'Connor acknowledges that much of what a writer reveals is comprised of material that is unconscious. She explains to her friend "A" that in an author's work "something of oneself gets through and often something that one is not conscious of" (CW 957). She admits that she "won't ever be able entirely to understand [her] own work or even [her] own motivations" (CW 944). She believes that "sin *occasionally* brings one closer to God" (CW 944; emphasis added). What is not stated, however, is that *occasionally* sin does not. O'Connor writes "A" that her writing is "first of all, a gift, but the direction it has taken has been because of the Church in me or the effect of the Churches teaching, not because of a personal perception or love of God" (CW 944). It is important to know, as O'Connor tells "A" that

> [t]he individual in the Church is, no matter how worthless himself, a part of the Body of Christ and a participator in the Redemption. There is no blueprint that the Church gives for understanding this. It is a matter of faith and the Church can force no one to believe it. When I ask myself how I know I believe, I have no satisfactory answer at all, no assurance at all, no feeling at all. I can only say with Peter, Lord I believe, help my unbelief. And all I can say about my love of God, is Lord help me in my lack of it. I distrust pious phrases, particularly when they issue from my mouth. (CW 944)

What comes out of O'Connor's mouth is also what comes from her pen, and what is not intentionally revealed is nevertheless seen, namely a struggle with acceptance. In a letter dated 23 December 1959, O'Connor tells Cecil Dawkins that "[w]hat the Church has decided definitively on matters of faith and morals, all Catholics must accept," and she goes on:

> [t]he Church has always been mindful of the relation between spirit and flesh; this has shown up in her definitions of the double nature of Christ [...]. The Church doesn't say what the [resurrected] body will look like [...] but [w]e are told that it will be transfigured in Christ, that what is human will flower when it is united with the Spirit. (CW 1117)

O'Connor's outlaw stories of freaks and of the grotesque form the corpus of her text and manifest aspects of her own illness. Dr. Arthur J. Merrill diagnosed O'Connor's disseminated lupus erythematosus in 1951 and recounted the effects of the cortisone, the loss of her hair and facial swelling which caused her to "feel like a large stiff anthropoid ape" (Fitzgerald 1245, CW 956) .

Upon her return to Georgia in 1952, O'Connor received two transfusions and an increase in the dosage of ACTH (Fitzgerald 1245). Lupus imposed increasing strictures upon her life, and O'Connor accepted this, in part, by adopting Teilhard de Chardin's notion of passive diminishment. Karl-Heinz Westarp, in an article on "Parker's Back," says that "the second part of *The Divine Milieu* exerted a particularly strong attraction on Flannery who because of her long illness had a deep understanding of suffering. By 'passive diminishments' Teilhard 'means those afflictions that you can't get rid of and have to bear" (97).

Throughout her letters, O'Connor affirms her Catholic beliefs. She writes "A" on 16 December 1955 to say she believes "the Host is actually the body and blood of Christ, not a symbol" (CW 976). Speaking about "The Temple of the Holy Ghost," O'Connor attempts to justify an acceptance of whatever God wills, be it deformity or illness and says that "the Church teaches that our resurrected bodies will be intact as to personality, that is intact with all the contradictions [...] except the contradiction of sin; sin is the contradiction, the interference, of a greater good by a lesser good" (CW 976). "Remember" she says, "When the nun hugged the child, in 'The Temple of the Holy Ghost,'

> the crucifix on her belt was mashed into the side of the child's face, so that that one accepted embrace was marked with the ultimate all-inclusive symbol of love, and that when the child saw the sun again, it was a red ball, like an elevated Host drenched in blood and it left a line like a red clay road in the sky [...]. As near as I get to saying what purity is in this story is saying that it is an acceptance of what God wills for us, an acceptance of our individual circumstances. (CW 976)

A letter to "A", written twenty-one days earlier, directly associates by sequence "A Temple of the Holy Ghost" and lupus, suggesting an unconscious connection between these two subjects. In psychoanalysis, an association of superficially disparate themes is taken as a means of communicating unconscious thought. O'Connor states that "'A Temple of the Holy Ghost' all revolves around what is purity" (CW 970). She says that "what you work hardest on is what you know least" (CW 970) and recounts her struggle in characterizing Hazel Motes in her novel *Wise Blood*. It was during the time she was working on this novel that she "came down with [her] energy-depriving ailment and began to take cortisone in large doses, and notes that "in that book I had spelled out my own course, or that in the illness I had spelled out the book" (CW 970). Like Virginia Woolf before her, Flannery O'Connor recognizes the fact that illness is a country and since her disease is one writ upon the skin, her text is, at once, a body of work, the short story, and the skin that maps her travels.

Considerable variance occurs in biblical references to the body, especially in the accounts in the Old Testament and that of the New, the former associating the body with sin, and the New which offers leniency and a promise of redemption. In Leviticus 21: 1-24, the Lord instructs Moses to

> [s]ay to Aaron that none of your descendants throughout their generations who has a deformity shall draw near, a man blind or lame, or one who has a mutilated face or a limb too long or a man who has an injured foot or an injured hand, or a hunchback or dwarf, or a man with a defect in his sight or an itching disease [...] he shall not come near the veil or approach the altar because he has a deformity that he may not profane my sanctuaries; for I am the Lord who sanctify them.

Roman Catholic manuals for three or four centuries contained passages labeled *De baptizandis monstris* that referred to deformities. A question arose as to whether deformed persons who may be missing a thumb or index finger, those who trembled and may spill the Precious Blood, those who, like O'Connor's Joy-Hulga, were missing a leg or who were mutilated and deformed were to be excluded from priestly services where they would be gazed upon by others. Juvenal in the first century A.D. believed that all men should aspire to *mens sana in corpore sano*. Saint Tertullian wondered if anyone deformed even possessed a reasonable soul and if the deformed were subject to resurrection. In Matthew 18:87, Jesus states that "it is better to enter into life crippled or lame than to have two hands or two feet and be thrown into the eternal fire." There seemed no consensus regarding deformity, but what was clear was the fact that the body was a site of contestation, both of deformity and of the divine.

Mark Taylor, in *About Religion*, explains how the figure X exemplifies the structure that Merleau-Ponty labels "the chiasmus." It involves a reversibility in which the outside is intertwined with the inside. In terms of language, it is an ordering of words so that one of two parallel clauses is inverted in the other, but for Christians, Taylor points out, this marking is "the sign of the cross where crucifixion becomes resurrection" (235). A linguistic and theological intertwining, in O'Connor's work involves what lies beneath the surface of what is seen as well as that which tends of be concealed. Peter Brooks shows that an inscriptive surface lends "a privileged insight into the ever-renewed struggle of language" to make the body mean when it is brought to writing (22). O'Connor's life is scribed both in and on "Parker's Back." O'Connor began writing the story in 1960, after a viral infection reactivated her lupus and forced her return to Milledgeville, Georgia. She was working on this story again, less than three weeks before her death. "I have drug another out of myself and enclose it," she wrote her friend and former editor Catharine Carver on 15 July (CW 1216). Ten days later, (only eight days before her death on August 3), she tells "A" in reference to "Parker's Back" that Caroline Gordon "didn't mean the tattoos were the heresy. Sarah Ruth was the heretic-the notion that you can worship in pure spirit. Caroline gave me a lot of advice about the story but most of it I'm ignoring" (CW 1218).

It is not without significance that Flannery O'Connor was, in her words, "puttering" with "Parker's Back" even as she lay dying. The story, then, is a diagnostic of her medical condition, and in conjunction with Parker's "leap forward into a worse unknown" (CW 666) serves as a literal and verbal passage that marks her journey from mortality to immortality, from living to dying, the latter a process that increasingly occupied O'Connor during the last year of her life when she corresponded with Maryat Lee about her medical condition.

From 21 May 1964 until the time of her death on 3 August, much of Flannery O'Connor's time was spent in Piedmont Hospital in Atlanta where on 28 May she adds a P.S. to a letter written to Louise Abbot that says: "Prayers requested. I am sick of being sick" (1210). She receives the Sacrament of the Sick, also known as Extreme Unction, from the parish priest on 7 July, and slips into a coma on 2 August. She died at midnight on 3 August of kidney failure, no stranger to the "temple" of death.

The inscriptions on Parker's Back, the tattoos that Sarah Ruth deems "the vanity of vanities" (CW 662) are, themselves, revelation. Irwin Howard Streight reads Parker's story as one of signs and significations, "about encountering the multifold texts that need to be interpreted and the difficulties and ambiguities of interpretation" (2-3). He points out that O'Connor's use of the word "botched" in relation to Parker is "doubly appropriate" for a "botch" is, both a "disorderly or confused combination" and "a skin disorder" (3). Parker's tattoos, Streight argues, are signs of embodiment, part of Parker's being or self; "the sign of the transcendental signified, the incarnate Logos on Parker's back orders and gives meaning to both the sacred and the profane [...]" (5). This acquisition of signification is what Sarah Ruth does not see in her seeing, and she would not know—though Flannery O'Connor might—that Leviticus 19:28 says that one should not gash themselves or tattoo themselves in mourning for the dead. O'Connor would also know that in the New Testament, the Word is made flesh and that it is this aspect of divinity that is revealed to man through the crucifixion itself. Jesus arose from the dead, and in order to fully reveal His resurrection, He tells the apostles in St. Luke 39-40 to "[b]ehold my hands and feet, that it is I myself; handle me, and see; for a spirit hath not flesh and bones, as ye see me have. And when he had thus spoken, he showed them His hands and His feet." Seeing, however, is not synonymous with believing. Sarah Ruth thinks that Parker has a chicken on his back when, in fact, the tattoo is that of an eagle. O'Connor notes that "[f]or the writer of fiction everything has its testing point in the eye, an organ which eventually involves the whole personality and as much of the world as can be got into it" (CW 807). Again contradictions are raised in O'Connor's discourse concerning sight. What is visible on the surface is only a part of what may be seen, and what may be known by way of the eye may not be trusted. Knowing is derived through the body as well as the eye, but appearance is deceptive.

Mark Taylor in *Hiding*, argues that the incarnation of the divine both materially and corporeally confers significance on the body, and he says that the New Testament encourages something that approaches tattooing. Paul concludes his Letter to the Galatians 6:17 with a plea: that "[i]n the future let no one make trouble for me, for I bear the marks of Jesus branded on my body." Though these words have usually been interpreted figuratively rather than literally, Taylor notes that some Christians have sought to imitate the stigmata of Jesus by incising their own skins (90-91). He cites an early account of Coptic tattooing in which a Christian pilgrim had a cross and the words *Via, Veritas, Vita* inscribed on his wrist. The man, it was said, prided himself "very much in beholding those Characters and in seeing them would often speak those words of St. Paul: I bear in my body the marks of Lord Jesus" (Taylor 91). Coptic tattooing exists today for decorative and therapeutic purposes. The embodied divine *marks* the passage from life to death and serves as a roadmap when "driving into a new country" (CW 672), the place that O'Connor moved toward in the last days of her life.

In his study of the tattoo, Taylor elaborates on how the marked or tattooed body is associated with death by confronting it and transcending it. "There's a point in the mystical experience," he says, "where the ego peels off and what's left is just an absolute kind of pure essence. Just prior to this, there's a moment of fear because the ego is really threatened, and the ego has to drop off" (131). The mystical experience is a sort of preview of death. The body becomes a ship of death, a vehicle that transports the self beyond the mortal body. For O'Connor, both her disease and her stories of it mete out this transition. Blood signifies the Lamb, the Christian Way, grace and redemption and, at the same time, registers disease. As Lappé points out, lupus erethematosus produces "a reaction at the skin surface—a thickening over the bridge of the nose or a rash-like tattoo in the form of a butterfly" (147). This is the cardinal sign, the tattoo-like markings of lupus that indicate an autoimmune disease process is occurring inside the body. Diagnosed in 1951, the disease killed O'Connor in 1954. James H. Buchanan makes several cogent observations regarding Flannery O'Connor's illness. He says it "started with a fever and an odd butterfly rash across her face" (131). It was at this time that Flannery O'Connor was staying in Connecticut with Sally and Robert Fitzgerald. It was when the rash worsened and "maculopapular spotting" spread to her breasts and back, then developed into painful ulcers that "began to punctuate her lips and soft palate," she began to realize, Buchanan says, "in some visceral and instinctual way–that she was desperately ill. It was late December 1950, and the Fitzgeralds drove her that afternoon to the train station" where she boarded the express to Milledgeville, Georgia (133). Buchanan explains that there are two types of systemic lupus erythematosus. The more gentle type "enjoy[s] teasing the skin with its round scaling papules that scar and tattoo the face like the markings of a wolf. The other type of lupus, which afflicted O'Connor is Disseminated SLE, and it is this type that Buchanan says "marches with its deranged immunoglobulins of death and destruction through the system, leaving fibrinoid necrosis and hematoxylin bodies in its wake" (134).

The "blood" and "body" of Christ made manifest in the sacrament and in O'Connor's disease prefigure the final revelation of O'Connor's stories. Speaking of her disease in a 28 June 1956 letter to "A," O'Connor says that "[s]ickness before death is a very appropriate thing and I think those who don't have it miss one of God's mercies" (CW 997). Such a diagnosis caused the patient to address her own mortality and, at the same time, give testimony by means of writing the body, the temple of the Holy Ghost.

Flannery O'Connor's diseased body scripted a long illness that called for increasing medical intervention. It disrupted her life in Connecticut and brought her home again to Milledgeville where she endured more and more bouts of hospitalization. Like the child in "A Temple of the Holy Ghost," she looked out "out over a stretch of pasture land" that edged "the dark woods" (CW 209).

When O'Connor was administered extreme unction on 9 July, she asked Janet McKane for a copy of Ernest Hello's "The Prayer to Saint Raphael," a prayer that addresses the transition from life to death. It petitions the Saint to "[l]ead us toward those we are waiting for, [...] lead us by the hand toward those we are looking for. May all our movements be guided by your light and transfigured with your joy" (qtd. in Buchanan 145). Buchanan notes that O'Connor received the Holy Eucharist on 2 August, and he writes that the reception of this last rite was "a fortuitous preparation "for her "migration" (147) to the life beyond. In the "Prayer to Saint Raphael" this is "the region of thunder, in a land that is always peaceful, always serene and bright with the resplendent glory of God" (qtd. in Buchanan 146).

The parchment upon which O'Connor's transcribed her illness is the dermatology and theology of her living body. Kathleen Spaltro writes that O'Connor understood her disability and "her consequent death as necessary precipitants of her spiritual growth" (33). In Christian theology, Donn Welton explains that

> Christ's death functions to terminate the reign of sin and death [...]. In becoming identified or "united" with Him the believer [...] becomes "dead" to and thereby "freed" from the demands of sin and death; and he or she becomes "raised from the dead" and thereby inducted into "the newness of life." (251)

The tattoos on Parker's Back, like those that mark Flannery O'Connor's diseased and dying mortal body are part of the process of providing life in the spirit. Tattoos are part of the discourse of living skin, and the short story form serves as a perfect vehicle for Flannery O'Connor to express the needs and concerns of a scribbling woman who wrestles with religion, with acceptance of God's will, and with her skin ego, with issues of life and death. "Parker's Back" and "The Temple of the Holy Ghost" are enfolders that bring to view the inner and outer aspects of being, of being ill, that like the short story form itself is often disjunctive, inconclusive, oblique and that resists closure while struggling to make meaning out of what is. She sums up her approach to the story in her essay, "The Catholic Novelist in the Protestant South" when she says that her own approach is

> very like the one Dr. Johnson's blind housekeeper used when she poured tea. She put her finger inside the cup. I think that if there is any value in hearing writers talk, it would be in hearing what they can witness to, and not what they can theorize about. I think it would be in hearing what some of their larger concerns are—the really important things that make details fall into place without too much sinister calculation on the writer's part. (CW 853)

Part of the difficulty of coming to terms with the layers of meaning in O'Connor's stories lies in interpreting the unconscious. If O'Connor, herself, failed to understand herself, the reader cannot satisfactorily rely on her word. It is necessary, then, to read closely and to approach the stories with a great deal of negative capability, because there is no final critical resolve regarding the meaning of O'Connor's work.

O'Connor's short stories "Parker's Back" and "The Temple of the Holy Ghost" elucidate a body of meaning that intertwines the superficial surface signification of the narrative with underlying layers of import. She attempts to communicate deep religious views and to understand them in relation to her physical condition and psychological conflicts. She conjoins the transgressive human body and the body of Christ and sees them as a means of redemption and an acceptance of her death.

Notes

1   Drs. H.H. L. Chan and W.K. Fung, writing in the *The Handbook of Dermatology & Venereology*, list the cutaneous manifestations of lupus erythematous as presenting urticarial patches, scarred patches with pigmentary changes. They note that the palms of the hands can be involved with atrophy, erosion or hyperkeratosis. During flare ups, the patient often develops a transient maculopapular butterfly rash on the cheeks.
2   Throughout this essay, CW indicates O'Connor's *Collected Works*.

Works Cited

Anzieu, Didier. *The Skin Ego.* Trans. Chris Turner. New Haven: Yale UP, 1989.

———. *A Skin For Thought: Interviews with Gilbert Tarrab on Psychology and Psychoanalysis.* London: Karnac Books, 1990.

Brooks, Peter. *Body Work: Objects of Desire in Modern Narrative.* London: Harvard UP, 1993.

Buchanan, James H. *Patient Encounters: The Experience of Disease.* Charlottesville: UP of Virginia, 1989.

Chan, H.H.L. and W.K. Fung. "Cutaneous Manifestation of Internal Disease." *Handbook of Dermatology & Venereology*. 2nd Edition. Eds. Sá Sabral, Luis Leite, and José Pinto. Hong Kong: Honk Kong Medical Journal, 1998. <http://www.hkmj.org.hk/skin/cover.htm>

Coles, Robert. *Flannery O'Connor's South.* Athens: U of Georgia P, 1993.

Fitzgerald, Sally. Chronology. *Flannery O'Connor: Collected Works.* NY: Library of America, 1988. 1237-57.

Foucault, Michel. *The Birth of the Clinic: An Archaeology of Medical Perception.* NY: Vintage, 1994.

Lappé, Marc. *The Body's Edge: Our Cultural Obsession With Skin.* NY: Henry Holt, 1996.

O'Connor, Flannery. *Flannery O'Connor: Collected Works.* Ed. Sally Fitzgerald. NY: Library of America, 1988.

Reesman, Jeanne Campbell, "Women, Language and the Grotesque in Flannery O'Connor and Eudora Welty," *Flannery O'Connor: New Perspectives*. Eds. Sura P. Rath and Mary Neff Shaw. Athens: U of Georgia P, 1996.

Spaltro, Kathleen. "When We Dead Awaken: Flannery O'Connor's Debt to Lupus." *Flannery O'Connor Bulletin* 20 (1991): 33-44.

Streight, Irwin Howard. "Is There a Text in This Man? A Semiotic Reading of 'Parker's Back.'" *The Flannery O'Connor Bulletin* 22 (1993-94) 1-11.

Taylor, Mark. *Hiding.* Chicago: U of Chicago P, 1997.

———. *About Religion.* Chicago: U of Chicago P, 1999.

Welton, Donn. "Biblical Bodies." *Body and Flesh.* London: Blackwell, 1998.

Westarp, Karl-Heinz. "Teilhard de Chardin's Impact on Flannery O'Connor: A Reading of 'Parker's Back.'" *The Flannery O'Connor Bulletin* 12 (1983) 93-113.

Cynthia Ozick's "The Pagan Rabbi" and the Seduction of the Storyteller

Beth Ellen Roberts

In her preface to *Bloodshed and Three Novellas*, Cynthia Ozick claims that the difference between novels and short forms is that the novel concerns itself with the consumption of the fruit of the Tree of Knowledge, while short stories begin "with the knowledge of nakedness" after the apple has been eaten (5). Ozick's story "The Pagan Rabbi" opens after the suicide of Rabbi Isaac Kornfeld, a respected Judaic scholar, who hangs himself by his prayer shawl from an oak tree in a public park, a perverse and decidedly non-kosher Garden situated next to "a bay filled with sickly clams and a bad smell" (4). Rabbi Kornfeld has not only eaten of the Tree of Knowledge—he had been seduced away from his studies of Talmud and Mishnah by books of Romantic poetry and Greek myth—but has had knowledge (in the biblical sense) of the tree by coupling with its indwelling dryad. Having concluded from the stories he read that Nature is inhabited by a multiplicity of "free souls" untethered to the material world, and literally embracing pantheism, Kornfeld seeks to release his own soul from his body in a misguided pursuit of divine knowledge. Both the stories that he reads and those he tells himself contribute to his death; and, in the story of the rabbi's unfortunate fall, as Ozick, an Orthodox Jew, raises concerns about the temptations of paganism and idolatry, she worries at the same time about the seductions of the storyteller.

In numerous essays, Ozick explicitly discusses her almost obsessive fretting over the dangers of idolatry inherent in storytelling. The lesson of her story "Usurpation" she describes as follows: "the point being that the story making faculty itself can be a corridor to the corruptions and abominations of idol-worship, of the adoration of a magical event" (*Bloodshed* 11). Noting that the concept of *yetzer ha-ra* (Hebrew term for an evil impulse or inclination) is "related also to the creative capacity; the desire to compete with the Creator in ordering being and reality," she declares forthrightly, "Literature is an idol"

(*Art and Ardor* 196). Idolatry implies the supplantation of monotheistic unity by pantheistic multiplicity; and, as such, the creation of stories inherently poses a threat to both Jewish writer and Jewish reader. In light of this danger, Ozick asks, "Why do I [...] lust after stories more and more and more?" (*Bloodshed* 12).

Ozick's use of the word "lust" insinuates that creativity represents a sinful sexual passion to be combated; but she knows that as sexual creation is necessary to sustain humanity, storytelling and invention sustain Judaism. Even in its most rigidly monotheistic forms, Judaism continually reinvents itself through the creation of *aggadah*, or legend, and *midrash*, or exegetical storytelling. Ozick's essay "Bialik's Hint" examines the paradoxical relationship between liberty and restraint within Judaism as exemplified by Chaim Nachman Bialik's assertion that *aggadah* and *halachah* (law) engage in a symbiotic relationship; *aggadah* arises out of *halachah* and vice versa. The trick is to encourage the creative without losing sight of the immutable. The foremost scholar of *midrash*, Jacob Neusner, explains that the technique:

> holds together two competing truths, first, the authority of Scripture, and, second, that equally ineluctable freedom of interpretation implicit in the conviction that Scripture speaks now, not only then. Joining the two, each in balance and proper proportion, Midrash as the process of mediation between the Word of God in Scripture and the world in which we live and serve realizes the continuity, in the here and now, of the original revealed Torah/Testament. (103)

In Jewish mysticism, transcendent authority and immanent freedom are represented by male and female aspects of God respectively, and discourse on the balance between the two tends to be highly sexualized. Telling stories which interpret yet differ from those told in the Torah then is a necessary exercise but fraught with danger; the loss of "balance and proper proportion" has the potential to seduce and destroy.

The creative capacity serves Isaac Kornfeld well as long as he uses it strictly for purposes of interpreting Torah. The unnamed narrator of the story, a childhood friend of Isaac Kornfeld's tells us that Isaac's imagination was praised by their teachers at yeshiva as "so remarkable that he could concoct holiness out of the fine line of a serif" (4). The narrator, who has become an atheist and married a gentile, claims that it was his own lack of imagination that caused him to leave the yeshiva; compared to Kornfeld he had no chance of distinction. "Now you," he recalls telling Isaac, "you could answer questions that weren't even invented yet. Then you invented them" (6). Kornfeld's brilliance is rewarded with a position as Professor of Mishnaic History and the publication of a brilliant book of responsa (8). The rabbi's reading, however, becomes promiscuous; he leaps from Saadia Gaon to Yehudah Halevi to

Dostoyevski and Thomas Mann (9). He begins to invent bedtime stories for his seven daughters, stories of dancing mice, talking clouds, and crying stones (13). A notebook found in his pocket after his death contains quotations from Greek and English poets, including Tennyson and Keats (16-17).

In turning to stories and poetry attributing spirit to Nature, Kornfeld pushes beyond the appropriate uses of the imagination. "The Pagan Rabbi" is usually read, quite correctly, as a midrash on the quotation from the *Pirkei Avot* (*Ethics of the Fathers*) that appears as an epigraph: "Rabbi Jacob said: He who is walking along and studying, but then breaks off to remark, 'How lovely is that tree!' or 'How beautiful is that fallow field!—Scripture regards such a one as having hurt his own being." However, critics who take this quotation as a statement of the story's point miss the fact that Judaism also encompasses an equal and opposite reaction toward Nature, one that Ozick addresses in her essay "The Riddle of the Ordinary," quoting a Talmudic saying: "Whoever makes a profane use of God's gifts—which means any partaking of any worldly joy without thanking God for it—commits a theft against God" (*Art and Ardor* 205). In this essay, she notes that such gifts "encompass every form of life and non-life. So there are blessings to rejoice in on smelling sweet woods or barks, fragrant plants, fruits, spices, or oils" and that *brachot* (blessings) are to be said for "trees in their first blossoming of the year or for their beauty alone" (205). We take joy in appreciating the beauty of nature and, she reminds us, "above all we are commanded to do it" (208).

Such pleasure in nature, however, creates the risk of pantheism; and Ozick goes so far as to associate Romantic poetry with idolatry, cannibalism, and genocide:

> "Tintern Abbey" assumes that the poet, in contemplating his own mind and seeking his own mood, inspired by a benign landscape, will be "well pleased to recognise / In nature and the language of the sense / [...the] soul / Of all my moral being." But the ecstatic capacity, unreined, breeds a license to uncover not only joy, love, and virtue, but a demon. The soul's license to express everything upon the bosom of a Nature perceived as holy can beget the unholy expression of savagery. It is not a new observation that the precursors of the Hitler Youth movement were the *Wandervogel*, young madcap bands and bards who wandered the German landscape looking for a brooding moodiness to inspire original feeling. (*Art and Ardor* 193)

Isaac Kornfeld justifies his own venture into pantheism by a rational process that leads him to a desire for understanding through inspiration rather than reason. Like Spinoza, he is widely read in philosophy, and the rabbi's inappropriate reading material leads him to the Spinozan heresy; coming to believe that spirit is immanent in all things, he concludes that "in God's fecundating Creation there is no possibility of idolatry" (21). He seeks *ecstasis* in his turn toward pantheism, mistakenly believing that freeing his soul from his body will lead to serenity: "To see one's soul is to know all, to know all is to own the peace our philosophies futilely envisage" (21). He fails to recognize that the attempt to know all is a usurpation of God's prerogative, despite the fact that he asserts that "To *see* the soul, to confront it—that is divine wisdom" (21). A body without soul cannot live, and Kornfeld's *ecstasis* leads to his death.

The union of body and soul balances the temporal and the atemporal, the individual and the universal; Kornfeld seeks a balance Nature and Holiness, immanence and transcendence, as well. His initial joining with Iripomonoeia, the dryad, in fact, heightens his sense of the balance between multiplicity and unity within himself. Having grasped the tree between the trunk and a branch, between its oneness and its ramifications, he calls to Nature, invoking both Lilith and the Shekhina (28–9). In an instant, he finds himself on the ground, experiencing an unmistakably post-coital satisfaction as if he had lain with his wife, yet feeling at the same time the victim of a "preternatural rapine" (29). He finds this sexual encounter, concurrently masculine and feminine, so exquisitely gratifying as to be "paradisal," and he explicitly relates the experience to the union of one and many in the juncture between the tree and the branch (29–30). He experiences "*at the same instant*, appetite and fulfillment, delicacy and power, mastery and submissiveness, and other paradoxes of entirely remarkable emotional import" (30). Christina Dokou and Daniel Walden suggest that the dryad's name derives from a combination of Iris, goddess of the rainbow, and the Greek "omonoeia," or "harmony of mind" (7), and this interpretation suggests that Iripomonoeia herself embodies the possibility of a conjunction between multiplicity and unity. Only when Isaac's soul attempts to extend the experience of this paradoxical (and necessarily ephemeral) union, removing it from the realm of the temporal to that of the atemporal, does the dryad pull the soul from the body in order to save herself from the eternal. The rabbi's death then results not from having abandoned monotheism for pantheism, but from having upset the balance between them.

Despite what she calls "a strong hostility to all mysticism as smacking on antinomianism and pantheism," Ozick admits that she is attracted to Jewish mysticism as "succulent matter for the magic of making fiction" (Rainwater 260); and she acknowledges within "The Pagan Rabbi" that, try as his rigidly orthodox wife might to blame Isaac Kornfeld's apostasy on Greek stories, the same dangers exist within the tradition of Jewish storytelling. Howard Schwartz, in his book *Reimagning the Bible: The Storytelling of the Rabbis*, identifies Isaac Kornfeld with Elisha ben Abuyah, known as Aher, a talmudic figure who read Greek books and sang Greek songs (192). According to the Talmud, Aher and three other sages achieved a mystical ascent into Paradise from which only Rabbi Akiba emerged unscathed; upon seeing an angel sitting on God's throne, Aher loses his faith in the unity of God and becomes an apostate (Schwartz 125). However, although he has been reading Greek mythology, Kornfeld finds justification for his belief in multiplicity within the godhead in numerous traditional Jewish tales. In addition to the Greek divinities, the rabbi cites the story in Genesis of the marriage of the sons of God with the daughters of men, stories of the demon queen Lilith, and the personification of the immanent aspect of God in the Shekhina.

By having Kornfeld use the examples of Lilith and the Shekhina to justify his pantheism, Ozick foregrounds the dangers inherent in the multiplicity of story telling, since both of these female figures result from imaginative exegesis of biblical text. Lilith was created to explain the discrepancy between the two different stories of God's creation of man and woman in Genesis 1:27 and Genesis 2:18-24. Schwartz emphasizes the multiplicity of both legend and demon, explaining that "the richly expressive legend of Lilith, which grew out of a single line of Genesis, gave birth to a myriad of legends" in which "the demons were believed to reproduce and proliferate endlessly" (72). The figure of the Shekhina arises out of the personification of a feminine-gendered noun meaning "the act of dwelling" (Patai 99). Early stories about the Shekhina were clearly allegorical, but, as Schwartz notes, in kabbalistic legend, "it is apparent that, at least from a mythological point of view, the *Shekhina* has become an independent entity" (94). According to Schwartz, adepts of Kabbalah were able to maintain an allegorical understanding of the Shekhina, upholding their monotheism, but "the danger of viewing the *Shekhina* as a separate deity was recognized, and that explains why the study of the kabbalistic texts was not permitted until a man had reached his fortieth year and was married" (94).

At the age of 35, Isaac Kornfeld illustrates the dangers of exposure to this material. In their introduction to *Rabbinic Fantasies: Imaginative Narratives from Classical Hebrew Literature*, David Stern and Mark Jay Mirsky explain that sexuality in the narratives of the *Zohar* represents both a forbidden danger and a path to enlightenment:

> It is the fascination of the mysterious, of the esoterically forbidden, of that which is off-limits to all but the uninitiated. Once entered, though, the realm of sexuality is there to be explored, not shunned; only by penetrating to its source can the mystical hero acquire the knowledge of perfection. Revelation thus comes to resemble sexual bliss; the imagination's own appetite for it becomes a cause for delight, not terror. (23)

One of these stories parallels "The Pagan Rabbi" in several ways: according to the *Zohar*, Moses left his wife Zipporah to engage in sexual relations with the

Shekhina, and the Talmud includes him among those who were honored by the taking of their souls through the kiss of the Shekhina rather than by the Angel of Death (Patai 141, 109). Isaac Kornfeld achieves his moment of mystical union with the Absolute; it is his desire to transform that union from the virtual to the actual that leads to his death.

Traditional Jewish literature also contains examples of stories which concern rabbis seduced by demonic tree spirits. One Talmudic *midrash* relates that Rabbi Akiba was overcome by lust when he saw a naked woman in a palm tree. Tearing off his clothes, he began to climb the tree; but when he got halfway to the top, the woman turned into Satan (B. Kiddushin 81a). Satan is generally associated with the *yetzer ha-ra*, and the link between lust, multiplicity, and the creative impulse is implied in the story. Conversely, Jewish folk tales also frequently depict demons as adherents to Jewish law, so that their unions with humans must take the form of legal marriage. In his collection of folktales *Lilith's Cave* (which credits Ozick as a contributor), Schwartz includes a 16th-century German story called "The Demon in the Tree" in which a rabbi's son playing in the woods sees a finger emerge from a tree. Thinking that the finger belongs to his friend, the man slips his ring on it and pronounces the wedding vow as a joke. Instead of his friend, however, a demon woman emerges from the hollow trunk of the tree and then disappears. The demon later asserts her status as the man's true wife.

"The Demon in the Tree" might be interpreted as a parable about the necessity of recognizing the proper balance between the authority of the Law and the freedom of Nature, between the unity of monotheism and the multiplicity of pantheism, between the eternal and the ephemeral. In the story, the demoness murders the first two wives of the rabbi's son on their wedding nights. The third wife, however, acknowledges the demon's claim as the man's true and legal spouse and leaves offerings by the tree to appease her. Understanding that the demon in the tree is a "daughter of Lilith" and knowing Lilith's role as a baby killer, the third wife when pregnant seeks out the demon in order to make a deal. In return for a vow not to harm the child, the wife promises the demoness that she will share her husband for one hour a day, when the sun is going down. "At that moment," according to the story, "the head of the demoness emerged from the tree, still looking exactly as she had when the young man was a child. She looked directly into the eyes of the bride and nodded. Then she sank back into the trunk" (106). For the next seven years, the demon not only spares the child, she protects the entire family from all danger; at the end of this period, she returns the original wedding ring and disappears forever. Through her flexible interpretation of the Law, in response to the demon's willingness to abide by some restraint, the wife insures that everyone lives happily ever after.

Isaac Kornfeld's wife, however, recognizes no such possibility of accommodation and winds up spiteful and alone. The *rebbitzin*, Sheindel, a woman who bitterly condemns her late husband for having "scaled the Fence of the Law" (24), represents the rigidly monotheistic, authoritarian side of Judaism, and Ozick emphasizes the character's inflexibility through her refusal to tell a story even for the purpose of comforting a grieving friend. When the narrator comes to her looking for answers about Isaac's death, she declines to tell the story of her husband's spiritual journey and subsequent destruction. Instead, she replies only to direct questions, and then only incompletely or obliquely. After the narrator insists that her husband was a great scholar and rabbi, Sheindel "spilled a furious laugh" and changes the subject (12). When the narrator insists that her husband sat and studied all kinds of books because he was a Jew, she replies bluntly, "He was not" (13). When pressed, Sheindel finally reveals that the rabbi wrote bedtime stories for his daughters —"stupid corrupt things," she calls them (15). Eventually, instead of telling the story, she gives the narrator Isaac's notebooks full of disconnected jottings and only later a letter from her husband which tells the tale.

At the time of Kornfeld's death, the narrator's flight from Judaism has left him unfulfilled; his wife is frigid, and he comes to view his work as a furrier as "an indecency" (6). Although he begins to tell the story as an account of his search for the cause of his friend's strange death, he eventually admits: "The fact was I had returned with a single idea: I meant to marry Isaac's widow when enough time had passed to make it seemly" (19). The return he speaks of is a return to the Kornfeld apartment in search of information about Isaac; but he is also looking to return to a religious life, looking to put together the pieces of both Isaac's death and his own life. Sheindel's rigid adherence to the Law and denial of the creative force, however, repel him. The narrator relates how Sheindel, born in a concentration camp, was saved from death when the electric fence against which the Nazi guards threw her miraculously lost its voltage at that exact moment. In response to her bitterness, he says, "I was marveling at her hatred. I suppose she was one of those born to dread imagination. I was overtaken by a coldness for her [. . .]. She was an orphan and had been saved by magic and had a terror of it" (14). At the end of the story, after reading Isaac's letter, the narrator again confronts Sheindel's contempt for her husband, incredulous at her lack of pity. When she tells him that Isaac was an illusion of a Jew, he responds "Only the pitiless are illusory" and leaves her for good (37). Sheindel's interpretation of a Judaism that consists only of rigid adherence to the Law thwarts the narrator's dream of marriage and (presumably) children; in rejecting multiplicity and thus the creative force, she rejects creation as well.

The irony is that Sheindel is already the mother of seven daughters who will, in their turns produce yet more children, multiplying more slowly than Lilith who is said to produce 100 demon children each day (Patai 223), but multiplying nonetheless. As Dokou and Walden point out, the narrator's description of Sheindel, years earlier, sitting still with babies in her arms and his picture of her spinning in the center of a dancing circle at her wedding "allude in a general manner to the prototype of the Greek fertility goddess" (13-14). In her 1972 essay "The Hole/Birth Catalogue," Ozick denounces valuing women only as childbearers on the grounds that "To make of the giving-birth a lifelong progression of consequences is to make a shrine of an act. It is a species of idolatry" (*Art and Ardor* 257); the fact that she feels a need to decry this association affirms its omnipresence. As Sheindel cannot realistically refute her own creative role, her denial of plurality within Judaism demonstrates that her pitilessness is indeed illusory. The narrator's account of Sheindel's wedding to Isaac suggests Ozick's recognition of the fecundity and multiplicity hidden within Jewish monotheism. Attending the wedding with his then-wife, a gentile, the narrator advises her not to take the segregation of men and women at the ceremony as an indication of sexlessness. "Count the babies," he suggests; "The Jews are also Puritans, but only in public" (7).

A worship of the plurality represented by the feminine has always existed within Judaism despite the public front of a pure monotheism portrayed as the masculine *Adonai* (Lord) in the Torah. In biblical times, the greatest threat to monotheism stemmed from the worship of fertility goddesses like Astarte (also Astoreth or Ishtar) and, according to Raphael Patai in *The Hebrew Goddess*, the figure of the Shekhina emerged as a transformation of these female deities into "the loving, rejoicing, motherly, suffering, mourning, and, in general, emotion-charged aspect of deity" (32). Isaac, in fact defines "gods" as "a collective word, showing much common sense, signifying what our philosophies more abstrusely call Shekhina" (27). His problem results from choosing these gods over God, not from recognizing that they exist; after all, God commands "You shall have no other gods before me" (Ex. 23), not "there are no other gods." Transcendent authority and the Law take precedence over and restrain the creative and fertile, reducing the danger inherent therein; by succumbing to the overt sexuality of Iripomonoeia, by throwing off the bonds of his marriage, Isaac destroys his own coherence.

Kornfeld's meditation on the Shekhina appears in the letter found in his pocket after his death, in which he relates the entire story of his turn towards pantheism, his coupling with the dryad, and his eventual death. Of all the characters in "The Pagan Rabbi," only Isaac who is attempting to balance unity and plurality is able to tell a story. Sheindel's refusal to tell her husband's story contrasts with the inability of Iripomonoeia to do so. Ozick emphasizes the difficulty of constraining the creative force associated with multiplicity, the feminine, and fertility through language. In her essay "The Seam of the Snail," Ozick recalls the difficulty in understanding her mother's scribbled memoirs, a mother she describes as "all profusion, abundance, fabrication" and that "she burgeoned, she proliferated; she was endlessly leafy and flowering. [. . .] she was so varied: like a tree on which lemons, pomegranates, and prickly pears absurdly all hang together" (*Metaphor* 108, 109). The memoirs, written with a "flashing and bountiful hand," presented numerous difficulties due to the fact that, "in the speed of the chase she often omitted words like 'the,' 'and,' 'will'" (108).

In "The Pagan Rabbi," the dryad literally plays with language, according to Kornfeld: "She either caught my words like balls or let them roll, or caught them and then darted off to throw them into the Inlet" (31). Her own speech, if it can be called that, he perceives "not as a series of differentiated frequencies," but as "a diffused cloud" (31). Like Iripomonoeia herself, who "must flash and dart," her words cannot be contained. Imagination, according to Ozick, "always has the lust to tear down meaning, to smash interpretation, to wear out the rational" (*Metaphor* 247), and the dryad's play with language does just that. This demonic aspect of the creative force can also be generative. Barbara Black Koltuv in her preface to *The Book of Lilith* writes that Lilith "hates to be pinned (penned) down by the Word," and part of the difficulty in obtaining a definitive picture of Lilith's qualities and activities stems from the multiplicity of stories told about this succubus. Each storyteller who has succumbed to the lust to create a new tale has only added to the confusion.

The changing styles in Isaac's letter reflect his transition from rabbi to pantheist to suicide. The letter begins with a scholarly analysis of and apologia for the recognition of divinity within Nature. The opening argument appears in the form of a proof of the immanence of God and, therefore, the impossibility of idolatry, followed by critical analyses of the relationships between body and soul and the reasons that Moses never transmitted his knowledge of the presence of other gods to the Israelites (20-23). The narrator recognizes the brilliance of the argument, comparing the understanding he receives from Kornfeld's reasoning to the unifying insight that allows us to comprehend the words represented by permutations of alphabetical symbols (23). The letter continues with a proof in the form of a narrative; the rabbi claims to have glimpsed a naiad when one of his daughters nearly drowned on a family outing (24-5). Having moved from the analytical to the analytical mixed with narrative, the letter then moves on to pure narrative as the rabbi describes his decision to search out a dryad in order to release his soul from his body, his meeting and subsequent affair with Iripomonoeia, and his despair when he finally accomplishes his goal and finds that his soul takes the form of an elderly scholar who refuses to look up from the tractate of the Mishnah that he reads to see the beauty of the flowers and greenery along his path. Kornfeld keeps writing as he ties his prayer shawl to a limb of the tree and hangs himself. Deprived of a unifying force, his writing disintegrates into asyndeton and fragments as it ends:

> ...body...
> ...fingers twist, knuckles dark as wood, tongue dries like grass, deeper now into silk...
> ...silk of pod of shawl, knees wilt, knuckles wither, neck... (37)

Deprived of a unifying force, cut off from continuity and history, he lives only as a temporal creature, and his writing changes from the past tense of the narrative he has been telling to a present tense that cannot be sustained.

Ultimately for Ozick, the telling of a story requires a delicate balancing act between liberty and restraint, an ability to face temptation without yielding to dissipation. According to Stern and Mirsky, the Hasidic approach to the imagination results from such a paradox: "The major challenge faced by the Hasid is to escape contamination by the feminine. Yet the closer the Hasid comes to such contamination, and the narrower his escape from it, the higher the degree of holiness he attains" (23). The storywriter must undergo a similar temptation. Ozick recognizes that "Literature, to come into being at all, must call on the imagination; imagination is the flesh and blood of literature;" however, "a redemptive literature, a literature that interprets and decodes the world, beaten out for the sake of humanity, must wrestle with its own body, with its own flesh and blood" (*Art and Ardor* 247). The seduction of the storyteller, for all of its dangers, Ozick concludes, is necessary for the rebirth of the people. Once we have eaten of the apple, the only hope is to keep eating.

Works Cited

Dokou, Christina and Daniel Walden. "The Pagan Condemnation and Orthodox Redemption of Rabbi Isaac Kornfeld." *Studies in American Jewish Literature*. 1996; 15: 6-15.
Koltuv, Barbara Black. *The Book of Lilith*. York Beach, ME: Nicolas-Hays, Inc, 1986.
Neusner, Jacob. *What is Midrash?* Philadelphia: Fortress Press, 1987.
Ozick, Cynthia. *Art & Ardor*. NY: Alfred A. Knopf, 1983.
———. *Bloodshed and Three Novellas*. NY: Alfred A. Knopf, 1976.
———. *Metaphor & Memory*. NY: Alfred A. Knopf, 1989.
———. *The Pagan Rabbi and Other Stories*. N.p.: Obelisk, n.d.

Patai, Raphael. *The Hebrew Goddess*. 3rd ed. Detroit: Wayne State University Press, 1990.

Rainwater, Catherine and William J. Sheick. "An Interview with Cynthia Ozick (Summer 1982)." *Texas Studies in Literature and Language* (Summer 1983): 255-65.

Schwartz, Howard. *Lilith's Cave: Jewish Tales of the Supernatural*. San Francisco: Harper & Row, 1988.

——. *Reimagining the Bible: The Storytelling of the Rabbis*. NY: Oxford University Press, 1998.

Stern, David and Mark Jay Mirsky, eds. *Rabbinic Fantasies: Imaginative Narratives from Classical Hebrew Literature*. Philadelphia: The Jewish Publication Society, 1990.

Breaking It Down:
Analysis in the Stories of Lydia Davis

Karen Alexander
Rutgers University

The most immediately striking feature of Lydia Davis's stories is their extreme brevity, a characteristic that contributes to some confusion regarding their generic classification. Two of her minimalist compositions, "Betrayal" and "A Mown Lawn," appeared in *Best American Poetry*, in 1999 and 2001 respectively, and three of her pieces are included in the 2003 anthology *Great American Prose Poems*. The concision of Davis's stories was no doubt a factor in their selection for these volumes. Her intensive focus on language and sensitivity to rhythm are also suggestive of poetry. She is said to be "admired by poets (particularly the Language poets), and indeed often shelved in the poetry section of bookstores" (Boddy 220). Nevertheless, she situates herself solidly within the tradition of fiction rather than poetry. Davis has also said that she considers herself a short story writer rather than a novelist (Ziolkowski), although she has published one novel, *The End of the Story* (1995). Six collections of her stories have appeared so far: *The Thirteenth Woman* (1976), *Story and Other Stories* (1983), *Break It Down* (1986), *Almost No Memory* (1997), *Samuel Johnson Is Indignant* (2001), and *Varieties of Disturbance* (2007). In addition to writing fiction, Davis is an active translator. She works primarily on French writers, including Maurice Blanchot and Michel Leiris. In May 2000, France honored Davis's translation efforts by proclaiming her Chevalier dans l'Ordre des Arts et Lettres. Her version of Proust's *Du Côté de Chez Swann*, with her rendering of the title as *The Way by Swann's* was published in Britain by Penguin in 2002 and by Viking in the United States in 2003 as *Swann's Way*.

Despite the fact that she insists on being identified as a short story writer, Davis delights in testing the limits of genre by formal means. She is interested in "confusing the distinctions" between poem and story, and in fiction that "enters other genres at the same time, so that a text can be partly autobiography, partly fiction, partly essay, and partly technical treatise" (McCaffrey 76). This tendency to sow confusion regarding genre should not be taken as an indication that she considers issues of genre unimportant. In fact, Davis's work sometimes takes a metafictional turn in which the nature of the story becomes an explicit thematic concern.

The title "Break It Down," given to one of her stories and a collection, is emblematic of Davis's fiction. Analysis is a compositional method for Davis, and thus a formal means of exploring genre. She breaks her stories into constituent elements in a variety of ways. Many proceed via analysis of a phrase, so that the logic or development of the examination determines the story's form. Her characters can often be seen resorting to analytic processes in futile attempts to come to terms with painful or confusing aspects of their lives. Logical analysis, as an attempt to understand the concept of the self and relationships between people and between language and the world, is one of her recurring themes. Davis's method of breaking down does not reveal the constructed nature of entities such as the self, but rather points to the sense of self and to emotion as things that elude analysis. The whole, it seems, is more than the sum of the parts into which it can be broken.

An American born in 1947, Davis belongs to the same generation as the short story writers Amy Hempel and Mary Robison, authors who along with Raymond Carver were at the center of the critical debate over minimalism in the 1980s. Like Davis's, many of Hempel's stories could be taken for prose poems, because of their poetically dense language and their brevity. One, "Housewife," from Hempel's collection *Tumble Home* (1997), consists of a single sentence. But Davis experiments in minimalist reduction of the story form more consistently than does Hempel: a number of the stories in *Samuel Johnson Is Indignant* contain two sentences or fewer. Both Davis and Hempel tend to refrain from naming or describing characters. A feature Davis's work shares with Robison's is the dividing of stories into smaller units. This is carried to extremes in Robison's novel *Why Did I Ever?* (2001), which is made up of 536 brief numbered or titled sections. Despite these similarities, Davis's work does not often come in for consideration alongside that of Hempel and Robison, perhaps because, while the others are generally thought to be practitioners of "neo-realism," Davis's concerns appear to be primarily with language and form.

Among contemporary authors, Davis cites as influences the short story writer Grace Paley and Russell Edson, whose work is usually designated prose poetry. But the most profound impact on Davis's work seems to have been made by Franz Kafka and Samuel Beckett. Critics and reviewers often note the Kafkaesque quality of her writing, a feature that is most evident in her earlier stories, a number of which are reprinted in *Samuel Johnson Is Indignant*. She has said that Kafka's parables and paradoxes inspired her to work in very short forms (Terzian). "Kafka Cooks Dinner" (*Varieties of Disturbance* 9–18) does not take the extremely brief parable form, but is an exploration of the existential discomfort of its eponymous narrator. A sense of unease with oneself is figured as confusion regarding species identity–human or dog?–in "The Dog Man" and "A Man in Our Town" (*Almost No Memory* 129–30), which are inspired by Kafka's own compositions such as "Investigations of a Dog" in which the distinction between human and animal is blurred.

In interviews, Davis frequently mentions Beckett, whom she claims to have first read at age thirteen, and whose picture she keeps on a bulletin board above her desk (McCaffrey 66; Prose; Ziokowlski). The Beckettian influence can be seen at work not only in the subject of "Southward Bound, Reads *Worstward Ho*," but also in the form the story takes (*Varieties of Disturbance* 68–71). An earlier version with a slightly different title ("Going South, Reads *Worstward Ho*," published in 2006) relates the experiences of a woman as she reads Beckett's composition on a bus journey. Davis revised the story for her new collection by removing the subjects of the sentences, specific indicators of time and place, the activities of the other passengers on the bus, and the places the narrator glimpses from the bus window. Although the original version is retained in footnotes, the new, minimalist rendering resembles Beckett's own text, a resemblance that Davis displays by juxtaposing her words to his: "Van turning, sun ahead, sun around and in opposite window, shadow on page, van pointing south and moving, reads: Longing the so-said mind long lost to longing. Dint of long longing lost to longing. Said is missaid. Whenever said said said missaid" (*Varieties of Disturbance* 70). One of the most noticeable features of Davis's writing is its tone. So distinctive and so common to her work is this particular tone that it could be called her signature. The rhythm and musicality of Beckett's language is a model for her in this regard (Prose). Sentence structure is the chief contributor to the similarity in sound between Beckett and Davis. For example, consider the following from *The Unnamable*:

> All this business of a labour to accomplish, before I can end, of words to say, a truth to recover, in order to say it, before I can end, of an imposed task, once known, long neglected, finally forgotten, to perform, before I can be done with speaking, done with listening, I invented it all, in the hope it would console me, help me to go on, allow me to think of myself as somewhere on a road, moving, between a beginning and an end, gaining ground, losing ground, getting lost, but somehow in the long run making headway. (316)

Just as Beckett's sentence proceeds by interrupting itself with brief qualifications, and then reverts back to a previous syntactical level, so does Davis's in 'Betrayal':

> And it happened that as she grew older still, and more tired, and then still older, and still more tired, another change occurred, and she found that even the mildest sort of companionship, alone together, was now too vigorous to sustain, and her fantasies were limited to a calm sort of friendliness, among other friends, the sort she really could have had with any man, with a clear conscience, and did in fact have with many, who were friends of her husband's too, or not, a friendliness that gave her comfort and strength, at night, when the friendships in her waking life were not enough, or had not been enough by the end of the day. (*Samuel Johnson* 5)

The way the sentence is put together reveals not only a close attention to its structure, but also sensitivity to its sound. "I hear the rhythms of the sentence," Davis says (Knight 457), but the sound is not that of her own speaking voice, which would interfere with the sound of the words on the page. So although there is a distinct voice in Davis's writing, one that is meant to be heard, it is to be heard only in the head.

Even though she is concerned with the musicality of her writing, Davis's language is often described as "flat." Her sentences seem to be constructed so that they end with a note of finality. Benjamin Weissman has remarked that she works by "piling each word like a rock to form a wall of subtle strangeness" (7). The last word of each sentence comes down with a clunk. For example, consider the opening of "Mothers": "Everyone has a mother somewhere" (*Break It Down* 79). There is no qualification in this sentence; what we have is briefly stated as a matter of fact. "Everyone" is echoed by "somewhere" in that both are compound words that include a quantifying element and an indeterminate indicator. Davis tends to eschew slang and colloquialisms, and chooses to repeat words and phrases rather than to vary them by substituting synonyms. Her language is so plain as to be remarkable. Marjorie Perloff calls it "at once totally familiar and yet rigidly defamiliarized" (211).

As noted above, Davis frequently divides her stories into smaller units. "Interesting" consists of seven discrete sections in which people are said to be interesting—or not. Each statement is then qualified in some way: "My friend is interesting but he is not in his apartment" (*Samuel Johnson* 48). "Cockroaches in Autumn" (*Break It Down* 84-87) has a similar structure, with twenty sections of no more than a few lines each. In this story, a series of images is presented without a traditional narrative structure or transitional passages linking them; they are joined solely by their shared subject. Each section is a carefully wrought observation of one aspect of the insects' behavior or a person's reaction to them. The economical structure has a poetic effect. By isolating each observation, Davis achieves a more intense cumulative result than would be the case had she adopted a linear narrative.

Davis occasionally gives titles to the brief units in her stories, and numbers as section headings are not uncommon in her work. An enumerative structure is sometimes implicit, as suggested by titles such as "Five Signs of Disturbance" and "A Few Things Wrong with Me" (*Break It Down* 165-177, 91-98). One of Davis's most successful uses of numbered divisions is in "The Family." Just over two pages long, "The Family" consists almost entirely of a sequence of forty-seven actions, most of which are not even allotted an entire sentence. The tone is flat, emotionless, and reportorial, resembling that of an anthropologist observing the social interactions of a family from another culture. The point of this story seems to be to demonstrate how a minimalist approach in which bare statement of events predominates still manages to yield information regarding emotional attachments and human interaction. In brief, fragmented, objective descriptions such as "(41) White woman carrying baby walks away with young black man and two girls while (42) older white man follows, holding crying black boy by hand" (*Almost No Memory* 80-81), we see at work the complex structures and bonds that form so many contemporary families.

Breaking things down into smaller units is a way for Davis to organize her stories, but one of her themes is the manner in which stories themselves help to organize experience. Stories are structured entities that offer ways of making sense of the mass of facts, events, emotions, and ideas that form the material of human life. Davis's writings about stories involve both the motivation of her characters to tell stories and meditations on the nature of stories. Some of her titles announce their thematic concern, including *The End of the Story*, "The Center of the Story," "Story," and "What Was Interesting." Her experimentally explicit writings about stories span a number of years. Davis's fascination is not just with stories, however, but with "storyness." She has remarked, "I guess it just simply doesn't interest me to tell a story and then to tell another story and tell another story [...]. [M]y higher value is on some sort of philosophical investigation" (Knight 533-534). This investigation is carried out as a result of a writer's painstaking thought about her craft, and her fiction displays her interest in what constitutes a story in content and form.

"The Universal Lady," published in *The Thirteenth Woman* in 1976, cannot get beyond a traditional storytelling opening without being sidetracked into analytical questioning of that very opening:

> There once was a woman. But was she really there, or was she perhaps some place else at the same time? And if she was there, was she there once or often, once or for a

continuing period of time? And if indeed she was, exactly how was was she? And was she a woman, or the woman, or the only woman? (29)

The words "there once was a woman" do not, for Davis, become simply an opaque formula that one utters and goes beyond, that one uses to begin a story without scrutinizing it intensely. The entire one-paragraph story consists of this process in which each term is analyzed in turn, and none is accepted without question.

"The Universal Lady" appears to be an instance of Davis's principle of "form as a response to doubt" at work. According to Davis,

> Doubt, uneasiness, dissatisfaction with writing or with existing forms may result in the formal integration of these doubts by the creation of new forms, forms that in one way or another exceed or surpass our expectations. Whereas repeating old forms implies a lack of desire or compulsion, or a refusal, to entertain doubt or feel dissatisfaction. ("Form as Response to Doubt")

Davis's refusal to pass without comment over the formulaic expression "there once was a woman" registers her doubt and dissatisfaction with storytelling forms, and manifests her desire to create new forms by subjecting the old to examination. This amounts to what Liam Callanan claims is her "attempt to remake the model of the modern short story." In "The Universal Lady," working through that doubt supplies the form of the story itself and initiates a continuing thread in Davis's writing.

"The Universal Lady" is the only story in *The Thirteenth Woman* that explicitly treats the nature of storyness and displays the self-conscious analyses found in some of Davis's more mature writings. But by the time *Story and Other Stories* appeared in 1983, these had become established features of her work. "Story," which also appears in *Break It Down*, is in two parts, a narration of events followed by a separate section in which the narrator engages in a search for the truth in the account she has given. She rehashes possible versions of the events, including what her lover has told her, and discusses their degrees of plausibility, ending with:

> Maybe the truth does not matter, but I want to know it if only so that I can come to some conclusions about such questions as: whether he is angry at me or not; if he is, then how angry; whether he still loves her or not; if he does, then how much; whether he loves me or not; how much; how capable he is of deceiving me in the act and after the act in the telling. (*Break It Down* 7)

The ultimate subject of "Story" is the narrator's quest for truth, or her effort to get the story straight, to sort the events into a coherent and plausible narrative. The events she relates prior to her concluding calculations serve only to make those calculations possible.

Story structure is the overt topic of "The Center of the Story," in which a woman writes a story featuring a hurricane, but "unlike a hurricane, this story has no center" (*Almost No Memory* 35). In a minimalist move, the woman tries to strip the story down to essentials, under the assumption that when there is less of a story, what remains must be central. The narrator goes on to discuss various elements of the story that the woman has decided to leave out, and her reasons for their exclusion. The story is disjointed and inconclusive; the search for the story's center is unsuccessful. This story is another instance of a new form arising in response to doubts about the efficacy of the old.

A similar process seems to be at work in "Killed by Monotony." The confusing scenario there is that a woman writes in her notebook about a conversation in which she tells of a letter describing a story about a young man who cites in his story an Isaac Babel story that mentions a story by Maupassant. The woman "senses that while one story within a story may add a certain richness to a story, too many cause that richness to fall away" ("Killed" 12). Effectively embedded narratives show up in "The Mouse" (*Break It Down* 43–48), which begins "First a poet writes a story about a mouse," and then switches perspective to a woman who is reading the story. This woman later has a real encounter with a mouse, and is reminded of another story about a mouse. Davis's skill is evident in this eloquent tale as she subtly links the elements of the various stories it contains. "The Mouse" also demonstrates Davis's way of telling a story while pretending to do something else, as the mouse vignettes lead up to a final image of the futility of a marriage.

Memory plays a prominent role in Davis's 1995 novel *The End of the Story*, a principal theme of which is the relationship between a story and its novelistic rendering. Davis begins her novel—and the narrator ends her story—with "the taste in my mouth of some cheap, bitter tea brought to me by a stranger" (9). This "ceremonial act" (231) is vaguely Proustian; however, it does not aid the narrator by bringing unbidden inspiration through involuntary memory. Davis's narrator is instead involved in the task of bringing order to bear on her voluntary memories. The order she seeks is narrative, and the ceremonial cup of tea provides her with an end to her story. A lengthy account of a woman's attempt to make sense of an unsuccessful love affair by putting it into novel form, *The End of the Story* marks the culmination of Davis's exploration of the nature of stories.

Despite the humor with which she sometimes treats the subject, and despite her remark in an interview that she doubts "that writing helps *anyone* to live" (McCaffrey 79), Davis obviously deems stories worthy of a philosophical "investigation of reality," which she sees as the "higher value" in her writing (Knight 534). This is not achieved by simply telling stories, but by subjecting the form of stories to doubt, by questioning their nature and analyzing them in the act of writing, in the stories themselves. "I'm always led by the possibilities of a form," Davis has said, "that's what is exciting to me" (Knight 546). In her analytical stories about stories, Davis succeeds in creating new forms, and in providing a refreshing perspective on the role of stories in our lives.

Davis often invokes systems of order in attempts to make sense of the self. In two sections of "Examples of Confusion," reflections lead to reflection, as a woman encounters her own image. "I think how remote I am," she says, "if that is me. Then think how remote, at least, that fluttering white thing is, for being me" (*Almost No Memory* 181). The confusion here is between her image and her self, but it is facilitated by language, in which one may refer to one's reflected or photographically captured image as "me." The confusion comes from a too literal belief in or too trusting a reliance on the system of language. In the next section the woman, who has been drinking, says:

> I stand up and look in the mirror and think: There she is. She's looking at you.
> Then I understand and say to myself: You have to say she if it's outside you. [...]
> In the mirror, you see something like your face. It's her face. (*Almost No Memory* 181)

The mistake here differs from that in the first section; it is the opposite mistake. But in both examples the woman has the sense that she is operating with a set of linguistic rules to reach a conclusion.

Part of the point of these stories is that excessive dependence upon ordering systems bears the risk of straying into absurdity. This is most obvious in "Once a Very Stupid Man." There, a woman in a café sits two tables from where a man with a beard is writing. Then

> two loud women came in to have lunch and disturbed the bearded man and she wrote down in her notebook that they had disturbed the bearded man writing at the next table and then saw that since she herself, as she wrote this, was writing at the next table, she was probably calling herself a bearded man. It was not that she had changed in any way, but that the words bearded man could now apply to her. Or perhaps she had changed. (*Break It Down* 140)

The woman's insecure sense of identity is worth noting, and may be an example of the existential discomfort Davis has suggested is part of human nature: "I'm tempted to say we're all very uncomfortable existentially or something in this life" (Moses). Although the woman's sense of self, not to mention the physical description combined with the spatial location, should be sufficient to pick out the referent of the phrase in question, she confuses herself regarding her own identity. As in "Examples of Confusion," the woman has erred in matching up language to world, but her mistake is, on some level, perfectly logical. Narrowly following this logical chain of thought leads her to entertain the absurd possibility that she is someone else, a bearded man.

In "Trying to Learn" the logical curiosities of personal identity merge with those of relationships between people. Here a woman experiments with the idea that her husband is really several different men in order to make sense of various aspects of his behavior and her reactions to them. She analyses him, breaks him down, considers fragments of the whole. Her belief in logic tells her that a patient man acts with patience, a serious man is serious, a playful man teases, and an angry one slams the door; this is at odds with the commonsense idea that one man can display all these behaviors at different times. She knows that she should realize they are all the same—it is this she attempts to learn—but she persists in wanting to treat them, for instance, by trying to protect the patient man from her anger. Although she tries to convince herself that the different men are in reality one and the same, "I can only believe I said those words, not to him, but to another, my enemy, who deserved all my anger" (*Almost No Memory* 82). The logic has been infected with her conflicting feelings, leaving her unable to reconcile analytical truths with the intuition of commonsense.

Rule-bound systems such as grammar, logic, and quantification are ubiquitous in Davis's fiction. The form of "Grammar Questions" is generated by an exploration of the correct way to speak about someone while they are dying and after they are dead: "When he is dead, everything to do with him will be in the past tense. Or rather the sentence 'He is dead' will be in the present tense, and also questions such as 'Where are they taking him?' or 'Where is he now?'" (24). The narrator goes on to consider whether the term "him" is the right one to use after death, or whether "the body" is more proper. It is eventually revealed that the "him" in question is the narrator's father, but the focus remains on language. This examination of grammatical issues surrounding the death of a parent is conducted in a dispassionate manner, though feelings with regard to the correctness or incorrectness of certain ways of speaking are mentioned: "I don't know if there is a 'he,' even though people will say 'he is dead.' But I see that it feels correct to say 'he is dead'" (24). Despite the fact that the questions are strangely humorous, a clear sense of emotion (sadness, distress, perhaps anger) emerges from this story's ostensibly merely formal analyses.

"Problem" describes in the barest possible terms, using letters in place of names, a complicated set of relationships among a group of people. Among them, "T takes money from U, W takes money from Y for herself and from V for their child, and X takes money from Z. X and Y have no children together" (*Break It Down* 154). It is easy to imagine someone else fleshing out this schema and expanding it into a novel, but for Davis the story is sufficiently interesting in the sparse logical expression she gives it. The algebraic form is enough to make a story, she seems to propose in this brief piece, one in which longing and love (to name only two emotions) remain discernible despite the cold, diagrammatic form in which the relationships are presented.

Characters in both "Finances" and "Break It Down" use quantification (unsuccessfully) in an attempt to comprehend their relations with others. The common problem of defining equality in a marriage is the subject of "Finances": "if they try to add and subtract to see whether the relationship is equal, it won't work" (*Samuel Johnson* 170). The man in "Break It Down" has resorted to a financial calculation because the pleasure and pain involved in a love affair are resistant to other means of quantification. "You can't measure it, because the pain comes after and it lasts longer." Since he cannot rectify the experience this way, he turns to the process of calculating its value in terms of the money he has spent, trying to figure out "how you can go in with $600, more like $1,000, and how you can come out of it with an old shirt" (*Break It Down* 30). Obviously, this analysis is no more satisfying.

Clearly, the idea that a mathematical process could lead to the truth about poignant and troubling concerns is absurd, but Davis's characters persist in their efforts to understand human nature by means of orderly systems such as language, logic, and mathematics. These stories show characters engaged in various forms of analysis, their minds actively seeking a way to make sense of painful experience, to subdue recalcitrant emotions through intellect. Their failure is both touching and apparent, for in it we witness our own struggles. And despite the futility of these attempts, we, like Davis's characters, doggedly pursue understanding by way of systematic analysis. We are doomed to repeat these analyses; it is part of the condition of being human to try to figure things out, Davis tells us. But her message is ultimately not so gloomy: through her analytical method and distinctive use of tone, we find that our very efforts are fascinating, sometimes absurd, and even humorous.

Davis chooses not to tackle social or political issues in her fiction. She describes the form of the short-short story, at which she excels, as that of a "parable that doesn't have a moral," a form she explicitly associates with Kafka (Davis, "AfterWord" 230). Nevertheless, there is a moral dimension to her work. Some stories acknowledge the power of words to wound, and thus the ethical issues inherent in the use of language. The relationship between the intention to hurt and the words that do the hurting is the subject of "Go Away" (*Almost No Memory* 120-121). In "The Other," the potential for a story to cause more damage even than actions is made clear. With the intent of annoying the person she lives with, a woman repeatedly moves household objects, and the other person repeatedly puts them back in place: "[T]hen she tells all this the way it happens to some others and they think it is funny, but the other hears it and does not think it is funny, but can't change it back" (*Almost No Memory* 115).

In "The Old Dictionary" (*Samuel Johnson* 67-70), Davis adopts the method of comparing the treatment of a person to that of other orders of being. The narrator describes a fragile old dictionary she considers so valuable that she uses it only when absolutely necessary. Even then she handles it with delicacy. By contrast, she thinks, she is not so careful with her son. She lists reasons for the difference; for example, his robust appearance does not indicate that he requires the care in handling she lavishes on the dictionary. Further comparisons are made, with houseplants and pets, and the woman reasons through the amount of attention and effort required to maintain these living things, in an effort to deal with her apparent shame at the lack of consideration she sometimes shows her son. Though Davis's method here is to apply the same analysis to the narrator's relationship with inanimate objects, plant and animal life, and people, the rather cold-sounding procedure yields a touching portrait of the fragility of human relations and the care we should use in handling them.

Breaking things down, analyzing them, is a powerful, if imperfect, means for grasping them as a whole. As Davis says,

> We can't think of fragment without thinking of whole. The word fragment implies the word whole. A fragment would seem to be part of a whole, a broken-off part of a whole. Does it also imply, as with other broken-off pieces, that enough of them would make a whole, or remake some original whole, some ideal whole? ("...Without Thinking of Whole...")

This recalls the efforts of Davis's characters to understand the nature of the self. The self may be a difficult concept to pin down as a whole; all we can see are aspects of it and this becomes even more apparent when we try to analyze it. Yet we believe and act as if the self is a whole and is something real. Davis's use of analytic procedures does not amount to committing murder to dissect. Instead, her work affirms the value of that which escapes the analytic structure she gives her stories, and reminds us that the importance of people and relationships with others may exceed the reach of the intellect.

Works Cited

Beckett, Samuel. *The Unnamable*. In *Trilogy: Molloy, Malone Dies, The Unnamable*. London: Calder, 1994.

Boddy, Kasia. "Lydia Davis." *The Columbia Companion to the Twentieth-Century American Short Story.* Ed. Blanche H. Gelfant. Columbia UP, 2000. 219-223.

Callanan, Liam. "Books in Brief: Fiction and Poetry." Review of *Almost No Memory. New York Times on the Web* 14 September 1997. 28 February 2003 <http://query.nytimes.com/search/fullpage?res=9B02E3DE1030F937A2575AC0A961958260>.

Davis, Lydia. "Afterword." *Sudden Fiction: American Short-Short Stories.* Ed. Robert Shapard and James Thomas. Salt Lake City: Gibbs M. Smith, 1986. 230

———. *Almost No Memory.* NY: Farrar, Straus and Giroux, 1997.

———. *Break It Down.* 1986. London: Serpent's Tail, 1996.

———. "Form as Response to Doubt" (excerpt from unpublished manuscript). *HOW(ever)* 4:2 (October 1987). Online archive. 28 February 2003 <http://www.scc.rutgers.edu/however/print_archive/alerts1087.html-form>.

———. "Going South, Reads *Worstward Ho*." *New and Used.* By Marc Joseph. Ed. Damon Krukowski. London: Steidl, 2006.

———. "The Dog Man." *The Paris Review* 97 (Fall 1985). 107.

———. "Grammar Questions." *Harper's Magazine* August 2002. 24-26.

———. "Killed by Monotony." *Conjunctions* 11 (1988): 11-12.

———. *Samuel Johnson Is Indignant.* NY: McSweeney's, 2001.

———. *Story and Other Stories.* Great Barrington, MA: The Figures, 1983.

———. *The End of the Story.* 1995. London: Serpent's Tail, 1996.

———. *The Thirteenth Woman.* NY: Living Hand, 1976.

———. *Varieties of Disturbance.* NY: Farrar, Straus and Giroux, 2007.

———. "...Without Thinking of Whole..." (excerpt from a talk given by Lydia Davis, November 20, 1986, at New Langton Arts, San Francisco). *HOW(ever)* 4:2 (October 1987). Online archive. 28 February 2003 <http://www.scc.rutgers.edu/however/print_archive/alerts1087.html-form>.

———, trans. *The Way by Swann's.* By Marcel Proust. London: Allen Lane-Penguin, 2002.

Hempel, Amy. *Tumble Home: A Novella and Short Stories.* NY: Scribner, 1997.

Kafka, Franz. "Investigations of a Dog." *The Complete Stories and Parables.* NY: Quality Paperback Book Club, 1983. 278–316.

Knight, Christopher. "An Interview with Lydia Davis." *Contemporary Literature* 40 (1999).

McCaffrey, Larry. "Deliberately, Terribly Neutral: An Interview with Lydia Davis." *Some Other Frequency: Interviews with Innovative American Authors.* Philadelphia: U of Pennsylvania P, 1996. 59-79.

Moses, Kate. "Not Tired of Thinking Yet" (Interview with Lydia Davis). *Salon* Magazine (June 97). 26 February 2003 <http://www.salon.com/june97/mothers/davis970620.html>.

Perloff, Marjorie. "Fiction as Language Game: The Hermeneutic Parables of Lydia Davis and Maxine Chernoff." *Breaking the Sequence: Women's Experimental Fiction.* Eds. Ellen G. Friedman and Miriam Fuchs. Princeton U P, 1989. 199-214.

Prose, Francine. Interview with Lydia Davis. *Bomb* 60 (Summer 1997). 25 February 2003 <http://www.bombsite.com/archive/davis/>.

Robison, Mary. *Why Did I Ever.* NY: Counterpoint, 2001.

Terzian, Peter. "How Proust Changed Her Life: Talking with Lydia Davis." *Newsday.com*. 4 Nov. 2001. 10 Nov. 2001 <http://www.newsday.com/features/books/ny-bktalk2446651nov04.story>.

Weissman, Benjamin. Rev. of *Almost No Memory*. *The Los Angeles Times Book Review* July 27, 1997. 7.

Ziolkowski, Thad. Interview with Lydia Davis (1997). *Index*. 2001. 25 February 2003 <http://www.indexmagazine.com/interviews/interview_davis.html>.

Silko, Le Sueur, and Le Guin: Storytelling as a "Movement Toward Wholeness"

Gayle Elliott

California State University, Dominguez Hills

> The divine art is the story. In the beginning was the story.
> Charles E. May, Short Story Theories

Leslie Marmon Silko, Meridel Le Sueur, and Ursula K. Le Guin seek in their work to resolve the contraries inherent in Western thought, striving to create a movement toward unity and wholeness by defining the world in terms of interrelationality. In addressing the modern dilemma of the divided self—in seeking narrative forms which express these dualities even while attempting to transform them—these women distinguish themselves, in spirit and in practice, as feminist writers. Marilyn Sewell describes both women's art and spirituality as "That which moves toward wholeness" (3). This movement toward wholeness is further delineated by theorist Caroline Whitbeck, who—in outlining a feminist ontology—argues for a reconceptualization of the "self-other opposition" in which our thoughts have traditionally been cast, proposing in its place a "self-other *relation* [...] assumed to be a relation between beings who are in some respects analogous" (62). These fiction writers, for whom the principles of coherence and complementarity are essential, depict the self not as separate and autonomous from the rest of creation, but as able to function meaningfully only in conscious relation to the larger systems to which the individual belongs. One cannot define oneself apart from community, culture, or nature—all are integrally connected.

The approaches used by Silko, Le Sueur, and Le Guin are consciously employed to achieve synthesis between fictive form and artistic assumptions that all, as sister writers, hold dear. All wish to convey through their work the importance of story, not only to the growth and enlightenment of the individual, but to the health and well-being of the community. My focus in this essay will be upon the themes and forms explored in their writing, suggesting that— even if their literary approaches are *not* unique to women writers—their relationship to their writing world *is*. Each of these writers circumscribes for her heroine a separate sphere for self-expression. The need for creative space, however defined, is articulated in each of their stories. Also, each emphasizes the importance of passing along the story she tells, not to preserve for herself a place in posterity, but as a means of establishing and maintaining essential human and cultural connections.

In "The Reading and Writing of Short Stories," Eudora Welty considers not only the story on the page but its genesis and afterlife, appealing not to the critic in her analysis, but to the mind and heart of its audience, assumed to be other writers. Welty describes writing as purely subjective: "How do we write?" asks Welty. "Our own way" (161). Reading, too, invites subjectivity, allowing a level of participation in which reader and writer share a mutually revelatory experience. Immersed in a story, we literally lose track of time, moving beyond ticking clocks—mechanistic, measured, and linear—to a world in which time becomes fluid. Past, present, and future intermingle, yesterday, today and tomorrow fluid and free-flowing. The Greeks distinguished between these qualities of time, terming ordinary, chronological time *kronos*, and the intuitive, eternal time of poetry, myth, revelation and dream, as *kairos*.

Story invites us to cross the threshold from *kronos* to *kairos* time, surrendering, temporarily, the left-brain dominance of the rational and verbal, merging with, and becoming absorbed in, a process of discovery which ultimately transcends language. Joseph Campbell describes the hero's journey as a "mystery of transfiguration"—a moment of spiritual passage which amounts to death and rebirth: "The familiar life horizon has been outgrown; the old concepts, ideals, and emotional patterns no longer fit" (6-7). This sounds a lot like James Joyce's notion of *epiphany*, a term which also describes a sudden illumination, after which the life of a character can never be the same. We do not arrive at moments of transformation by rational or deliberate means, however, but by surrendering ourselves to the processes of the unconscious, which introduces in a series of symbols and images a language which we interpret not by analysis but by feeling.

A mystic experiences awareness of the divine not through effort but through grace. We allow ourselves the same surrender as a story unfolds, considering it not from the outside but from within. By so doing, we trust that "Everything That Rises Must Converge" (to borrow from Flannery O'Connor): alternate realities exist, co-mingle, and intersect. We come to knowledge not seized by the intellect but entered into by intuition. Welty describes the great stories of the world as those that seem new even when they are old "because they keep their power of revealing something" (159). Stories resonate because, in a moment of intuitive possibility, *kairos* and *kronos* meet. The writer makes manifest a world which joins the seen and unseen. If in the presence of a true storyteller, we find ourselves changed.

The short story, then, proves the ideal form for these women writers, who strive in their work to integrate disparate aspects of self, and, indeed, to define self not only in individual but in broader, interdependent terms. Each, in "moving toward wholeness," provides a mirror in which opposite aspects of the same reflection meet and, potentially, merge, resisting the dualities that characterize Western thinking (male/female, spirit/body, culture/nature) as well as the hierarchical power structures which emerge from such divisions. As Margaret Atwood observes, fiction enables the reader to more clearly see herself and her world. But literature "is not only a mirror, it is also a map, a geography of the mind" (18). The women writers I discuss here are intent upon refashioning our psychological maps, reconstructing the interior and exterior world not in terms of binary oppositions, but in terms of integration and identification instead. (Le Guin, in "Sur," takes this remaking of maps literally.)

Feminist writers, including Silko, Le Sueur, and Le Guin, find support in this undertaking from what may appear an unlikely source—the very scientific community which each at times critiques. Berkeley physicist Fritjof Capra, too, decries the dilemma of the divided self, referring to the "crisis in perception" which pervades Western thought. Capra maintains that bifurcatory models have become outmoded; while Western thinking still privileges "scientific" technologies and habits of analysis, the scientific community itself has moved beyond a mechanistic Cartesian paradigm which conceives of the universe as a huge machine, giving over, instead, to a view of a living universe in continual evolution—a single, organic whole "whose parts are essentially interrelated and can be understood only as patterns of a cosmic process" (Capra 78). Capra's systems view, which focuses upon the interrelatedness of living systems, foresees a fundamental change in thinking that can occur if we consider ourselves not in competition with, but interdependent to, other living things.

Silko, Le Sueur, and Le Guin anticipate Capra's holistic "systems" view of life and to create narrative forms which accommodate, even celebrate, interdependence. Each of these women writers seeks a new (non-Cartesian) way of thinking, writing, and being, a new way of envisioning the images of personal, social, and artistic transformation. The concept of the universe as an interconnected web of relations is one of two major themes that occur throughout modern physics (Capra 87) as well as in the fictional worlds constructed in one manner or another by each of these women writers.

Capra's description of this "web" seems particularly well-suited to Silko's Yellow Woman tales, for in the Laguna Pueblo tradition, all stories are woven in the mind of Grandmother Spider. Vital to the reconciliation of binary opposites (goodness/evil, victor/victim, reason/instinct) is the recognition that the tensions between seemingly opposite poles can be considered interactive and dynamic, part of a process that establishes continuity and relation, even within areas of difference. Silko, Le Sueur, and Le Guin mediate the difference between polarizing point of view, recognizing that the story emerges from a multiplicity of perspectives.

Asked to consider what distinguishes black from white writers, Alice Walker states: "It is not the difference between them that interests me but, rather, the way black writers and white writers seem to me to be writing one immense story—the same story, for the most part—with different parts of this immense story coming from a multitude of different perspectives" (5).

The Landscapes of Desire:
The Feminine Creatrix in Leslie Marmon Silko's "Yellow Woman"

Leslie Marmon Silko, too, sees within storytelling the conjunction of a multitude of viewpoints. "Within one story there are many stories coming together," she says of the oral traditions of her culture ("Language" 64). Silko's storytelling skills are part of her birthright, the natural inheritance of her Laguna Pueblo tribe, whose traditions shaped not only her own stories but her deepest notions of personal and cultural identity. Linked as she was with the Laguna Pueblo lands and with the ceremonies and rituals passed to her from her ancestors, Silko's stories establish her place within her culture, her family, and within an ancient oral storytelling tradition as well. Much of Silko's work (*Ceremony*, for instance, as well as, to a lesser extent, "Yellow Woman") propounds Silko's view of American culture as technologically-based and exploitative of nature. Silko takes exception to the Darwinian notion that life consists of continuous competition and struggle for survival, believing, with Capra, that "all struggle in nature takes place within a wider context of cooperation" (Capra 34). And Silko, like Le Sueur and Le Guin, evokes magic and myth to break the bounds of realism and traditional fiction, commenting upon the creative impulse and the possibilities within the art of storytelling.

Silko's writing—decidedly female-centered, situated in a "motherworld"—provides feminist readers and writers with a powerful literary model. Silko begins *Ceremony* not with prose fiction but with poetry, suggesting the rhythms of long-familiar oral tales passed from one generation to the next in recitative Laguna Pueblo tradition. In interweaving those lyrical forms more commonly associated with poetry, story, and song with traditional prose, Silko blurs the boundaries between literary genres, interlacing written and "spoken" accounts to emphasize that it is the two, *together*, that complete the story. The images of creation invoked by Silko—those sacred myths central to the Native cosmology upon which her people depend for spiritual survival—are feminine in origin and are, according to legend, engendered by *vision*. Writes Silko:

> Ts'its'tsi'nako, Thought-Woman,
> is sitting in her room
> and whatever she thinks about
> appears. (*Ceremony* 1)

As noted by Paula Gunn Allen, Silko establishes in *Ceremony* a mythic landscape (continued in "Yellow Woman") which identifies Ts'eh—the *feminine* creative and life-producing power—as the matrix within which all else is created. At the same time, Silko stresses the power of image, hinting that reality may depend, in part, upon the way it is construed: the manner in which we think about and construct our stories may, in fact, determine their outcome. Silko as writer, then, links herself closely with Thought-Woman and with the invisible world of the imaginary, articulating the part Silko herself will play in the story to come:

> [Thought-Woman] is sitting in her room
> thinking of a story now
>
> I'm telling you the story
> she is thinking. (*Ceremony* 1)

In layering the central story of Tayo, Silko's protagonist in *Ceremony*, with cultural myths repeated from generation to generation, Silko becomes an active part of the very tradition she perpetuates, identifying herself—and the stories she tells—with the storytellers who have preceded her. She also honors a source beyond her own imagination: all stories emerge from the mind of Ts'its'tsi'nako, Thought Woman, Grandmother Spider, Spider Woman. In these poems, Silko recognizes and thanks Ts'eh, the singer of the song and, ultimately, the creative force at the center of the novel and the source from which all stories are born. Although Silko's protagonist in *Ceremony* is a man, the images in the novel are all in some way connected with the universal feminine principle of creation. Language emerges from the mind of Ts'its'tsi'nako; everything exists as a result of Thought Woman's naming.

In her Yellow Woman stories, Silko furthers this (feminine) tradition of bringing together Laguna Pueblo tales, continuing to illuminate the multifaceted nature of Yellow Woman. Silko explores the many shapes assumed by Yellow Woman in her tribal culture, eventually adding her own versions to the story, in the process revising and reshaping the traditional myth. In *Storyteller*, Silko retells in a number of forms the story of Yellow Woman's meeting with a spirit-man, a ka'tsina spirit from the mountains. Silko's contemporary accounts feature a variety of plotlines and outcomes told in various tones and voices. Sometimes Yellow Woman is kidnapped; at other times she seeks the mountain spirit on her own. Always the encounter alters her, and sometimes she returns to her family and tribe with new spiritual insight as a result of her experience.

In "Yellow Woman," Silko continues to explore this woman-centered myth, the heritage of what she describes as a matriarchal culture. In this version of the story, the unnamed narrator temporarily abandons her family (husband, mother, grandmother, infant) and gives way to the wilderness of her own longings and desires. Her search is not precipitated by logic or design; she simply crosses the river that separates her pueblo from the mountains. It seems natural that the protagonist's search for self must lead her away from domestic life and back into the lands of her heritage. This modern Indian woman, who aligns herself temporarily with the Yellow Woman of myth, recognizes intuitively that hers is a self divided, partially alienated from her people (she's a mixture of Anglo and Pueblo descent) and also from the land and traditions that once sustained them. The schism within her—between the Anglo/Judeo-Christian and Laguna Pueblo cultures—marks a similar division within the Native American people. This psychic/spiritual split is inscribed, in a variety of forms, throughout the story, and to resolve it, the protagonist must surrender to an ancient calling that will, ultimately, draw her back to herself. As the story begins, Silko's protagonist has obviously been intimate with a stranger whom she's met by the river.

> "Do you know the story?"
> "What story?" He smiled and pulled me close to him as he said this. I was afraid lying there on the red blanket. All I could know was the way he felt, warm, damp, his body beside me. This is the way it happens in the stories, I was thinking, with no thought beyond the moment she meets the ka'tsina spirit and they go. (*Fiction 100* 1244)

This man and woman experience one another in two dimensions: in ordinary, "real" time as well as in the timelessness of myth, enacting roles already familiar. Ultimately, the narrator's participation in the Yellow Woman story will reconcile her—though transformed—with her life in the pueblo. She begins her narrative by confiding what it feels like to awaken next to the "spirit-man."

"My thigh clung to his with dampness, and I watched the sun rising up through the tamaracks and willows" (1243). The dampness suggests not only their recent sexual encounter, but also the river beside which they've become lovers. The flow of the river—which has, the night before, reflected within it the feminine image of the moon—conveys not only sexual longing, but also the protagonist's awakening to the currents and capacities within her own female body. The call she's answered has been the call of desire—not just for a sexual encounter, but for a more sensual and deeper connection with her ancestral lands. It is the landscape with its "small brown water birds," "narrow fast channel," "washed green ragged moss and fern leaves," and "white river sand" that Silko describes most vividly. The narrator herself is left nameless, merging with the mythical identity of Yellow Woman, whereas the land is described, or named, in impeccable detail. And, in the narrator's first encounter with the ka'tsina, she has no need to identify him, either. However, in the morning, she becomes more curious. "'Yellow Woman,' he said," continuing their story-making of the night before.

> "Who are you? I asked.
> He laughed and knelt on the low, sandy bank, washing his face in the river. "Last night you guessed my name, and you knew why I had come." (1243)

The Yellow Woman stories offer young women the liberating prospect of a female character who focuses upon her own needs and desires and survives her transgression. As Paula Gunn Allen notes in *Spider Woman's Granddaughters*, the Yellow Woman story belongs to the woman. "Kochinnenako [Yellow Woman's tribal name] is a role model, whose stories do not necessarily imply

> that difference is punishable; on the contrary, it is often her very difference that makes her special adventures possible, and these adventures often have happy outcomes for Kochinnenako and for her people. This is significant among a people who value conformity and propriety [...]. It suggests that the behavior of women, at least at certain times or under certain circumstances, must be improper or nonconformist for the greater good of the whole. (182)

The protagonist's domestic life in the pueblo is too mundane to allow for such spiritual exploration. When she returns home at the end of the story, she relates to the reader the inane conversation she overhears inside: "[M]y mother was telling my grandmother how to fix the jello [...]" (1249). Silko's narrator steps out of her domestic role for only the briefest moment, but, as a result, she experiences the reality of her relationship to the Yellow Woman stories related by her grandfather, to the myths from which they originated, and—

because of this new knowledge of herself and her traditions—to the lands of her ancestors, to her own body and desires.

The Yellow Woman of myth—as the protagonist knows well enough—goes off with the spirit-man and then, mysteriously, returns home. Although she and Silva, the stranger, have played at being Ka'tsina and Yellow Woman, the narrator has felt herself long distanced from the stories of her people. "The old stories about the ka'tsina spirit and Yellow Woman can't mean us," she says (1244). The elders repeat such stories, but they're about people who lived and died in ancient times. The narrator feels removed from their source and their power. Yet the narrator can't help speculate about this lost woman of myth: "I was wondering if Yellow Woman had known who she was—if she knew that she would become part of the stories" (1244). And what of the narrator's own disappearance? As she eventually returns home—making her way not along the pavement, as she'd come, but instead along the river, as she and Silva had gone—she chooses the old pathway, claiming for herself the cultural tradition she's been exploring, for upon her homecoming she extemporaneously contributes her own version to the Yellow Woman story. "I decided to tell them that some Navajo had kidnapped me, but I was sorry that old Grandpa wasn't alive to hear my story because it was the Yellow Woman stories he liked to tell best," she says (1249). Silko herself, by renewing the traditional Yellow Woman stories in a contemporary setting and by connecting them with the old, identifies herself with her narrator and continues the storytelling tradition she continuously affirms.

"The Slow Time of Making" in "Annunciation": Growth Cycles and Organicity in the Fiction of Meridel Le Sueur

It is worth noting that, although only Silko is Indian, both her own and Meridel Le Sueur's work are influenced strongly by the world view, legends, and imagery of North American Native traditions. Both women recognize the usefulness of reclaiming ritual and myth to restore equilibrium, both to nature and to the human spirit. Indeed, it might be said that the tensions between the two opposing forces described by Silko in *Ceremony*, Ts'eh, the feminine (creative) life force and the mechanistic death force of the "witchery," surface again in Le Sueur's "Annunciation." A highly lyrical story, Le Sueur portrays a world both richly metaphorical and darkly literal. The protagonist is a young wife deeply content with her first pregnancy, and she wants nothing more than to fully experience the flowering of new life within her. She is, however, surrounded by poverty and despair, often broke and with little or no food to nourish the developing child in her womb. The story takes place during the depression years, and the narrator, alone all day in a one-room apartment while her husband searches for employment, finds herself starkly aware of the dispossessed who surround her. Even her pregnancy—the source, for her, of deep joy and a transfiguring new knowledge—is opposed by her husband, Karl. "'Why don't you take something?' he kept saying. 'Get rid of it. That's what everybody does nowadays. This isn't the time to have a child. Everything is rotten'" (Le Sueur 1631-32).

Yet the wife's pregnancy has altered her perceptions, and in her husband's absence, she struggles to find a means of expressing this change. The story begins with a dedication, "For Rachel," the unborn child to whom the narrator/mother-to-be is addressing a series of notes. "Ever since I was going to have a child I have kept writing things down on these little scraps of paper," confesses the narrator (1628). Coinciding with the budding of new life within her, then, is an impulse toward self-expression, the life force and the creative impulse one. "There is something I want to say," she writes, "something I want to make clear for myself and others" (1628). Though her attempts to write are recent and halting, the narrator has a growing sense of the importance of words, and absorbed as she is in her pregnancy, she wants suddenly to pass on insights deemed significant not only to herself, but to others as well.

The narrator is aware, simultaneously, of the new life quickening within her and of the stirrings of a previously undiscovered desire for articulation. Sensing a profound change, occurring on two levels, she attempts to record not only the depth of the experience but the agency by which it has occurred:

> There is the pear tree I can see in the afternoons as I sit on this porch writing these notes. It stands for something. I sit here all afternoon in the autumn sun and then I begin to write something on this yellow paper; something seems to be going on like a buzzing, a flying and circling within me, and then I want to write it down in some way. I have never felt this way before, except when I was a girl and was first in love and wanted then to set things down on paper so that they would not be lost. (1628)

What the narrator has discovered in the pear tree, of course, is a metaphor, not only for the unfolding of new life within her own body (a personal experience) but also of the gestation of an innate, creative propensity within humankind in general (a more universal insight). The narrator recognizes in the progress of her pregnancy the emergent life cycles—the *growing* cycles—of other living things: plants, animals, humans. "Straight out from the [porch] rail so that I can almost touch it is the radiating frail top of the pear tree that has opened a door for me. If the pears were still hanging on it each would be alone and separate with a kind of bloom upon it. Such a bloom is upon me at the moment" (1630). Le Sueur's protagonist experiences a moment of transcendence in which she perceives the potential of such bloom in everyone in her midst: the woman who runs the boarding house, "the woman next door, the girls downstairs" (1630).

Yet the outward circumstances of people's lives often prevent what should be a natural interior process—toward growth and self-expression—from coming to fruition. When the narrator goes for her daily walk in the late afternoons, she sees in her neighborhood park the tired and care-worn, the "old men and tramps [who] lie on the grass all day," the hungry people exhausted and out of work (1629). "People are ready to flower," she observes, "and cannot" (1629). It is by virtue of her quiet contemplation of the pear tree—ready to blossom, as she is—that her perception of the world has been transfigured. "Many afternoons I sit here," she notes. "It has become a kind of alive place to me" (1630).

Still, the narrator faces the concept of death at every turn. In the room next to hers, a sick woman lies, waiting to die. Her husband is forever angry with her for refusing to abort her unborn child. "'Everybody does it,' he kept telling me. 'It's nothing, then it's all over'" (1631-32). Then there is the unidentified woman who offers this unsolicited comment: "'I hear you're going to have a child,' she said. 'It's too bad.' She is the same color as the dead leaves in the park. Was she once alive too?" (1636-37). Even the trees along the old city sidewalks seem heavy and waiting to die. "Night leaves hang from them ready to fall, dark and swollen with their coming death" (1635). If Le Sueur celebrates the ongoing cycles of life, she also acknowledges that the circle leads, eventually, back again to death.

Yet the narrator's identification in "Annunciation" is with the thriving of new life: "I feel like a tree swirling upwards, too, muscular sap alive [...]" she exults. "And dark in me as I walk the streets of this decayed town are the buds of my child" (1635). Because Karl talks only of death to her, she stops speaking to him. More and more, writing becomes a source of comfort and revelation: "[...] I had got the habit of carrying slips of paper around with me and writing on them, as I am doing now. I had a feeling then that something was happening to me of some kind of loveliness I would want to preserve in some way" (1631).

Writing becomes a conversation carried on between the narrator and the unborn child, the narrator's expression in words another means of aligning herself with the life force, with the possibility of creation. The awareness of the pear tree has heightened the narrator's awareness of her surroundings in general, and she no longer feels separate from them, but as if she's participating in a single, organic system. Le Sueur's language—the very structure of her narrative—reflects the circular, organic progress of the story, as the flourishing pear tree becomes a repeated and central symbol of continuity and life. This notion of organicity, in structure and in theme, might be said to be another marker of feminist writing, and the concept seems particularly suited to a story like Le Sueur's. Susan Lohafer points out that "[Eudora] Welty is an organicist" (30), and, according to Welty, "Stories grow. They come into being within the deepest recesses of the nourishing spirit" (30). Le Sueur is in perfect agreement, seeing her own work in terms of its "organic growth and unfolding." In "Annunciation," the structural patterns emerge from the shape of the emotions expressed; the story expands and swells even as the branches of the pear tree do the same.

> I have sat here in the pale sun and the tree has spoken to me with its many tongued leaves, speaking through the afternoon of how to round a fruit. And I listen through the slow hours. I listen to the whispering of the pear tree, speaking to me, speaking to me. How can I describe what is said by a pear tree? Karl did not speak to me so. No one spoke to me in any good speech (Le Sueur 1636).

But if no human being has spoken to the narrator in any true speech, she has, through the mediation of nature, received an annunciation nevertheless. The narrator has learned to heed voices that whisper both within and beyond her, the voices of nature, affirming life, and, attuned to the silences as well as to the murmurs of the natural world, the narrator has achieved a new way of knowing. Contemplating the pear tree, "hanging in ripe body" (1636), the mother-to-be acknowledges: "My child when grown can be looked at in this way as if it suddenly existed [...] but I know the slow time of making. The pear tree knows" (1636). Le Sueur's world vision merges with her narrative vision as well: the world—and the story—is a circle, movement within it cyclical, and all "true" knowledge comes from interrelatedness.

Desire Pure as Polar Snow:
Exploration without Footprints in the Fiction of Ursula K. Le Guin

Ursula K. Le Guin's "Sur," a first-person narrative, begins with an account of an expedition to a land whose bounds are imaginary as well as geographical. Le Guin, in her "report" of the "Yelcho Expedition to the Antarctic (1909-1910)," bids her reader to consider the following query: What would happen if *women* had discovered the South Pole? Le Guin sets off to answer this question, gathering together a modest group of Latin American women as the traveling companions of her undauntable narrator. Indeed, Le Guin's female explorers arrive in Antarctica a full year before Amundsen and Scott, but they decide not to mention their own adventure, realizing how disappointed the men would be to be outdone by this small contingent of women. "We left no footprints, even," reports the narrator (Le Guin, "Sur" 2022).

The women recod the story of the expedition to pass along eventually as a family heirloom. As the narrator puts it, "Although I have no intention of publishing this report, I think it would be nice if a grandchild of mine, or somebody's grandchild, happened to find it one day" (2008). The explorer's journal is then compared in value to other items tucked away in the attic in the family's leather trunk: "Rosita's christening dress and Juanito's silver rattle and [the narrator's] wedding shoes and finneskos" (2008). These are all equally important—as material possessions *ought* to be—not because of their significance to posterity or their monetary value, but cherished because of past association with loved ones. It is enough, suggests Le Guin, to experience life on its own terms and for its own sake; public recognition—the elevated status of hero—need not be the impetus toward adventure or its prime motive force. Discovery should be a cooperative venture, undertaken for its intrinsic rewards, not a mad race to an artificially fixed finish line.

In "Sur," Le Guin challenges assumptions about competition and conquest, proposing instead of an antiquated model—Man against Nature—a new, less proprietary ethos. She calls into question many of man's assumptions about exploration and appropriation, attempting to resolve in the process the binary oppositions discussed earlier in this essay. In "Sur," Le Guin is intent upon delineating a different approach to the "taking" of land, a woman-centered ethic of cooperation rather than domination. In her version, women come, look, then leave, content with the *experience* of exploration, with the camaraderie amongst sister travelers, with the isolate beauty of the Antarctic, with the startling vision of penguins greeting them in Arrival Bay. The women, *being* women of their time, have no scientific training and have no wish to accumulate data. Although the narrator professes respect for the explorers who ventured into polar regions with such scientific goals foremost in mind, she describes *her* purpose as far more limited: "observation and exploration" (2010). The narrator, in fact, visits the South Pole after years of reading and dreaming on the subject, and finally, filled with longing, not for public distinction but for personal fulfillment, she arranges an expedition so she can see with her own eyes

> that strange continent, last Thule of the South, which lies on our maps and globes like a white cloud, a void, fringed here and there with scraps of coastline, dubious capes, suppositious islands, headlands that may or may not be there: Antarctica. And the desire was as pure as the polar snows: to go, to see—no more, no less. (2010)

Le Guin's female explorers risk the Antarctic wilderness not for public but for private reasons, not to add to the store of scientific knowledge but to their own personal knowledge instead. Ultima Thule is described in a footnote as "an imaginary island [...] thought by ancient geographers to mark the edge of the world" (2010). This expedition, then, takes place in two realms: the geographical world and the imagination. This is a voyage not confined simply to the known boundaries of cartographer's maps, but that extends also into the landscape of the imaginary. In both venues, Le Guin prompts women to venture as far as they dare—even to the edge of the world! She also urges women to reject the hierarchical relationships imposed by men upon expeditionary forces.

While the women in this story acknowledge patriarchal traditions of hierarchy, they consider appointing leaders only as a last resort. Such titles and such ordering hold no appeal for them. When such choices *are* made (in case of emergency in which a single voice is needed), they are made democratically, by the group as a whole, not imposed externally, as military personnel are ranked. Le Guin is realistic about honest disagreement, even grumbling, amongst co-workers and fellow expeditioners. The women simply regard such contention as natural; thus, they settle disagreement by consensus, effectively creating cooperation where competition might otherwise exist.

Le Guin, like Silko and Le Sueur, also addresses the bifurcation in Western thinking. In fact, in recounting the inception of "Sur," retracing its engendering images, Le Guin reports watching a PBS version of Shackleton's expedition. The following is his own account of failing to reach the South Pole ninety-seven miles short of his goal: "Man can only do his best. The strongest forces of Nature are arrayed against us." Le Guin admits: "I sat there and thought, Oh, what nonsense!" What Le Guin objects to is the notion that Nature mustered its forces to defeat Shackleton's poorly laid plans. She can't help but direct a question to Shackleton himself: "Indeed, what did you ask for?" What is inflated, according to Le Guin, is the military image, "what is pernicious is the identification of 'Nature' as enemy" (*Dancing* 173).

> We are asked to believe that the Antarctic continent became aware that four Englishmen were penetrating her virgin whiteness and so unleashed upon them the punishing fury of her revenge, the mighty weaponry of wind and blizzard. [...] Well, I don't believe it. [...] Nobody, nothing, "arrayed" any "forces" against Shackleton except Shackleton himself. He created an obstacle to conquer or an enemy to attack; attacked; and was defeated—by what? By himself, having created the situation in which his defeat could occur (*Dancing* 173).

Le Guin's women explorers do not fight with, but live in harmony with, nature. Since they have no need to prove themselves, no competitive desire to be *first*, they build ice caves in severe weather and remain snugly within them until it is safe to travel. They build a sense of community and live life fully, even in the Antarctic, establishing companionship not only with one another, but with their environment as well. One woman even makes ice sculptures, purely for her own and the others' enjoyment, of course, since they can never be transported home. Once they embark upon their journey, the women delight in naming various mountain peaks and other landmarks, but—since they're not recording the names for posterity or otherwise communicating their discoveries in any public sense—the names, mostly feminine, are contributed in a spirit of fun. A glacier is named for Florence Nightingale, a mountain termed "Throne of Our Lady of the Southern Cross" (2019). The women leave no markers or monuments, since they have no wish to stake any claims. Their expedition isn't external, to prove something to the world; it is an inner embarkation, fulfilling a desire to see and to know. In the end, the expedition is turned not into a public, recorded history, but into stories passed around the various families of its participants, sometimes exaggerated, referred to by the narrator as "other fairy tales" (2021). The discoveries made by Le Guin's intrepid explorers, recorded chiefly in their own imaginations and hearts, are never made known to the world at large. Le Guin observes: "But achievement is smaller than men think. What is large is the sky, the earth, the sea, the soul" (2015). What connects them is the awareness that all are, in some respect, interrelated. Leslie Silko and Meridel Le Sueur would undoubtedly agree with Le Guin, who believes that

> [T]o attain real community, [the ego] must turn inward, away from the crowd, to the source: it must identify with *its own* deeper regions, the great unexplored regions of the Self. These regions of the psyche Jung calls the "collective unconscious," and it is in them, where we all meet, that he sees the source of true community; of felt religion; of art, grace, spontaneity, and love. (*Language* 63)

Silko, Le Sueur, and Le Guin all call upon their own unique cultural experiences while at the same time identifying universal values and concerns, particularly the suggestive and curative powers of myth and legend, which depend upon (and, indeed, unite) both the familiar, external landscapes of "person and place" as well as the inner realms of the imagination. All emphasize the limitations imposed by language even as they see language as potentially liberatory; they also challenge the boundaries between "fact" and "fiction." The narrative technique of each embodies her views on the nature of language, for the aim of these women writers—that of interconnectedness to one's personal, cultural, and familial traditions as well as, ultimately, to nature, self and community—resonate as particularly feminist.

bell hooks, rejecting "the notion that the self exists in opposition to an other," writes of black women: "We learned that the self existed in relation, was dependent for its very being on the lives and experiences of everyone, the self not as signifier of one "I" but the coming together of many "I"s, the self as embodying collective reality past and present, family and community" (31). Silko, Le Sueur, and Le Guin, too, conceive of a more expansive sense of self, embracing a movement in the collective imagination from a lone, individual narrative to a more comprehensive human story. The first-person narrator approaches wholeness when she discovers for herself that her own story merges, in the telling, with that of a far more inclusive narrative voice: the "I Am that I Am" which affirms that all the world's stories—at their source—meet and converge.

Works Cited

Allen, Paula Gunn. *Spider Woman's Granddaughters*. Boston: Beacon Press, 1989. 182.

Atwood, Margaret. *Survival: A Thematic Guide to Canadian Literature*. Toronto, Ontario: House of Anansi, 1972.

Bates, H.E. "The Modern Short Story: Retrospect." *Short Story Theories*. Ed. Charles E. May. Ohio UP, 1976. 73-74.

Bolen, Jean Shinoda. *Crossing to Avalon: A Woman's Midlife Quest for the Sacred Feminine*. NY: HarperCollins, 1994.

Campbell, Joseph. *The Hero with a Thousand Faces*. Princeton: Princeton UP, 1949.

Capra, Fritjof. *The Turning Point*. NY: Simon & Schuster, 1982.

hooks, bell. *Talking Back: Thinking Feminist, Thinking Black*. Boston: South End Press, 1988.

Le Guin, Ursula K. *Dancing at the Edge of the World*. NY: Harper, 1989.

———. *The Language of the Night: Essays on Fantasy and Science Fiction*. NY: Berkeley, 1985.

———. "Sur." *The Norton Anthology of Literature by Women*. Ed. Sandra Gilbert and Susan Gubar. NY: W.W. Norton, 1985. 1932-42.

Le Sueur, Meridel. "Annunciation." *The Norton Anthology of Literature by Women*. Ed. Sandra Gilbert and Susan Gubar. NY: W.W. Norton, 1985. 1628-1637.

Lohafer, Susan. *Coming to Terms with the Short Story*. Baton Rouge: Louisiana State UP, 1983.

O'Connor, Frank. "The Lonely Voice." *Short Story Theories*. Ed. Charles May. Ohio UP, 1972.

Silko, Leslie Marmon. "Language and Literature from a Pueblo Indian Perspective," *English Literature: Opening Up the Canon*. Ed. Leslie A. Fiedler and Houston A. Baker, Jr. Baltimore: Johns Hopkins UP, 1981.

———. "Yellow Woman." *Fiction 100*. Ed. James Pickering. NY: Penguin, 1977. 1243-1249.

Walker, Alice. *In Search of Our Mother's Gardens*. San Diego: Harcourt Brace, 1983.

Welty, Eudora. "The Reading and Writing of Short Stories." *Short Story Theories*. Ed. Charles May. Ohio UP, 1972. 159-77.

Whitbeck, Caroline. "A Different Reality: Feminist Ontology." *Women, Knowledge and Reality*. Ed. Ann Garry and Marilyn Pearsall. Boston: Unwin Hyman, 1989. 51-76.

Contributors

KAREN ALEXANDER is Senior Editor for *Signs: Journal of Women in Culture and Society*. She completed her Ph.D. at the University of London in 2005 with a thesis on minimalism in American literature. She is coeditor, with Mary Hawkesworth, of *Feminist Perspectives on War and Terror*, forthcoming from the University of Chicago Press in April 2008. Her other publications include "The Abstract Minimalist Poetry of Robert Lax" in *Interval(le)s*, and she is currently researching gender issues in 1980s debates on the American short story.

WINNIE CHAN teaches colonial and post-colonial Anglophone literature at Virginia Commonwealth University. She is the author of *The Economy of the Short Story in British Periodicals of the 1890s* (2007). Her current project, *Imperial Gastronomy*, examines the relationships among food, the British Empire, and post/colonial identities.

ROBERT COLEMAN is the director of the Honors Program at the University of South Alabama. He has published on nineteenth- and twentieth-century United State literatures, critical theory, and composition. He is currently working on a book on the southern novelist, James Branch Cabell.

VANESSA HOLFORD DIANA is Associate Professor of English and Women's Studies at Westfield State College in Westfield, MA, where she teaches courses in multicultural American literature and women's studies. Her work on fiction by nineteenth- and twentieth-century women writers of color in the United States has appeared in various collections, reference volumes, and journals, including *Speaking Their Minds: 19th Century Black Feminism and the Legacy of Feminist Theory*; *Voices of America: Interviews with Contemporary American Writers*; *Approaches to Teaching Louise Erdrich: MLA Pedagogical Series*; *Encyclopedia of African American Literature*; *Asian American Short Story Writers: A Bio-Bibliographical Critical Sourcebook*; *In Process*, and *MELUS (Multi-Ethnic Literatures of the U.S.)*.

CONTRIBUTORS

GAYLE ELLIOTT, an essayist, fiction writer, and literary scholar, has published her work in literary journals such as *Writers Forum* and *The Journal of Modern Literature*; she is currently at work on a bildungsroman entitled Gulf Stream, for which she received a fiction grant from Sandra Cisneros' Macondo Institute. Last June, she was invited to read her fiction and serve as a panelist at the International Conference on the Short Story in English at the University of Lisbon in Portugal. She is also working on a nonfiction book, *At the Table of the Goddess: Learning to Partake of Life's Feast*. One of the chapters, "Borders of the Self and the Sacred: Healing Our Writer Selves," began as a seminar at the Macondo Institute, a session which she co-presented with Cisneros. Elliott teaches at California State University Dominguez Hills in Los Angeles, where she teaches courses in the Power of Myth, the Hero/Heroine's Journey, Creative Writing, and Literature.

SCOTT D. EMMERT is Associate Professor of English at the University of Wisconsin, Fox Valley where he teaches composition and American literature. He has published articles on Theodore Dreiser, Edith Wharton, Jack London, and Ambrose Bierce and is the author of *Loaded Fictions: Social Critique in the Twentieth-Century Western* (1996) and the co-editor of *Upon Further Review: Sports in American Literature* (2004).

ELLEN BURTON HARRINGTON is Assistant Professor in the English Department at the University of South Alabama. Her work examines gender in the sensation and detective fiction of Charles Dickens, Wilkie Collins, and Arthur Conan Doyle, as well as the influence of these genres and criminal anthropology on the work of Joseph Conrad. Recent publications include articles in *Clues*, the *International Journal of Cultural Studies*, *The Conradian, Storytelling, The Journal of the Short Story in English,* and *Conradiana*. She is currently continuing work on Conrad's heroines.

SUSANA M. JIMÉNEZ-PLACER teaches North American literature and culture at the University of Santiago de Compostela in Spain. She wrote her dissertation on the Mexican stories of Katherine Anne Porter, and published a book on this topic: *Katherine Anne Porter y la revolución mexicana: de la fascinación al desencanto*. She has written several articles and papers on different aspects of Porter's work. Since 2004, she has been a member of a research project on "Ghosts, Gender and Subjectivity," and now her research focuses on this topic.

RACHEL LISTER currently teaches at Durham University in England, where she gained her Ph.D. Her research interests include modern American women's fiction, regionalism, narratology and form. She specializes in American short stories and short story sequences, and her thesis examines the juncture between form and gender in the modern American short story sequence. Publications include an essay on Grace Paley's formal poetics in the Faith Darwin stories and a comparative study of masculine immobilization in the short story cycles of Eudora Welty and Joyce Carol Oates. Among her forthcoming publications are essays on Louise Erdrich's later novels, trends in contemporary American women's fiction, and formal and narrative strategies in A. S. Byatt's *Matisse Stories*.

MIRIAM LÓPEZ-RODRIGUEZ teaches in the Department of English at the University of Málaga, Spain. She is a member of the research group working on American Studies there and was co-organizer of the international conferences on American theatre held in May 2000, 2002, and 2004. Her doctoral dissertation on Louisa May Alcott was published by the University of Málaga. She held a Fulbright Fellowship to study the Sophie Treadwell Papers at the University of Arizona, Tucson. She has co-edited *Staging a Cultural Paradigm: The Political and the Personal in American Drama* (2002), *Women's Contribution to Nineteenth-Century American Drama* (2004) and *Broadway Bravest Woman: Selected Writings by Sophie Treadwell* (2006).

BETH ELLEN ROBERTS is an independent scholar in Chattanooga, TN. Her first book, *One Voice and Many: Modern Poets in Dialogue* appeared in 2006. Much of her research has focused on mysticism, especially kabbalah, in literature, and that work has led recently to an interest in philosemitism among non-Jewish modern writers.

MARGOT SEMPREORA is an Associate Professor of English at Webster University, St. Louis, where she teaches courses in United States literature, modern drama, and British and American women's literature. Her areas of research and publication include the short fiction of Kate Chopin, Alice Dunbar-Nelson, and Ernest Hemingway, as well as the adaptation of fiction into film. As part of Prison Performing Arts of St. Louis since 2001, she has taught the plays of Shakespeare and Sophocles in three Missouri adult prisons.

RUTH STONER is Associate Professor of American Literature in the Department of English Philology at the University of Málaga, Spain, where she specializes in nineteenth-century literature by women. Her dissertation exploring the popular fiction of Rebecca Harding Davis has been published by the University of Málaga. She has published a number of articles on Davis and other women novelists and playwrights in Spanish academic journals as well as in the American journal *Legacy*. She is currently working on a book titled *Rebecca Harding Davis's Gift to Women* as well as an anthology titled *Mary Wilkins Freeman: Playwright*, which was made possible through a research grant from the Real Colegio Complutense at Harvard University.

SUE BRANNAN WALKER is the chair of the English Department at the University of South Alabama and Poet Laureate of Alabama. She has eight published books of poetry, edited five national literary anthologies, edited a collection of critical essays on the work of Marge Piercy, and published numerous critical articles. She is known for her work on Carson McCullers, Flannery O'Connor, and James Dickey.

SUSAN PROTHRO WRIGHT, Assistant Professor at Clark Atlanta University, has published articles and book reviews in *Western American Literature, CLA Journal, MELUS, MP: An International On-line Feminist Journal, The Mark Twain Encyclopedia*, and *Southern Literary Journal*. She is past president of and remains active in the Charles Waddell Chesnutt Association. Wright teaches undergraduate and graduate courses in American and British literature and serves as the English Department's Undergraduate Coordinator.

Index

A
African Americans, characterization of, 47-59, 86, 96
Alcott, Louisa May, 37-45
Allen, Paula Gunn, 101, 182, 184
American Indian, 15-25, 116, 120, 183; see also Native American story
Anzaldúa, Gloria, 90
Atwood, Margaret, 28-29, 34-35, 180

B
Baym, Nina, 3, 7-8
Beckett, Samuel, 167-68
Bennett, Arnold, 61, 68, 71
Brooks, Peter, 144, 148

C
Capra, Fritjof, 180-81
Chinese American story, 99, 104-09
Chopin, Kate, 47, 50, 74-83
Christianity in story, 23, 33, 103, 113-26, 143-53, 183

D
Davis, Lydia, 165-75
Davis, Rebecca Harding, 28-35
detective stories, 61, 63-67, 69
"Diva Citizenship," 109
Doyle, Arthur Conan, 61, 63-65, 69, 70-71
Dunbar-Nelson, Alice, 86-96

E
Eliot, George, 2, 29
epiphany, 5-8, 138, 179

F
Frank, Joseph, 5-6

G
gothic story, 17, 23, 38-41, 45

H
Hawthorne, Nathaniel, 9-10, 23, 28-9
hooks, bell, 94, 192

I
Iser, Wolfgang, 129-30, 132, 134, 135, 138

J
Judaism in story, 154-63

L
Le Guin, Ursula K., 178, 180-81, 188-92
Le Sueur, Meridel, 178, 180-81, 185-88, 191-92
literary orality, 19-20
local color story, 47, 48, 57, 82n2, 87, 89
Lohafer, Susan, 6, 8, 65, 83n8, 188

M
Matthews, Brander, 5
May, Charles, 6, 28, 34, 35, 43-44, 78, 178
Meade, L. T., 60-72
midrash, 155-56, 159
Milton, John, 114, 118, 120, 126n3
Moore, Alice Ruth, see Alice Dunbar-Nelson

N
narrative twinning, 98-99, 102, 104, 108, 109n1

Native American story, 15-25, 98-104, 109-10, 178, 180-85, 190-92; see also American Indian
Naturalism, 34, 74-83

O

O'Connor, Flannery, 142-53, 179
Ozick, Cynthia, 154-63

P

Poe, Edgar Allan, 4-5, 35, 64-65
Porter, Katherine Anne, 112-126, 128-39

R

Rohrberger, Mary, 5-6, 8, 13n9, 130

S

Silko, Leslie Marmon, 178, 180-85, 190-92
Shaw, Valerie, 20-21, 25, 130
short-short story, 174
silence in narrative, 89, 95, 100, 102, 128-39
"skin-ego," 143
Spofford, Harriet, 15-26
Stuart, Ruth, 47-59
Sui Sin Far, 98-99, 104-10

W

Walker, Alice, 181
Welty, Eudora, 128, 130, 144, 179, 188
Woolf, Virginia, 1, 71, 147

Z

Zitkala-Ša, 98-104, 109-10